GIVE YOURSELF
MORE

A science-backed, six-part plan for women to hit their weight-loss goals by defying diet culture

Georgie Fear, RD, CSSD, and K. Aleisha Fetters, MS, CSCS

Foreword

Lisa Lewis, ED, CADC-II, Licensed Psychologist

On Target Publications
Aptos, California

Give Yourself MORE

A science-backed, six-part plan for women to hit their weight-loss goals by defying diet culture

Georgie Fear and K. Aleisha Fetters

Foreword by Lisa Lewis

Cover art by Nebojsa Adamov

Copyright © 2020 Georgie Fear and K. Aleisha Fetters
Foreword © 2020 Lisa Lewis

ISBN-13: 978-1-931046-31-2 (paperback)
ISBN-13: 978-1-931046-28-2 (epub)
First printing April 2020

On Target Publications
P O Box 1335
Aptos, California 95001 USA
otpbooks.com

Library of Congress Control Number: 2020934177

ALSO BY GEORGIE FEAR

Lean Habits for Lifelong Weight Loss

The Racing Weight Cookbook (with Matt Fitzgerald)

ALSO BY K. ALEISHA FETTERS

Fitness Hacks for Over 50

The Womans Guide to Strength Training (with Betina Gozo)

CONTENTS

PART 3

THE MORE METHOD:
HOW TO GIVE YOURSELF EVERYTHING YOU NEED TO THRIVE
(AND HIT YOUR GOALS WHILE YOU'RE AT IT)

PART 4

MAINTAINING YOUR MORE:
TROUBLESHOOTING AND COMMUNITY

FOREWORD

Big and strong. Healthy and happy. When I was a little girl, that's what my parents, my pediatrician, and I all wanted for me. "Eat your spinach so you can grow up big and strong!" "Get to bed so you can rest and get big and strong!" I can remember the words so clearly—and I can remember when they were redacted from my daily instructions and directives.

Something happens to girls just before puberty. The encouragement to get big and strong is rescinded—by parents, peers, schools, society, and the media. Suddenly, it's time to be careful. Time to watch: our weight, shape, size, and appearance. Most unfortunately, it's time to flip our motives from growing up big and strong to slimming, shrinking, and occupying as little space as possible.

Boys don't endure the same change in messaging. Tweens and teens are left with these "facts:" boys should be big and strong, girls should be small and slim. And from then on, the "rules" muddle the clarity of our self-concept, malform self-esteem, and murder self-confidence, self-assurance, and self-worth.

Some girls and teens develop eating disorders, anxiety disorders, or mood disorders. Other girls use drugs, alcohol, or sex to distract themselves from food, or hunger, or their thoughts and feelings toward themselves. Some girls strive for "perfection," always in pursuit of LESS. Lots of other girls avoid mental illness and substance use, but all girls—all—must reckon with the reality of societal standards for women.

In addition to this cacophony of societal nonsense, all of us must also reckon with regular old life. So alongside the directive to work hard at smallness and less-ness, girls and women must also learn to cope with stress, at school, at home, and in relationships. As we develop coping strategies for life's stresses and challenges, many of us experiment with using food—or the restriction of food—as a way to cope. Eating, or starving, can distract us from, numb, or even kill emotional pain. It can be a powerful (and effective) analgesic.

Although eating, or starving, in order to regulate our emotions can be effective for a short time, the consequences far outweigh the benefits. The strategies themselves cause problems just as bad or even worse than those that they were meant to cover up, and indeed, this is the definition of maladaptive coping strategies.

Within the pages of this book, Georgie and Aleisha shine a light on the origins of confusion and misuse of food and methodically review the beliefs, practices, and cycles of self-abuse and -sabotage that reinforce emotional eating and the pursuit of LESS. What sets this book apart is its focus on what to do about all of this—how to unlearn the habit of eating or restricting—for emotional regulation, and how to replace that maladaptive coping skill with healthy, adaptive, effective strategies.

Many of us missed out on observing and learning healthy emotion regulation skills, stress management, and self-care from those around us when we were young. For many of us, emotional eating was a resilient, resourceful, effective strategy at a time when we had no other alternatives! But today, we have so many alternatives. Chapters of them. Georgie and Aleisha present these alternatives to you, and invite you to sample strategies for managing life and all of its stressors that will help you to be healthier and happier.

Big and strong. Healthy and happy. I use these words often with my clients in private practice, in consultation, and at workshops and speaking engagements. I see that women need to be reminded of this original goal—and that making it a part of life's pursuits is energizing, engaging, and empowering. Even if you are not personally interested in being physically big and strong, you are most definitely interested in being psychologically big and strong. That is the definition of resilience: possessing strategies and capacity to endure stressors and cope effectively.

My wish for the reader is to get back to our original goal: Becoming big and strong. Healthy and happy. I wish that reading this book, metabolizing the information inside, and practicing the habits and skills presented to you will set you free from whatever beliefs, emotions, or habits hold you down, and keep your focus on working toward LESS. My wish for you is to find ways to give yourself MORE.

Lisa Lewis
ED, CADC-II, Licensed Psychologist

INTRODUCTION
RUNNING ON LESS AND
WHY WEIGHT "LOSS" DOESN'T WORK

Lose. Shrink. Carve. Whittle. Cut.

For many of us, body goals are all about loss. We strive to become smaller, take up less space, and obliterate this stretch mark and that arm flab. We believe that, to feel truly visible, we must first erase much of our bodies.

Indeed, for the more than 56% of U.S. women who try to lose weight[1] every year, "wanting to feel better about themselves" is a top reason for wanting to shed pounds.[2] "Improving appearance" follows closely behind. Many women pursue weight loss with happiness as the end goal,[3] believing that looking better is an assumed prerequisite for feeling better about themselves. (By better, we mean smaller.)

But treating weight loss as the embodiment of self-improvement is a losing proposition. The very act of trying to lose weight makes us unhappy. In fact, in one study, every single person who went on a diet reported being less happy four years later.[4] And get this: The least happy of the bunch were those who "successfully" lost weight. They were twice as likely to suffer from depressed moods compared to those who either maintained or gained weight. According to another analysis, five years after losing weight, nearly half of women have regained more than one-fourth of the weight—and the average regainer is heavier than she was before she ever started dieting.[5]

We aren't happy with our results, and it's because we aren't happy with ourselves.

When our motivation to eat healthfully or exercise depends on the intensity with which we want to erase parts of our bodies, what can we do but suffer? This bid for loss keeps us in a constant deficit, running on less than empty. In fact, researchers point to the fact that the greatest barrier to weight loss isn't sitting too much or eating the "wrong" foods—it's a faulty mindset.[6] And unfortunately, according to one survey, 90% of people don't consider psychological well-being to even factor into the weight-loss equation.[7, 8, 9]

But let's be clear: Mental and emotional health are inseparable from physical health. They are the root of every healthy behavior.

As health professionals, we (Georgie and Aleisha) witness this play out time and time again. Women come to us frustrated with their "failed" weight-loss attempts—tired of their eating habits, disappointed with their lack of consistent exercise, and, above all, confused.

They often say, "I know what I need to do to lose weight." But they also admit that they struggle to make themselves do it. No matter how much they say they want to lose weight, they can't seem to eat healthfully or exercise with any consistency. They believe their inability to lose weight proves there's something "wrong" with them. They question their willpower and call themselves lazy. Such internal narratives are not only counterproductive; *they're wrong.*

NEGATIVE EMOTIONS ARE LOUSY MOTIVATION

Behavioral scientists know that negative motivation, whether it's hatred of our thighs or fear of future health issues, is a fleeting impetus for change. Negative self-evaluation doesn't inspire us to thrive; it encourages inertia. If we think of ourselves as lazy or unhealthy, we'll do what lazy or unhealthy people do. Research repeatedly shows that negative emotions erode impulse control and guilt fosters self-destructive behaviors; when we're "bad," we believe we deserve punishment and suffering.[10, 11] When we disapprove of ourselves, we feel like we don't deserve better. Furthermore, negative moods reduce our cognitive abilities. When we're down on ourselves, we're literally in too bad of a mood to learn how to make healthier decisions.

Weight stigma—the belief that size is inversely proportional to worth—is a pervasive social problem that results in psychological distress, increased binge eating, disinterest in exercise and healthy eating, and weight gain.[12, 13] Experts in health psychology and behavior change have found that self-criticism and judgment are anything but conducive to healthy habits. Research shows that people

> You've probably noticed a ton of quotation marks around words such as "wrong," "should," "fix," and "clean." That's because they might be a regular part of your vocab, but they belong in the trash. You deserve a kinder, more productive relationship with your body, habits, and goals.

who believe their body type affects their worth exercise less—regardless of their body shape or size.[14] And people with type 2 diabetes are less likely to follow their doctor-recommended diets and exercise routines if they have poor self-esteem.[15]

Dieting, exercising, or trying to form even the healthiest of habits to "fix your flaws" is like willingly sitting for a 24/7 teardown from a nasty panel of critics. *This week, let's explore every single mistake you've ever made and, while we're at it, what's up with your hair?*

Think of it that way, and no wonder you're too busy to work out, you can't seem to white-knuckle your way through the latest deprivation diet (conveniently masked as a detox or clean-eating strategy), and the words "get fit" sound like torture.

They're rooted in a mindset that desperately needs to change, for our bodies, health, and lives. We have built careers around helping women overturn the belief that successful weight loss is simply about exerting more effort and mustering more willpower. We teach women to start meeting their real needs, and we watch transformation happen. But there are millions more women out there than the ones we can coach one on one, and we feel all women deserve to hear: Wellness isn't about giving yourself LESS.

MORE, MORE, MORE

Give Yourself MORE is all about changing that losing mindset so you can change your body and life for the positive. It asks, what if you stopped trying to subtract from your life (and erase your so-called "faults"), and started adding to it? What if your priority wasn't on shrinking portions, cutting carbs, or burning calories, but giving yourself MORE—more of what you need to thrive physically, mentally, and emotionally?

The answer: You would learn to live more fully, love your body, and take up the space you deserve, mentally, emotionally, and physically. You'd create healthy habits that would last a lifetime because they'd fill you up rather than drain you. You would lose weight and keep it off—by defying diet culture.

According to research, when dieters aren't focused solely on weight, they not only feel better, they become healthier and enjoy more sustainable weight loss.[16] Dropping the hyper-focus on shrinking frees up cognitive space and energy to learn how to navigate emotions, nurture supportive relationships, and discover forms of exercise that are actually enjoyable.

Additional research links rigid one-size-fits-all approaches with both weight gain and disordered eating, and those that value "listening to and trusting your body" with weight loss.[17] Studies show that the most effective diet and exercise plan is the one you can stick with over the long term; low-carb, low-fat, and "clean" eating plans all yield similar weight-loss results—until you drop the ball... because who would want to carry it forever?[18, 19]

Scientists have recently proposed a novel theoretical framework called the "upward spiral theory of lifestyle change." Integrating scientific data on psychology and health outcomes, they stress that the most effective exercise and diet interventions are founded in positive emotional experiences. In fact, they say that thinking a behavior is *enjoyable* has a far greater impact on human health behavior than the belief that the behavior is *beneficial.*[20]

This gets to the heart of self-determination theory, the prevailing framework of human motivation. Its central tenet is that **intrinsic**, internal goals and rewards elicit greater, longer-lasting motivation compared to **extrinsic**, or external factors like obtaining the "perfect" body. What's the most intrinsic of motivations? Pure, unadulterated enjoyment.[21]

Meanwhile, psychologists repeatedly find that when it comes to habits, it's more effective to think of adding one or replacing an unwanted one than taking one away.[22, 23] People are more successful when working toward gains as opposed to losses: adding grams of protein to a meal plan as opposed to removing calories, trying to lift 10 more pounds rather than weighing 10 fewer. This requires us to turn diet messaging on its head, because healthy living's consistently defined in the negative: "Don't sit on the couch, avoid sugar, cut calories, and don't you dare eat that dessert or drink that wine."

Cultivating an attitude of MORE isn't as easy as saying, "I'm not going to seek LESS anymore." Nope. It's also going to require honesty, introspection, and vulnerability.

After all, how many times in our lives have we asked ourselves what we really, truly want or need? It can even be hard to know, because we haven't thought about it in so long… or ever. Learning to stop trying to subsist on LESS goes against everything we've been told about our value as women, losing weight, and what health looks like.

It won't all be hard work, though. We're going to have some fun with it. We'll flip the bird to that no-fun, no-pleasure, no-satisfaction methodology, and start meeting our needs to create healthy, vibrant bodies and lives.

You won't do this on your own. We and every other woman making her own journey into MORE will be right here with you. (Join the *Give Yourself MORE* Facebook group for support!) Together, we'll explore how we became LESS seekers. We'll look critically at how our mindsets manifest in our relationships with our bodies, workouts, meals, friends and family, hobbies, and even free time (wait, what's that?). We'll pinpoint the areas of our lives in which we all deserve MORE, and then embark on an actionable, sustainable path toward yours.

Give Yourself MORE is about seeking the positive: claiming more space, both physically and emotionally, satisfying our appetites, choosing nutritious foods, prioritizing joy, resting more, being more authentically, unapologetically us.

Through this easy-to-follow program, you can expect to improve your mental and physical health, strength, stamina, body image, and learn to live more authentically and fully. Let's stop trying to not be "too emotional" and give ourselves permission to have feelings, opinions, and needs. Let's honor our bodies and learn to embrace them for all they are and do, not just for how they look.

Yes, we promise both weight loss and improved body image, but here's the thing: Weight loss should be an effect of, rather than a cause for, an improved body image. Your weight doesn't determine your worth.

But if you want to lose weight, rest assured yours is a valid goal and doesn't mean you don't love or appreciate yourself. It's often implied that loving your body and wanting to change it are mutually exclusive. But, when we love something, we want what's best for it. When we truly love our bodies, we want to care for them and ensure their health and well-being.

Starting now, you're going to learn how to be more generous with yourself and treat your body in the way it deserves. The results will blow you away.

Imagine:

- Emotional and binge eating being things of the past
- Confidence to stride down the sidewalk with self-assured grace, whether you're wearing haute couture or your college sweatpants
- No longer worrying what people at the gym—or anywhere, for that matter—think of you
- Waking up feeling rested, keen to get out of bed, and full of energy
- Having so much fun getting stronger that you look forward to your workouts
- Never again feeling the urge to sneak food or eat in secret
- A shorter to-do list and more opportunities for meaningful experiences with others—and even "me time"

All of these things happen when you give yourself MORE. And they're just the start. Together, let's discover all that you can gain by embracing your MORE.

PART 1

ALWAYS STRIVING FOR LESS:
HOW WE BECAME "LESS" SEEKERS
AND HOW IT'S HURTING OUR HEALTH

CHAPTER 1
HATING OUR BODIES INTO LESS

By and large, we women want to physically shrink. Honestly, becoming smaller might be one of our most pervasive lifelong pursuits. That's a pretty depressing reality. Seriously, don't we have better things to do and be?

According to one nationwide study, the average U.S. adult tries to lose weight more than 15 times throughout their life,[24] and market research suggests that the average dieter makes four to five attempts in a *single year*.[25] While some women follow flat-belly meal plans or try to burn fat in the gym, others strike "skinny arm" poses, and pretty much everyone has learned to keep their stomachs perpetually sucked in. Belly breathing? That's for at home; most women are not inflating their middles in public.

But why do we want to downsize? Why, no matter how compact we get, are we still unhappy with our bodies?

In this chapter, we'll explore how we've internalized messages about "the perfect body" and its value. We'll also dive into how, when we don't match this image, we consider it a reflection of personal defects or unworthiness—a self-defeating belief that makes it impossible to make healthy lifestyle changes, lose weight, and keep it off.

Consider this the foundation of giving yourself MORE.

INTERNALIZED SMALLNESS

The definition of what's feminine or beautiful is exceedingly narrow. Despite culture, location, and time in history, they've always been intricately linked with power dynamics. As Naomi Wolf writes in *The Beauty Myth*, "A woman's appearance is more often called to her attention for a political reason than as a constituent of genuine attraction and desire."[26]

Think about it: The eyes alone don't see natural female anatomy—a full waist, touching thighs, or cellulite—as unfeminine or undesirable. Empirically, they aren't aesthetically displeasing. But we're imprinted in cultures that convince us they are.

In turn, we women have spent centuries working to downsize our bodies in whole or in part. Methods have included corsets, foot binding, rib removal, waist trainers, Spanx, diets, liposuction, pills, exercise, CoolSculpting... the list goes on and on. And as time has progressed, the focus has gotten tighter and tighter. Maybe in just the last few years or decade, you've felt the increasing pressure. After all, what the average woman pinpoints as the "ideal" or "most attractive" female body is medically underweight.[27, 28] Yikes.

RAISED FOR LESS

The pressure to downsize might be at an all-time high, but it was long ago that we learned that our worth rested in our appearance. Even as toddlers, when we received compliments, they were far more likely to be that we were pretty, cute, or adorable than that we were fun, funny, or smart. Within our first years of life, our nails were painted, ears pierced, and we had so much fun putting on our mothers' makeup. Beauty culture welcomed us with open arms.

But, throughout it all, we didn't just learn that beauty was the goal. We also learned that our size and weight were threats to it.

When do you remember first wanting to lose weight? Some estimates indicate that more than half of girls ages six to eight want to lose weight, and by 10 years old, 80% of young girls have been on a diet.[29, 30] In one study that followed a group of 496 adolescent girls for eight years, 12% of the girls suffered from some form of eating disorder.[31] Sadder still, most young girls say they feel better about themselves when they're actively slimming, according to research.[32]

Our homes certainly play a part: There's a powerful connection between our mother's body image and our own. Indeed, research shows that by age five, girls who've observed their mothers diet are more likely to be concerned about their own weight than are girls whose mothers haven't tried to lose weight.[33] When our mothers, sisters, and aunts said they were "too big," "too fat," or needed to "drop two dress sizes," we listened, just as our daughters, sisters, and nieces listen to us now.

We not only kept tabs on their analysis, we considered how our own bodies ranked in the evaluation. This analysis is the heart of social comparison theory, which explains that much of what we think about ourselves and our worth comes from how we think we stack up against everyone else. And when our family members—female or male—commented on women's bodies, they likely made it clear that women belonged in one of two camps: desirable or fat.

It's telling that, when little girls ask their mothers if they're fat, the immediate response is "No! You're not fat! You're beautiful!" Even that reassurance reiterates the idea that a person couldn't be both.

As kids, the body images and weight stigmas of those around us were instrumental to forming our identities, senses of self-worth, and aspirations. We were sponges, taking in and absorbing everything around us to make sense of the world and our places in it. We looked not just within our homes, but everywhere we went—school, sports practice, the mall.

However, it's possible that the greatest influence on girls' desire to become ever-smaller is from women they never even meet. Characters in cartoons, shows, movies, and now YouTube are among young girls' greatest female idols. Research shows that these female characters are nearly twice as likely to have an uncharacteristically small waist compared with their male counterparts.[34, 35]

Aleisha can attest to the impact these images have over young girls. As a child, she was obsessively envious of Ariel's waist, and spent an inordinate amount of time sucking in her stomach and jamming her hands into her sides, and trying to get her hands to wrap all of the way around her waist. It never occurred to Aleisha that the cartoon mermaid's body was altogether impossible (not just for the fins) and unhealthy. After all, Ariel's waistline was roughly the same diameter as her neck!

SOCIAL COMPARISONS AND SOCIAL MEDIA

Images influence our thoughts more than we realize, and research shows that women are significantly more likely to internalize societal appearance standards than are men.[36] When we see these images, within a fraction of a second—sometimes even before we consciously register it—we make a social comparison. We compare our bodies to what we see in front of us and use it to appraise our own standing. Psychologists consistently show that when it comes to these social comparisons, women are more prone to making upward rather than downward comparisons.[37] Basically, every time we look at another woman, we find something to devalue ourselves.

While past research has focused on how traditional forms of media, such as magazines, TV, and music videos spur women's body dissatisfaction, social media is a whole new body-dissatisfaction-fueling beast. Social media doesn't *just* allow us to compare ourselves to celebrities and models; it also encourages us to compare ourselves to other "real" women.

But that doesn't mean the images haven't been altered. Free online image-editing apps offer to slim waistlines, thighs, or stretch the entire body into a leaner look, and they have hundreds of thousands of users. (And if you aren't at least playing with filters on Instagram, what are you even doing?)

Indeed, research shows that women's Instagram use is strongly linked with a tendency of self-objectification. The more frequently women view fitspiration images on Instagram, the more apt they are to internalize appearance-related ideals and base their worth on how they compare to others.[38]

> A depressingly hilarious series of studies shows that when researchers tell heterosexual women that men prefer women with larger bodies, they automatically feel better, and more secure in their bodies.[39]

Think about it: When you scroll through your social media feeds, how do you feel? What emotions do you experience as you look at other women's photos? What do you think about your body and yourself?

BODY SHAME, ON TAP

Our experiences teach us that smallness is the goal, and that largeness is hated. The prevalence of weight stigma has increased in past decades to the point that it's now on par with that of racial discrimination, especially among overweight women.[40] Hiring discrimination against women who are overweight is extremely prevalent.[41] Women say their most common stigmatizing situations include receiving nasty comments from family members and children, encountering physical barriers and obstacles such as public spaces being too small, others making negative assumptions like having low expectations because of their size, and hearing inappropriate comments from doctors.[42]

Every one of these situations hurt women, but the fact that not even the healthcare and wellness fields have a healthy perspective on women's bodies is especially disheartening. Research has shown that physicians view obese patients as less self-disciplined and more "annoying," and report less desire to help them than to help thinner patients.[43] One systematic review of weight stigmatization reveals that most physiotherapists think that people with increased weights are "noncompliant" and "unmotivated."[44]

Clients have told us far too many stories recounting doctors dismissing their medical complaints and concerns. In most cases, women explain that doctors completely ignore the symptoms and concerns for which appointments were scheduled, with the doctor instead wanting to talk about weight loss. Alternately, some patients feel that physicians cut diagnostic processes short, seemingly prematurely, to conclude that excess weight is to blame for their headaches, issues sleeping, or gastrointestinal troubles. Health only worsens when women become hesitant of seeing doctors.[45, 46, 47]

Gyms and fitness studios blatantly punish those who enter overweight. In fact, Aleisha recalls a friend of hers leaving a gym in tears, unable to enter the facility through its turnstile. And, once in a gym, larger women are likely to get unsolicited advice for diets, suggestions to stick to walking on the treadmill, and unwelcome looks from both staff and fellow exercisers.

Remarks like, "You're so inspirational" call out overweight women who exercise as exceptional, a reminder that if a woman is overweight, she's presumed to hate exercise, be lazy, or have some character defect.

In one of the least surprising findings ever, a 2017 study confirmed that experiencing stigma at a gym is associated with developing negative attitudes toward the gym.[48] Of course it does! Who would feel eager and positive about going to a gym where people give you dirty looks or stare at you? The same study found that when women experience stigma at a gym, they typically respond with maladaptive coping behaviors such as avoiding exercise, hiding in baggy clothes, and trying to rapidly lose weight with unhealthy strategies like crash diets.

Signs and pamphlets—in gyms, family medicine exam rooms, chiropractic waiting rooms, dermatologist offices—advertise weight-loss medications and procedures. Advertisements in pharmacy windows or spa storefronts promote the latest fad-diet pills or slimming gimmicks. For some women, it's impossible to get a Pap smear or skin-cancer screening without being told to shrink. Attending the gym means becoming a target for disparaging "helpful" comments from a personal trainer, and even picking up your prescriptions comes with another reminder that *you're not okay.*

How can the effect on mental health be anything but terrible? Since weight bias is a reality of everyday life, it's understandable that we absorb these attitudes as our own. In fact, one large-scale study estimates that about 40% of U.S. adults internalize weight bias, and 20% do so to a very high degree.[49] This internalized stigma results in people devaluing themselves or applying negative stereotypes to themselves because of their weight.[50] "I'm lazy" is the most common refrain we hear women using to tear themselves down.

WOMEN AREN'T JUST VICTIMS, WE'RE ALSO ACTIVE PARTICIPANTS

As much as we suffer from body hatred, we women are often the ones perpetuating it.

29

Women's magazines—staffed almost entirely by women—provide a strong example. Although, in past decades, women's magazines have arguably done more to popularize women's rights and welfare compared with even "feminist" publications, they still echo many negative messages about how we should exist in our bodies.

An analysis of the top women's health and fitness magazines reveals that their pages contain more messages about body shaping and weight loss than actual health.[51] Another analysis supports this, and adds that their performance-related content appears far less frequently than appearance- or health-related topics do.[52]

In short, women are usually the people who write headlines covering ways to shrink, and the ones who edit women's photos. It's largely women hanging airbrushed images of celebrities on a wall and debating which will sell the most copies.

Doing so, unfortunately, has been the key to these publications' survival. After all, nearly every headline and article you'll ever read, whether it's in print or online, is based on what will perform—what women will buy or read. Online publications afford some of the best examples, with search engine optimization companies often determining editorial content. They even outline article topics, headlines, subheadings, what words and "burn fat" catchphrases to use most frequently, and questions to be answered—based entirely on what women are Googling.

Meanwhile, in all forms of media, it's not actually articles read or episodes watched that turn a profit or keep companies afloat; it's advertisers, a vast number of which propel body hatred. After all, selling stuff hinges on keeping women dissatisfied with themselves and desperate for solutions.

Women drive 70 to 80% of all consumer purchasing through a combination of buying power and influence in determining what their households buy. They form the backbone of the $72 billon weight-loss industry, despite a greater percentage of men being medically overweight or obese compared to women.[53, 54, 55]

Some digital marketing experts estimate that we see and hear 4,000 to 10,000 ads every single day.[56, 57] Although many of those ads don't directly sell weight-loss programs, diets, or tools, they still reinforce the idea that for women, size is intimately linked to beauty, worth, love, and happiness.

Similarly, on social media, women are both the leaders and the followers. "Fitspiration," which is overwhelmingly female-driven, reinforces the over-valuation of physical appearance and endorses extremes in food restriction and exercise.[58] When encouraging behavior change on social media, influencers consistently use attractiveness more frequently than health or happiness as motivation.[59] The motivation is, again, social comparison. We don't look like the beautiful images we see online. "So let's do something to fix that," they urge.

Often, even the women in these posts don't look like their idealized selves. As prevalent as photo-editing is among everyday women, it's seemingly mandatory—and far more extensive—for women who use the platforms to earn a living. Influencers have entire teams of people fine-tuning every curve and erasing every trace of cellulite.

The bottom line is that these images don't make us feel good about ourselves, no matter if we're the creator or consumer. Either way, they convince us that our bodies are not ideal.

Our bodies are flawed, we think. And with that mindset, our bodies will stay flawed to us, no matter how we change them.

NEVER SMALL ENOUGH

What we think about our bodies actually has very little to do with how we look. We tend to think our bodies are too big and our frames carry too much fat, regardless of our body mass indexes (BMIs) and body-fat percentages. In fact, more than one-fourth of the women trying to lose weight at any one time are already at a healthy weight or underweight.[60]

The reason is human nature. Our minds don't make judgments based on absolutes, but through reference points, à la social comparisons. And, in addition to asking ourselves, "Do I rank higher than the women around me?" we also ask, "Do I rank higher than I did yesterday?" No matter what we do or achieve, we think we need to do more. This plays out in all aspects of our lives. For instance, psychologists have found that regardless of how much money we make, we think we need more to finally be happy.[61]

So when women hit their weight-loss goals, they often discover their quest to downsize is far from complete. They want to lose more, or begin to focus on this or that "trouble spot." The work is never done and they're never happy with their bodies. This isn't just true for women who are critically underweight or suffer from clinical body dysmorphia or eating disorders.

To a certain degree, this tendency exists in all of us.

HOW POOR BODY IMAGE
GETS IN THE WAY OF OUR GOALS

Just as societal weight stigma encourages us to see our very cells as problematic, poor body image degrades our health. This internalized weight stigma—believing that if we have weight to lose, we're lazy, unmotivated, or don't have what it takes—has a massive effect on health and the quality of life that health affords us.[62]

In fact, people who have high levels of self-directed weight stigma are three times more likely to have metabolic syndrome (a combination of high blood pressure and blood sugar, excess abdominal fat, and unhealthy cholesterol or triglyceride levels) than are people who have low levels of internalized stigma.[63] That's irrespective of BMI, depression, and demographics. Internalized weight stigma, and weight stigma alone, is the crap-tastic factor to blame.

IS YOUR HEAD IN THE GAME?

The more negatively you feel about your body, the lower your confidence and self-esteem, placing you in the worst position to grow in a positive direction. For you to feel motivated and make meaningful behavioral changes, you need to feel like, "I can do this!" Self-determination theory describes this feeling as competence, and asserts that it's critical to developing intrinsic, lasting motivation.

Some psychologists value this feeling so highly that they've developed an entire theory around it: self-efficacy theory. This states that self-efficacy—our confidence in our ability to do what's needed—determines how much effort we put toward our goals, and for how long. It also notes that feelings of self-efficacy influence how we react when faced with challenges and stressors as we pursue our goals.[64]

If you have below-the-floor levels of self-efficacy, you're likely to see difficult tasks like losing weight not as opportunities to crush it, but opportunities to fail, dwelling on your personal deficits and the obstacles in front of you. You might quickly give up on diets and exercise plans, feeling that slip-ups are a sign of failure and personal weakness, rather than opportunities for growth.

Research shows that perceived lack of competence is a major deterrent to exercise, even for people who are highly motivated,[65] and that feeling less-than-confident in your abilities is a high predictor that you won't see your goal through, whether you're trying to adopt healthy eating habits, hit the gym, or learn to play the ukulele.

RISKY BEHAVIOR

Even if pursuing smallness didn't have enough potential ramifications on its own, achieving the "ideal" body can be outright impossible depending on our genetics. But that doesn't stop us from trying.

The pressure to push past natural biology keeps many women in a state of constant war with their bodies. Poor body image and body image distortion—that feeling of never being small enough—are linked to use of extreme weight-loss methods such as vomiting and taking laxatives and weight-loss pills.[66]

It's estimated that 20 million U.S. women will have an eating disorder at some point in their lives.[67] In one study of 4,023 women ages 25 to 45, 31% of women *without a history of anorexia or binge eating* said they've purged in an effort to influence their weight.

Nearly half of female dieters have used weight-loss supplements,[68] which, contrary to what you might think or hope, aren't approved by the Food and Drug Administration (FDA) for efficacy or safety. Their potential side effects include increased blood pressure, muscle weakness, headaches, vomiting, nausea, dizziness, abnormal heart beats, stroke, heart attack, seizures, and death.[69]

Each year, weight-loss supplements are to blame for about 4,000 emergency room visits from women—more than three times as many as from men.[70] But women keep buying the pills.

SEARCHING FOR BODY LOVE

In the last few years, body acceptance has become quite the buzzword, largely in an attempt to buck the standards that keep us wanting to be smaller. For that, we applaud it. However, body acceptance often has two major flaws:

1. It tends to dispute the fact that body composition is linked to physical and mental health, and that excessively high or low levels of body fat are detrimental to both.

2. It often says that having aesthetic goals for our bodies is a bad thing.

In regard to that first point, no research has ever shown that health is truly irrespective of body composition. Yes, BMI—a ratio of height to weight—isn't a great indicator of individual health, and your levels of lean versus fat mass aren't a 100% predictor of your overall health, but neither is your blood pressure, bone mineral density, blood glucose, or estrogen levels. But health isn't immune to these factors and, most importantly, every woman in every body deserves the best health possible.

And in our work with thousands of women, we've found that it's more than possible to both love our bodies and want to change them. If we truly love something, we want what's best for it. Giving our bodies the health and vitality we desire can and sometimes does include weight loss.

Second, we're here to tell you that it's okay and perfectly healthy to have aesthetic goals. It's okay to want to change the physical look or feel of our bodies. If we really want to lose weight, cool. If we want a smaller waist or to lower our body-fat percentage, okay. We just need to understand which goals are actually *someone else's,* and learn how to pursue our goals in ways that honor our bodies.

We're not saying you have to or should lose weight. We're also not saying you have to or should abandon weight loss as a goal.

You can also dye your hair green and get a tattoo if you want to do that with your body… it's *your* body!

What we're saying is that *you* get to choose what you want to do with your body. And most of us need help learning how to love our bodies, determine what we actually want for them, and pursue our goals in ways that allow us to thrive.

CHAPTER 2
EXERCISE, PUNISHMENT, AND LOOKING "LIKE A MAN"

With so much cultural value placed on smallness, it's really no surprise that most women see exercise as nothing more than a means to a smaller end. And if exercise's overriding goal is smallness, its mission is to burn calories—the more, the better.

The unfortunate reality is that this focus on *burning, burning, burning, always burning* deprives women of so much of what exercise has to offer—physically, mentally, and emotionally. A focus on loss prohibits us from discovering everything we can gain through movement.

In this chapter, we'll explore how using exercise to counteract calories, punish ourselves for splurges, and seek smallness sucks the joy out of exercise—and our results along with it.

FORM OVER FUNCTION

Our bodies were made to move. Literally. We have a whole muscular system devoted it. That's its jam.

But in our society's culture of LESS, the commercial fitness world prioritizes reduction in size over actual health, strength, or function. Boutique fitness studios market themselves based on the number of calories they torch in an hour; watches beep at us if we haven't hit our calorie-burn goal for the day, and in many women's publications, "fitness" often just means "exercise for weight loss."

You probably know the drill. When you work out (or think you should work out), what's your reasoning? If in the last chapter, you identified yourself as having internalized some messages around the ideal body, appearance is likely your number-one concern.[71] You're anything but alone. According to research, most women report that weight control is the top reason they exercise. Mood is down on the list, and enjoyment is in dead last.[72] "Looking better" is certainly a top reason that women reach out to Aleisha for training.

While it's totally normal and okay to have aesthetic goals for your body (something we'll get into more in Chapter 9), appearance is only one of your body's many attributes. And it's far from the most important one.

What about your body's function and ability to get you out of bed each morning and move you through your days; to enable you to hug, laugh, kiss, and have sex; to travel the world and maneuver down windy, crowded, cobblestone sidewalks?

Even if your body isn't perfect-looking (whatever the hell that is), it can help enable a full, meaningful life. And while weight is an inaccurate indicator of happiness, being functional in daily life and able to do the things you want to do is huge for your quality of life, life satisfaction, and happiness.[73]

ROBBED OF GROWTH

Seeking smallness discourages building strength, and all of the benefits that come with it.

Your strength and levels of muscle mass on your frame are major players in your health and longevity. Research shows that your muscles are more indicative of your overall health than your BMI is, and that low strength is more accurate at predicting heart disease than high blood pressure is.[74, 75] Sarcopenia—severe age-

IT'S HAPPENING AT EVERY LEVEL

Similarly, in athletics, women's smallness is often prioritized over health—and, head-scratchingly, even over performance. In 2019, Mary Cain, once one of the fastest young women in history, shared that the coaching staff in the now-defunct Nike Oregon Project pressured her thinness to the point that she cut herself and contemplated suicide. She reportedly lost her period for three years, broke five bones, and suffered from increasingly worse times in her races.

"I got caught in a system designed by and for men which destroys the bodies of young girls," she says in her viral op-ed. She explains that her training staff expected her five-foot, seven-inch frame to weigh a medically underweight 114 pounds, with her coaches weighing her publicly in front of her competitors, and admonishing her when she didn't make weight.[347] Her body wasn't allowed the space it needed and deserved. And without that space, it couldn't thrive.

Meanwhile, countless other world-class athletes struggle to reconcile their strength and femininity. "I like the way I feel when I get some muscle... but yet, in the back of my mind, I get scared that I'm gonna get big... I get scared of looking too much like a guy, like having too much muscle," said one softball player in a study titled *Living the paradox: Female athletes negotiate femininity and muscularity*. Other studies show that while female athletes are proud of their bodies and feel good when they're strong, they also fear increasing in size. Researchers conclude that "sportswomen develop two identities—athlete and woman." [348]

That sounds like a pretty spot-on observation, especially when you read what coach Tomasz Wiktorowski had to say to *The New York Times* several years ago about former tennis player Agnieszka Radwanska, who was then listed at five feet, eight inches and 123 pounds. "It's our decision to keep her as the smallest player in the top 10," he said. "Because, first of all she's a woman, and she wants to be a woman."[349]

So, if she weren't the smallest female player on the court, would she cease being a woman?

related muscle loss that affects one in three adults ages 60 and older—contributes to fat gain, low mobility and function, and early death.[76, 77] Without regular, intentional exercise, the process of strength and muscle loss can start in women as early as their 20s and 30s.

The potential mental and emotional benefits of building strength are just as great. For women, being able to take both athletic and everyday feats of strength in stride nurtures a greater sense of self-confidence and self-efficacy in all areas of life. As is shown in research, higher levels of strength correlate with better cognitive function and mental health. [78, 79, 80]

Unfortunately, the majority of women have been taught that strength isn't for them, that it's for men. One study that examined the first 200 Google Image search results for "burn fat" and "build muscle" tells how tightly the two fitness pursuits are tied to gender. As you might guess, women are more likely than men to show up in "burn fat" searches. And when searching "build muscle," men appeared 10-plus times more often in Google Image results than women did. 75% of the "build muscle" image results depicted only men, and a mere 7% depicted only women.[81]

One troubling reason: A lot of women actually don't think they *need* to be strong, according to one study. In it, women commonly said they were afraid of lifting too much weight and becoming bulky (a concern you've likely heard or even voiced before). Some women talked about starting weight training, feeling like they were gaining better function in everyday life, and then stopping because they started to get "too big."[82]

Many women actively fear going up a pants size, even if it's because they're packing on muscle to help them run faster, take the stairs without getting winded, and even lengthen their life spans. This mindset—that moving through life with greater ease isn't worth the risk of any increased size—is more than troublesome. It's disturbing.

Within the last decade, a lot of well-meaning fitness professionals have encouraged women to get into resistance exercise by assuring them that no, "Strength training won't make you bulky." They coach their dumbbell classes with promises of long, lean muscles. On Instagram, they post videos of slim celebrities lifting big weights and pushing heavy sleds. "See, strength training will make you skinny!" Many trainers say women can't build muscle as effectively as men can.

But here's the truth: It takes a lot of time, effort, goal-specific training, and even a caloric surplus (gasp!) to really Hulk out. That's the case regardless of biological sex. And when using the same training program, women can increase their bodies' muscle mass percentages just as well as men can.[83] It's just that women, on average, have smaller starting levels of muscle mass: In absolute terms, a 10% gain on 20-inch biceps is always going to be greater than a 10% gain on 12-inch arms.

Even more important to emphasize the fact that, *it's okay for women to want to build bulk!*

"Toned" doesn't have to be the glass ceiling of strength. And, because it's big a pet peeve of ours, we're going take it down here and now. Muscle tone has nothing to do with muscle shape or size; it refers to muscles' levels of resting tension.

What the fitness industry peddles as "toning up" is just a sexist synonym for muscular hypertrophy, the exact same muscle growth that makes bodybuilders huge. With so-called "toning," women work toward fat loss as they build muscle. After all, if you also lose fat, you'll be able to see your muscles without adding inches to your frame. You become more compact, and, for ladies, that's allowed.

Everything about what the fitness field promotes as the ideal feminine body is similarly contradictory. Terms such as "firm but shapely," "fit but sexy," and "strong but thin" illustrate how for women, everything comes with a giant "but."[84] Basically, strength and muscle are cool on women as long as their bodies are still small—or even smaller than they were before picking up a weight. And still, that pairing is tenuous.

MALE TERRITORY

Understandably, many women perceive that there's some sort of masculine monopoly on strength. Unfortunately, that belief is really good at intimidating women out of traditionally male-dominated spaces. For example, in co-ed obstacle-course races, women are often the minority. Mixed martial arts disproportionately attract male practitioners, and the weight room... ha!

In the gym, it's telling that many women call the stretching space the "girls'" area and the weight room the "boys'" area. In the squat rack or on a weight bench, a woman can easily feel like an imposter, alone and on display. While research shows that women are less comfortable in any part of the gym compared to men, they're especially so when using free weights and weight machines.[85]

That discomfort is at its highest when women are just starting strength training, most likely surrounded by guys who've been lifting weights since they were in their teens. (Rhetorical question: Why aren't women taught this stuff!?!) Plus, as we just mentioned, men have greater *starting* levels of muscle.

Imagine one possible resulting scenario: A woman walks into the weight room, new to lifting. She starts doing squats with a 20-pound dumbbell. She looks around, and sees men squatting—or even bench pressing—bars with multiple 45-pound weight plates on the ends. Remember how we love social comparisons and hate things that we don't think we're good at?

Research shows that evaluation concerns—worrying that we'll be or are being judged—dominate our strength workouts.[86] We think: *Am I making a fool of myself? What if I fumble with the weights? These guys have to be judging me. I don't belong here.*

This makes for an extremely crummy, disempowering experience. For some women, it simply doesn't feel worth it. They understandably prefer to stay in their comfort zone. A survey conducted by Fitrated.com found that 64.9% of the 1,000 women surveyed had avoided a gym due to anxiety or fear of judgment.[87]

Some women continue to strength train. Some enter the weight room only to grab a set of dumbbells and take them to the stretching area where women feel they fit in. It's not uncommon for women to change their gym memberships or go the gym during certain hours to avoid specific men. Others join female-only gyms or work out at home, in hiding.

These can feel like necessary steps to protect ourselves emotionally or even physically. Sometimes they don't just feel necessary; they are. No matter where you are or what you're doing, your safety deserves to be your number-one priority.

However, shrinking back from male spaces also reaffirms to both men and women that we don't belong. When we enter the weight room and find that we're the only woman in it, of course we feel out of place! Maybe we even wonder if strength isn't for women. Maybe only smallness is.

EXERCISE AS PUNISHMENT

Our internal dialogue can be brutal in an infinite number of ways. Our most vicious trains of thought often revolve around imagined crimes and self-induced punishments.

"I've been bad lately. I should get to the gym."

"If I ate this donut, how long would I need to run?"

"I'm fat. I need to work off this weight."

"No pain, no gain."

Heck, we even say a lot of these messages to others! After all, they're already littered across boutique workout studios, fitness articles, and social media. They're so pervasive that often, we don't notice them all that much.

However, statements like these both reflect and reinforce the belief that exercise is a form of punishment, atonement, or way to afford food, celebratory dinners, rest, "lazy" days spent on the couch with a good book, and everyday pleasures. *Exercise makes our bodies a little less gross and us a little more worthy.*

This attitude toward exercise—and more generally, movement—takes something that should nurture and fuel our bodies and uses it to put them down. It sucks all the joy from activity.

Remember when swinging on monkey bars, climbing ladders, and crawling through tunnels was fun? Remember how good it felt to run so fast you thought your legs might fall off?

That was back before push-ups and horribly named "suicides" were used as a form of punishment in gym class. It was before websites told us what we'd have to do to "work off" different foods... before trainers told us that for a workout to be beneficial, it must reduce us to quivering piles of near-vomiting sweat. And the next day, we better be sore.

It's sad how much the equivalency of pain and gain has permeated female consciousness. Often, when women come to Aleisha wanting to start a training program, they talk about how their past workouts have left them nauseated the rest of the day or limping in agony for a week.

They hate the pain, but admit they're reluctant to believe that, without it, they can reach their fitness, body-composition, and aesthetic goals.

Let's say this loud and clear:

> *Treating exercise as punishment is*
> *emotionally and physically abusive.*

It damages our body images, mental health, and relationships with both exercise and food. It inflicts pain—pain to which we'd never subject a loved one.

In both the short and long term, it has the potential to cause grave physiological harm. In fact, women's pursuit of pain has gotten so intense that emergency rooms are reporting a disturbing trend: cycling-class rhabdo.

Rhabdomyolysis is a potentially life-threatening syndrome in which muscle damage is so severe that proteins from within the ruptured cells flood the bloodstream and can cause kidney failure.[88] Women are increasingly pushing themselves so hard in cycling classes that they're putting their lives at risk.

While quality exercise isn't always going to be easy, there's a difference between putting in work and pushing ourselves to, or even chasing, pain. There's a difference between using the gym to challenge ourselves and to atone for our bodies or actions. Treating exercise as punishment has absolutely zero beneficial effects.

THE RESULTS ARE IN

Together, these factors do a superb job of keeping us from enjoying movement. It creates a toxic relationship between a body and its natural ability to move, flex, stretch, and bend. It's a primary factor in keeping us women from achieving our fitness goals.

The relationship plays out in two main, completely opposite ways:

1. Avoiding or having trouble maintaining a regular exercise habit

2. Excessively or compulsively exercising

AVERSION TO EXERCISE

When people exercise out of a feeling of obligation or "having to," they're unlikely to stick with their routines for very long.[89] Behavioral psychologists call these "shoulds" extrinsic motivators. They're rooted in external factors and, although these can sometimes prod people into action, they have little staying power. Eventually, external, extrinsic motivation gives way to internal, intrinsic motivation—the most intrinsic motivator being enjoyment. We do what we want.

Many women enter into exercise from a position that's as far as it can be from pure, intrinsic enjoyment. They hate it. So, spoiler alert: They don't stick with it very long, and become really adept at coming up with reasons they just can't or don't have time to work out. We all have legit time limitations, but more often than not, what we say is keeping us from the gym is just a front for a bad relationship with exercise.

Moreover, some women don't just avoid the gym, workout classes, and structured exercise; they avoid all movement. When women's experiences with exercise are coupled with feelings of un-enjoyment, hate, unhappiness, and suffering, some women begin to associate even routine movement—walking from the car into the supermarket, taking stretch or movement breaks at work—with drudgery.

Many have never even thought of going on a walk just for fun.

EXCESSIVE EXERCISE

On the opposite end of the spectrum, this ever-burning, crime-and-punishment mentality can keep some of us constantly churning our wheels. There are always more calories to burn and meals, snacks, and desserts to negate!

Excessive and obsessive exercise aren't healthy in any way. They can close us off from the world outside the gym, keeping us from meaningful life experiences. When women become fixated on exercise, they regularly skip social events in order to get in their workouts, worry on vacation about the exercise they're missing, or drop once-fulfilling hobbies to devote every non-working moment to their fitness pursuits.

They may exercise every day or almost every day, ignoring the body's physiological need for recovery, and increasing their risk of stress fractures and overuse injuries. At minimum, they continually get less and less from their workouts as their bodies fail to recover.

Up to 5% of all women and 69% of female athletes lose their periods, in part, because of excessive training.[90] Some develop Relative Energy Deficiency in Sports (RED-S) syndrome.[91] This medical condition involves inadequate energy intake, secondary amenorrhea (absent menstrual periods), and low bone density. Consequences range from osteoporosis and injuries to cardiovascular, mental-health, and immune-system impairment. RED-S is typically a result of excessive exercise, low-calorie diets, and an unhealthily low body-fat percentages.

Remember, though, that what the average woman thinks of as the "ideal" body is clinically underweight, so this medical condition overlaps with some women's current goals.[92]

CHAPTER 3
RUNNING FROM EMOTIONS

Many of us identify emotional eating as blocking our weight-loss progress. It's a stumbling block we trip over again and again and again. However, other than "stop," experts rarely address what we should do about this situation.

In fact, many of us fear that being emotional eaters can't be changed and it's just the way we are. Thankfully, that frightening thought is simply untrue.

While our individual differences in mental health and mood inclination can be linked with genetics, all of our emotional experiences (including using food to modify how we feel) are the result of our mental processes. That means we aren't stuck with our emotional processing in the same way we're genetically programmed for a given hair and eye color (hair dye and contact lenses aside).

Coping with emotions in healthy, productive ways is a set of skills; it's learnable and changeable. We can change the way we process feelings, and end emotional eating. We can learn how to lift ourselves when we're down, stay calm when our emotions are intensifying, and take action despite anxiety or fear.

It's not your fault if no one taught you these skills as a youngster, modeled them throughout your formative years, or reminds you as an adult to tap into them when life feels brutally hard. We're going to teach you how in this chapter, and we promise it's never too late to learn.

WHAT EMOTIONAL REGULATION SKILLS?

Emotional regulation skills are the behaviors and strategies we use to manage, inhibit, or enhance our emotional experiences.[93] We can perform them consciously and unconsciously. They come in two varieties: **adaptive** (helpful for adjusting to the world and thriving) and **maladaptive** (more harmful than helpful). For optimal well-being, we want to have a wide variety of adaptive emotional regulation skills and regularly use them over less-effective, maladaptive ones.

When young, we form many of our emotional regulation skills as we interact with our parents or caregivers. If all goes well, we observe adults managing their emotions in healthy ways, such as talking about their feelings or heading outside for a walk to improve a low mood. In turn, we learn to use these adaptive emotional regulation skills for ourselves. Sometimes we fine-tune them later in life, as a result of working with a mental health professional or even through books.

However, not all of us learn healthy emotional regulation skills as children, or even well into adulthood. Our parents might not have spent enough time with us to imprint their emotional regulation skills on us, or they might have not possessed adaptive skills themselves. The type of bond we have with our main caregivers can also impact how we learn to manage our emotions.[94]

If no one teaches us adaptive emotional regulation skills, our normal day-to-day feelings can become painful, confusing obstacles. In the face of suffering, it's natural and understandable that we'll do just about anything to cope. This can lead to maladaptive behaviors, such as avoiding experiences or emotions, abusing drugs or alcohol, or turning to food for comfort.

We can also learn maladaptive behaviors from observing our role models perform them. For example, we might have frequently seen our moms hide in bed with food. We might have grown up placating a parent's substance abuse issues to avoide outbursts or violence. These maladaptive behaviors aren't good for us or for the people we love. But good people can develop them as a natural way to solve the problem of emotional pain and survive.

Given the option, none of us would choose to have maladaptive behaviors. We're all doing the best we can with what we have.

HOW DEFICITS IN EMOTIONAL REGULATION DING OUR HEALTH

Limitations in adaptive emotional regulation are linked to mental health problems including anxiety, depression, disordered eating, and substance abuse.[95, 96] This may be because emotional regulation ability affects how well we recover from what happens to us. For example, after negative experiences such as maltreatment or a traumatizing event, a person with better-developed emotional regulation skills may be able to heal and cope to a greater extent, whereas a person with fewer resources may experience more long-term psychological effects.

Emotional regulation abilities not only impact mental health, but also influence physical wellness. The combination of stress and ineffective emotional regulation produces abnormal cortisol levels, and is linked to unhealthy lifestyle behaviors including emotional eating, a sedentary lifestyle, reduction of physical activity, lower fruit and vegetable intake, and sleep problems.[97, 98]

When our mental wellness suffers, the hormonal signature of uncontrolled stress impacts our bodies, and our other healthy lifestyle behaviors typically take a hit.

You may have experienced some of these effects yourself. Recurring worries can banish a good night's sleep, elevate blood pressure, and worsen digestive ailments. Feeling overwhelmed by stress, suffocated with anxiety, or deflated by hopelessness can make it all but impossible to go to the gym. After a devastating day, few of us are up to getting groceries or cooking dinner.

And practically everyone has had a friendship or romantic relationship strained when someone shuts down in the face of conflict or isn't able to communicate how they feel or what they want.

All of these effects negatively impact our long-term health.

THE TIES BETWEEN
EMOTIONAL REGULATION AND EATING BEHAVIORS

Not everyone who lacks emotional regulation skills goes on to develop an eating disorder, and not everyone with an eating disorder has difficulty regulating emotions. Still, a 2019 meta-analysis of 96 studies found a consistent link between deficits in emotional regulation abilities and eating problems, including eating disorders.[99] In fact, in a 2016 study, patients undergoing treatment for eating disorders had greater problems regulating emotions than did patients undergoing treatment for other psychiatric illnesses:

> *"Patients with EDs [eating disorders] demonstrated significantly more difficulty in terms of their overall ability to regulate emotions, their ability to accept emotional responses, their ability to accomplish goals in the midst of emotional states, their ability to attend to and acknowledge the significance of emotions, and their ability to influence emotional states."[100]*

Ample evidence shows that emotional dysregulation plays a pivotal role in binge eating, in which people eat large amounts of food and feel unable to stop.[101, 102] Binge eating is tightly linked with obesity, and is the most common eating disorder, making it a research topic of prime importance.[103, 104]

Escape theory asserts that binge eating is primarily a way to flee self-awareness.[105] Self-awareness occurs when we turn our attention to ourselves. Automatically, we compare our current selves to our ideals, or what we want ourselves to be. As you can imagine, a painful gap can exist between reality and what we want.

What do we do with this discomfort? There are three potential responses: We might change our ideal, so that the current version of ourselves isn't so far off. We might work on changing ourselves to move closer to our desired state. Lastly, we might flee from the painful self-awareness altogether, turning away from or blocking those thoughts. Escape theory proposes that binge eating is a manifestation of the third option; people binge eat to avoid thinking about themselves, and for a short while, escape pain.[106]

A framework known as the affect regulation model explains things slightly differently, positing that people binge eat to change their mood (*affect* is another word for mood).[107] The affect regulation model is broader than escape theory. It encompasses binge eating that results from sadness, loss, frustration, anger, overwhelm, loneliness, anxiety, or other uncomfortable feelings—not specifically self-awareness.

This model doesn't contradict escape theory, so both coexist. As far as both theories are concerned, overeating and binge eating serve as a maladaptive emotional regulation strategies. Even if a woman doesn't think her food habits fit the definition of a binge, difficulty dealing with emotions contributes to weight gain and obesity through a more common behavior: emotional eating.[108]

Emotional eating is defined as using food to cope with negative emotions. It fits perfectly in that affect regulation model we just mentioned. Emotional eating is closely related to binge eating, and the same factors fuel both habits.

Emotional eating is incredibly prevalent. Think about it: Consuming more food than we usually do or eating unhealthy foods when we feel sad, mad, or disappointed is so commonplace that the modern woman perceives it as normal.

While occasionally using food to impact our emotions is harmless, high levels of emotional eating can lead to uncontrollable weight gain. Patients seeking weight-loss surgery report high levels of emotional eating, and even after undergoing major life-changing procedures to facilitate weight loss, they don't just stop emotional eating. They typically cut back for the first 12 months following surgery, and then slowly but surely resume emotional eating.[109] It's a habit people can't just stop through pure desire, dedication, or willpower.

Fittingly, mounting evidence shows that emotional skill development is a crucial part of successfully addressing both binging and emotional eating.[110] When they don't include emotional skill development, treatment methods and programs such as behavioral weight-loss counseling, diet programs, cognitive therapy, and medication are ineffective for many women. Some women feel better for a short time and relapse when life gets hard.[111, 112]

Sadly, few weight-management programs and experts integrate emotional regulation skills into their treatment approaches, opting instead to focus on food, food, and food. Many womens' personal histories include receiving food directions, recipes, diet programs, and eating advice ad nauseam—and no direction on how to skillfully deal with your feelings.

Using food to manage emotions also creates problems that reach beyond excessive caloric intake. Relying on eating as a standalone coping mechanism prevents us from using healthier, more effective adaptive strategies. We become likely to forego exercising when we're feeling blue, and choose instead to stay home with a pint of ice cream. It's easier, it's faster, and we don't have to get sweaty.

This creates a cycle of being unhappy, seeking comfort in food, and feeling stuffed—again and again. With each cycle, it becomes more of a habit—more automatic—and we get less practice with other options. Because of disuse, we lose what adaptive emotional regulation skills we once had. Our friendships can fade and become distant, instead of strengthening as they can when we share our tough times with pals.

Perhaps scariest of all, the people we love watch us, and we cannot avoid our impact on their behaviors. Imagine a preteen daughter responding to a tough day at school. She thinks, *When mom's sad, she gets a tub of ice cream. Might as well give it a shot.*

Sadly, eating isn't even very effective as a coping mechanism. Almost universally, episodes of intensely negative moods follow binge eating and emotional eating. While eating causes an immediate, short-term bump in feel-good neurochemicals, as soon as the eating ends, a steep drop occurs.[113] Acording to a 2011 meta-analysis of 36 studies, after a binge, people actually feel considerably *worse* than they do immediately before.[114]

> Difficulty is not a sign we're doing anything wrong.
> It's a sign we're alive.

Binge eating consistently makes women feel worse, but they keep on doing it in a bid to feel better... how does that work? This seeming contradiction comes down to recall bias, a fancy term for the human tendency to remember things inaccurately or to omit details of past experiences.

For example, in interviews, women say that binge eating gives them relief from negative feelings and thoughts. However, when researchers capture data on people's moods before, during, and after binges, it's apparent that any emotional relief binging provides is slight, brief, and immediately replaced by guilt and shame as awareness returns.[115] Women tend to forget the negatives, leading them to believe that food was more effective than it really was, and look to food for future comfort.

SUPPRESSING EMOTIONS

Another way we commonly deal with unwanted emotions is by suppressing them. Emotional suppression is an attempt to control a feeling by simply not acknowledging it.[116] All emotional regulation strategies get easier the more we engage in them, which, in this case, might not be in our favor.

Once emotional suppression has become automatic, we may not even notice ourselves doing it.

Here are some examples of ways we suppress or avoid emotions:

- Saying, "Nothing's wrong; I'm fine" when we're actually upset
- Working long hours when things are difficult at home
- Pretending to like someone or something we don't, or pretending to not like something we really do
- Fake smiling
- Avoiding our past errors and mistakes
- Not objecting when someone says something we disagree with or feel offended by
- "Keeping our mind off things" with the Internet, gaming, TV, shopping, etc., without purposely addressing our feelings at other times
- Not voicing our ideas or making suggestions at home or at work
- Coming up with reasons to not feel angry at someone who hurt us

As you can see, these are all things that are exceedingly common. They're things *we all do* some of the time. And in some circumstances, suppressing an emotion—like not laughing at a funeral or choosing to remain composed when a client pushes our buttons—is a wise idea. However, the more we suppress our feelings, fighting to contain a wider swath of our emotional selves, the worse it is for us and those around us. Don't buy into the "good vibes only" mantra, okay?

How is emotional suppression maladaptive? What's its harm? Suppressing feelings consistently results in negative outcomes such as decreased mental and physical health.[117] Emotional suppression impedes goal attainment. We encounter depressed moods, more fatigue, lower self-esteem, and less life satisfaction. We exert less effort toward our goals, feel less support from others, and have less success.[118]

Given all the negative outcomes, it's puzzling why we so often suppress our emotions. The shortest explanation may be because it seems normal, or because we believe it serves social purposes, such as improving our likeability.[119] Not surprisingly, we most often use emotional suppression when we're around other people, particularly when we want to get along with them.[120]

The irony is that we practice emotional suppression to enhance our relationships, but in reality, it poisons them.[121] Emotional suppression results in feeling less acceptance and warmth from others and less satisfaction in our relationships.[122, 123] Instead of making us feel supported, it makes us feel disconnected.[124]

Emotional suppression predicts loneliness, which some experts are calling a public health crisis for its link to heart disease, suicide, and early death.[125] Much like emotional eating actually leaves us feeling worse, keeping our feelings inside to come across as more likable make us lonely.

Life experiences have tacitly discouraged and sidetracked us from learning how to properly express and deal with emotions.

When, as children, we became upset, our parents may have told us to "stop crying" or "be quiet," rather than treating our emotions as meaningful. And let's not forget that parenting is a tough job! Mothers and fathers can become flustered and upset at their children for being, well, childish. Even toddlers can pick up that their crying is making someone either yell at or walk away from them. Receiving the message that our feelings are unimportant or aversive to others, especially if that message is never counteracted with emotional encouragement, paves the way to actively hiding our feelings.

Social interactions outside the home can further dissuade us from being emotionally forthcoming as adults. Internalized labels of being "too much" or "too emotional" encourage us to bear our struggles privately and reject opportunities to freely communicate.

Gender norms—unspoken rules that communicate what personality traits are desirable or acceptable based on gender—call for women to be agreeable, concerned with attractiveness, caring toward others, sexually reserved, and generally pleasant.

Expressing our disagreement with someone in the office, even in the most professional manner, is likely to get us labeled "a bitch." Indicating our needs when they inconvenience others often results in people thinking we're selfish. For women, being outspoken is commonly seen as a flaw that increases the challenges of attracting a mate, a concern that's supposed to be among a woman's most important goals. (Men battle their own toxic societal expectations, too, learning to suppress "feminine" emotions and encountering their own health risks as a result.)

Even if when, as children, we felt intense emotions, we cried freely and ran to our parents' encouraging arms, by our early 20s, we learned not to let our feelings be so plainly seen.[126] Instead, when we experience emotional pain or anger, many of us find ourselves keeping it all in. We post a smiling photo on Facebook and head for the pantry to silently eat cookies in an attempt to quell normal human feelings. We consider letting our spouses know they hurt our feelings, then decide there's no use in that. We disagree with a new friend's statement that, "Some people shouldn't wear shorts that short," but smile anyway.

THE FITNESS AND FOOD INDUSTRIES AREN'T HELPING

It's a common saying in psychology that food is one of the least effective but most commonly used antidepressants, while movement is the most effective antidepressant, and far too rarely used.

In fact, while physical activity offers a promising strategy for mood regulation and emotional well-being, marketing and society as a whole keep us from reaping those benefits by framing activity as a thing we do only for physical reasons.

Girls learn from an early age that exercise is primarily a way to improve appearance and pursue smallness.[127, 128] As we discussed in the previous chapter, perceiving physical activity as an obligation to fix appearance or undo caloric intake can leach all the joy out of the process, leaving us less consistently motivated to move.

On the flip side, the food industry directly benefits from a society in which we use eating to manage emotions. It sells more snack foods, more ice cream, more chips, and more chocolate if we turn to these "treats" to help us cope with unwanted emotions. Naturally, it exploits our emotional vulnerabilities in subtle ways, especially when it comes to low-nutrition, high-pleasure foods.

Here's a perfect example: ice cream. A Mega Ice Cream Facebook post from January 2020 states, "Vanilla ice cream is duct tape for the heart."[129] An Ambassador's Ice Cream post dated August

2019 reads, "You deserve a treat for surviving this week! Reward yourself with our guilt-free vegan ice cream."[130] Perry's Ice Cream has a flavor called Bad Breakup, playing on the cultural motif of women eating ice cream after breakups.

Ben & Jerry's has a blog post on their website titled "6 Times Ben & Jerry's Has Been There For You" that shows a tub of Phish Food (a flavor of ice cream) along with crumpled tissues, and a teary woman crying into one.[131] The text reads "When the rain starts to fall, like it's been there before, Phish Food will be there for you. Cuddle up and let off some steam... it's a great listener."

While companies certainly intend for such ads to be humorous, they still perpetuate the association between having a bad day and eating ice cream. As a result, when we think of bad days, we automatically think of, and crave, ice cream.

Other industries also benefit from us choosing to buy things when we feel bad. Clothes, jewelry, makeup: The countless number of advertisements we see in a week has a significant impact on our emotional regulation strategies.

Every advertisement is certainly not going to cause harm to every woman who views it. (And we also love ice cream!) But for a woman who lacks social support or has uncertainty over what to do with her emotions, the ubiquitous nature of these messages can further reinforce emotional eating habits while downplaying its adverse consequences.

A SOURCE OF NEGATIVE FEELINGS: SELF-DEFEATING BELIEFS

We all experience negative moods from time to time, as a natural consequence of existing in the world. We'll be disappointed and unhappily surprised at times. We'll be treated unfairly. We'll lose things, break things, contract illnesses, and encounter endless difficult situations and people.

The amount of negative emotions we endure as a result isn't fixed. Rather, core beliefs influence how we process everything that happens to us, especially how we personally fit into it all.[132]

Core beliefs—also called schemas—are deeply held ideas about ourselves, others, and the world; we tend to see them as absolute and universally valid.[133] We can learn them in the context of our childhoods. Rational and healthy core beliefs can mean that we suffer less as a result of life's adversities, while self-defeating core beliefs can cause us undue burden and suffering. Having maladaptive beliefs is linked to automatic negative thinking patterns, and causes greater distress in the wake of trauma.[134, 135, 136]

Sounds pretty rough. So, what are these beliefs that make life so much harder? Self-defeating beliefs often manifest in perfectionism, absolutist thinking (also called "black-or-white thinking"), and the imperative need to please everyone all the time. They can take the form of scripts for how we "should" be, or how life is "supposed" to work. Unrealistic expectations for ourselves are common maladaptive beliefs.

Here are some common self-defeating themes, along with examples of how they pop up in our lives.

- **Perfectionism:** If I can't do something perfectly, I'm not happy. It's completely right or it's useless garbage. When I make a mistake, I'm horrified.

- **Needing Universal Approval:** If anyone is upset with me, ever, I'm highly distressed. I need to be liked. I need to make people happy.

- **Invariability:** I should be in a good mood every day. I am supposed to have the same high-level energy and productivity every day. I must always be better than I was before, never worse.

- **Proper Conduct:** Don't speak highly of yourself—it's bragging. A normal life means getting married and having children. Only weak people ask for help.

- **Beliefs about Ourselves:** I have no self-control. I have a flawed personality. I'm lazy. I'm a quitter.

- **The Way The World Should Be:** There's a right and a wrong way to do things. Things ought to be fair. We get what we deserve in life.

- **Universal Values:** A woman should always put time and energy into looking her best. Everyone ought to prioritize exercise and being fit. No one should spend money on fancy cars.

- **Need for Achievement:** I need to do great things to be a good person. I'm not valuable unless I accomplish something today. I haven't accomplished enough.

As you read through these, you can probably already tell that such beliefs are unhelpful, at least in most situations. They stress us out. They make us perpetually unsatisfied. They can take away our freedom to decide how we want to live our lives. They cause guilt. They make us feel like we aren't good enough.

It's not hard to find ways that the diet field has encouraged these self-defeating beliefs; body dissatisfaction lies at the root of the industry's survival.

Perfectionism fuels the design (and collapse) of most meal plans and diets. Perfectionism keeps women in the weight-loss market even when they already inhabit perfectly healthy bodies. (There's always something that could be more perfect.) It can also cause analysis-paralysis, and justifies buying more diet and exercise programs because the previous one wasn't quite perfect.

The need for achievement causes us to train hard when we're better off resting. Hunger for constant approval nudges us to post fitness stats on social media, and possibly causing our friends to feel the sting of their own need for achievement.

And if the whole process of micromanaging your food or killing yourself at the gym causes you to feel unwell—physically or psychologically—self-defeating beliefs about seeking help being a weakness prevent millions of people from consulting a professional when a professional's support is exactly what they need.

Meanwhile, beliefs concerning proper conduct often hold women back from exploring all the options the world has for them. "Women of my size can't _____" is a common example. So is "Where I come from (or in my family), everyone _____." Think about it: How often have you sat out on the fun, restricted your fashion or career options, limited your intimacy, or not explored a type of movement because it didn't seem "proper" or like what the world would accept of you?

In future chapters, you'll probably encounter many ideas that challenge your existing self-defeating beliefs. That's a good thing. You don't have to keep your old beliefs. You also don't have to adopt the alternatives we offer. What you do is completely up to you.

We hope you choose to let go of unhelpful ideas, welcome new concepts that resonate, and retain beliefs that strengthen and empower you.

CHAPTER 4
CUTTING CALORIES,
MACROS, AND FOOD GROUPS

If there's one way the weight-loss industry has overwhelmingly convinced women to pursue LESS, it's with diets. The field's take on weight loss bears little semblance to reality.

It's like a game of "telephone." One person whispers a message to the next person, and over the chain of a dozen or so whispers, the original message becomes drastically, ridiculously different. The biological truths that presumably started the diet game of telephone probably started like this:

"Fat tissue is a form of excess energy storage. When we consume less energy than we're burning, these stores shrink."

But, over time, millions of whispers have oversimplified and distorted that message into false, misleading, and sometimes dangerous translations. And the chain of whispers isn't just one long line of people passing messages; it's branched and forked, with people listening in on others' conversations, everybody hearing simultaneous and conflicting messages, and some people speaking to thousands or millions of people at once.

Most of the messages we now hear sound very different from the original facts, having been shaped into things that sound better, faster, and simpler. We get sound bites like "500 calories per day and HCG shots," "no carbs," "cut out the grains," "1,200 calories are enough," "just don't eat for 18 hours per day."

It's all about less, less, less.

And going wholeheartedly for less, less, less gets us… very little. A focus on cutting calories, macros, and entire food groups neglects the fact that *entire people* are involved. People are not as simple as calories-in, calories-out systems. We have thoughts and preferences, nutrient needs, flavor desires, and hair we'd like to not fall out, thank you very much. And focusing on restriction forgets to take all of this into account to our mental and physical detriment.

ARE ANY FOODS OKAY TO EAT ANYMORE?

The more we're exposed to articles and headlines from the diet industry and pseudoscienctific health gurus, the more we can get the feeling that no foods are safe. Warnings abound about pesticides in fruit and vegetables, lectins in beans, hormones in meat and milk, mercury in fish, gluten in wheat, and arsenic in rice. Fear-mongering headlines caution that genetically modified corn or soy processed foods and palm oil are dangerous. It's enough to make us afraid to eat at all!

Orthorexia nervosa is a new, scarily common condition characterized by an unhealthy obsession with healthy eating.[137] Often, women who develop orthorexia began, as so many of us do, limiting their diets to improve their health. However, as they adopt more and more food restrictions, physical and mental health suffers. Malnutrition results, as well as mood and social problems such as anxiety, obsessive thinking, and social isolation.

The meteoric rise of this "new" disorder should make us reconsider the way the world talks about nutrition. Over the last 20 years, most diets, articles, and books pertaining to "nutrition" have become more concerned with what we *aren't* eating than the actual nutrients we're providing our bodies. This landscape of alarm not only leads to orthorexia, but also to generalized confusion and worry.

An unfortunate consequence of this gloomy food environment is that it can be used as a reason to reject all nutrition advice—even common-sense guidelines. After all, if legumes and yogurt are going to kill us, why not just eat donuts? (FYI, Aleisha loves donuts. She also loves legumes and yogurt.)

At its most basic, food nourishes. It fuels. It provides the raw materials from which we build bones, organs, and every cell of our bodies. We need to obtain enough essential vitamins, minerals, energy, fiber, fatty acids, and amino acids from our diets to have good health. However, even in a society plagued by excess food consumption, many people would benefit from getting more nutrients from their food. With all our focus on nutrient-deficient foods, we've fallen into another trap of LESS, shortchanging ourselves on the health-promoting nutrients.

A CLOSER LOOK AT HOW OUR BODIES ACTUALLY "DETOX"

We'd like to remind you not to fall for claims that any food helps you "detox," and please don't buy into any type of cleanse. Those two words should send you running. Claims used in the marketing of detoxes and cleanses often revolve around the idea that your body is chock-full of dangerous substances that you need to clean out... with their product, of course.

The truth? Your kidneys, liver, respiratory system, and other organs are helping you break down and excrete waste products and harmful compounds from your body 24/7. Your body has a multitude of pathways to break down waste products and harmful chemicals we encounter in our environment. Our bodies even continually monitor our DNA and repair it if it becomes damaged, for example, by ultraviolet light.[138] (Argh, we forgot sunscreen, again!)

The techniques and products sold as detox regimens don't en-hance these capabilities whatsoever. They don't cleanse your blood in any way; your body is already constantly filtering it. They don't nourish your cells in any way; the foods you eat and the oxygen you breathe already do that. Your organs definitely don't need you to withhold food so they can reset. They have performed this self-cleaning operation for millennia and they're superb at it.

Want to see an expert in action? Look no further than your liver. Your liver is a superhero. Your liver is the Serena Williams of breaking down chemicals, able to handle just about anything in-coming, and it definitely doesn't need your help. You don't offer Serena Williams herbal tinctures to help her do her job better. You show respect, offer water, and stay out of her way.

Some unscientific health gurus make your body's naturally oc-curring compounds sound as scary as possible. You might read, "Formaldehyde, a chemical used in embalming fluid, is in every-one's body; you need a cleanse to get rid of it!" Or, "That juice product exposes you to methanol or wood alcohol! It's dangerous!"

But how much of that's actually true?

Many things that sound scary or dangerous are completely nor-mal to detect in low amounts in living things. Meanwhile, you've probably heard that water, salt, or essential nutrients like potas-sium can kill you if you have enough of them.

It's true, because the deadliness of any chemical—even ones that we consider healthy—depends on the dose. Formaldehyde is, in fact, carcinogenic at high levels.[139]

Our bodies actually produce formaldehyde in small amounts during normal metabolic reactions. When we eat methanol-containing produce, specialized enzymes turn the methanol into formaldehyde, then formic acid, which then becomes carbon dioxide and water. That's why it's present in everyone's bloodstream, not because environmental sources are silently killing us.[140] Now that's not so scary, is it?

Now, in large enough doses, methanol is poisonous too and can be fatal. Methanol poisoning causes nausea, abdominal pain and vomiting, central nervous system suppression, and damage to the kidneys and retinas.[141] Since small amounts of methanol occur in healthy foods like fruits, vegetables, and fruit juices,[142] does that mean we should avoid these foods, and share the memes so our families can also beware?

No. While drinking windshield wiper fluid is a terrible idea and can cause methanol poisoning, Internet warnings about apples, juice, or diet soda poisoning you with methanol are completely absurd and a bit humorous if we get out a calculator: It's estimated that for a 154-pound adult, a dose of 14.7 grams of methanol is enough to produce harmful effects.

Eating a kilogram (2.2 pounds) of apples produces 500 milligrams or one half of a gram of methanol.[143] Thus, to get methanol poisoning from apples, you'd need to eat 64.68 pounds of apples. We think you're going to be okay, even if you go a bit nuts during Honeycrisp season. A liter of fruit juice averages 140 milligrams per liter.[144] To ingest a toxic dose of methanol you'd need to drink 27.7 gallons of juice in a very short time period. The overload of fluids would kill you long before you'd get methanol poisoning.

What about sugar substitutes? According to the World Health Organization, one-tenth of aspartame is converted to methanol, so a packet of Equal sweetener produces 3.7 milligrams of methanol.[145] It would take 3,973 packets of Equal, all ingested at once, to give you methanol poisoning. So please, don't give someone dirty looks for putting two in her latte.

Looking at diet soda might be a more realistic illustration, since some people really do drink a lot of it. A human study found that consuming 4,800 milligrams of aspartame, the amount of aspartame contained in 2.25 gallons (9 liters) of diet soda over eight hours didn't produce a measurable increase in blood methanol or its metabolites.[146] That makes sense, since it would take 147 grams of aspartame to cause methanol poisoning, and 2.25 gallons of diet soda only amounts to 4.8 grams of aspartame.

The take-home message is that we aren't all walking sacks of consumed poisons. You don't need to detox yourself with herbal teas or celery juice, or take capsules to cleanse your body. Your body's already remarkably equipped to get rid of harmful chemicals as part of its everyday processes.

(Yes, people certainly can be poisoned by pollutants in the environment [such as exposures to paint dust, asbestos, or lead], or by consuming things that are adulterated [like homemade or bootleg alcohol]; if one of those things happens to you, see a doctor for treatment, not the supplement store.)

CRASH-AND-BURN DIETS

In today's sea of diet messaging, weight loss has become synonymous with deprivation and extreme restrictions. Given that high level of assumed unpleasantness, coupled with our desire for instant gratification, speed is a huge selling point for many weight-loss diets.

For example, consumers with high levels of urgency (and low levels of skepticism) can do the Military Diet, which claims they'll lose up to 10 pounds in a week.[147] The Five-Day Bikini Blitz Diet comes with promises of up to 14 pounds of weight loss in a single week.[148] And if those are too slow for you, Haylie Pomroy is happy to sell you her solution called "The Burn," which she describes as "an ingenious diet programme that offers dramatic physical transformations in as little as three days."[149]

Not to be outdone in the race for instant slimness, the Holly-wood 48-Hour Miracle Diet says you can shed 10 pounds in just two days. Part of the miracle, apparently, isn't eating any actual food, just drinking one-half cup of orange liquid five times per day for 48 hours.[150]

Many of these weeklong-or-less plans are centered on a set meal plan, which just lays it all out: On day one you eat this, on day two you eat this, and so forth. Sometimes it's simply the same menu every day. These often go (frighteningly) viral on social media. There's so little food involved that people can actually display an entire week's menu in a social-media-sized image. Other rapid weight-loss plans set a calorie limit such as 500 per day, or require you to pass on actual food in favor of special cookies, shakes, or juices, like in the previously mentioned Hollywood Diet.

Most women who embark on these sorts of quick-acting crash diets recognize that they're going to be short-lived. And they will be. Even the creators know this. When asked how the Five-Day Bikini Blitz Diet works, creator Zoë Harcombe explained, "It works because everyone can maintain something for a short period of time, like five days."[151]

She has a point. Natural forces to resist starvation kick in swiftly. If a diet's imposed caloric deficit, the difference between energy intake and energy expenditure, is sufficiently large to provide rapid weight loss (more than two pounds per week), the battle will start within hours.

It's a showdown: Dieter versus Appetite.

Within hours of beginning a crash diet, the hunger sets in. It doesn't matter how much water you drink, you're going to be hungry. Your energy will be low, and you're likely to feel colder than normal. You'll be hyperaware of what people around you are eating. Within days, sleep disruption, fatigue, headaches, and constipation join in, and sooner or later you'll quit. You can lose several pounds in the first week; however, most of those pounds come from water loss—and they come back just as quickly.

Such swings in body fluid are largely due to changes in the level of glycogen the body has stored. Glycogen is a carbohydrate molecule, and our bodies stockpile it in the liver and muscles for energy. With each gram of glycogen that our bodies store, they also store 2.7 grams of water.[152] Therefore, when we drastically reduce carbohydrate or calorie intake on a diet, we burn the glycogen, free up the stored water, and pee it out. Body weight returns to baseline once we resume normal eating.[153]

THE LIE OF "LIFESTYLE" DIETS

Other dieting methods make less extreme promises, and often bill themselves as "lifestyles" that women can easily follow forever. But as we'll see, that's rarely, if ever, a reality. But we'll come back to that.

Some of these diets allow a certain number of calories or "points" consumed. Depending on the size of the resulting deficit and the quality of the foods you do eat, you may experience a great deal of physical symptoms, such as hunger, fatigue, dizziness, hair loss, disrupted gut biome, digestive complaints, vitamin or mineral deficiencies, and immune-system suppression.[154, 155, 156]

But no matter the specifics of the diet, some costs are universal. It takes time and mental energy to count up the calories or points in a meal, and often the information isn't available, leaving the dieter to guess. Additionally, following most diets will be at odds with many of your established eating practices and social behaviors, forcing difficult decisions in order to follow the diet rules. "Can't go for drinks, I'm on a diet." "No fries with that, I'm on a diet."

If we avoid spending time with people to minimize our exposure to temptations, diets can negatively impact our social relationships. Being in a significant caloric deficit and the associated feelings of lethargy can make it hard to enjoy being physically active. These elements can add up to a significant toll on mental and emotional health.

Other diets focus on restricting what you're allowed to eat. They might involve lists of approved and non-approved foods. The big idea is that you eat from the "thumbs up" or "good" list and say no to foods on the "thumbs down" or "bad" list. Prohibited items typically include calorically dense, low-nutrition foods like cake, potato chips, ice cream, sugar-sweetened soda, and white bread. Commonly, nutritious foods are banned as well. For example, some diets forbid grains, dairy products, fruits, and beans.

Many diets offer a pseudoscientific rationale for these restrictions, but at their core, they're really just a means to cutting calories. So, yeah, if you regularly overeat pasta, cutting out grains will indirectly help you lose weight.

Or will it?

One of the key flaws in this diet design is its assumption that designating a list of banned foods will actually result in those foods becoming absent from women's food-choice landscapes.

That just doesn't happen. We know those foods still exist. We pass them in the grocery store, sit across from them at meetings, and read them listed on menus.

Over and over, the choice keeps presenting itself as a fork in the road. *What I want to do* sits on the left, and *follow the diet* sits on the right. We have to choose one or the other. Since the diet is an external entity—a faceless, impersonal concept we have agreed to follow—it feels like a drag. We want our authority back.

We know that all it takes to alleviate the stress is deciding not to follow the diet. And that's where it goes. At some point, we choose the path on the left, and go off the diet.

Depending on how long we lasted on the diet, we may have lost weight. We may return to the diet on and off for months or even years, typically with decreasing enthusiasm and adherence. If the diet was a temporary thing, our weight loss will also be temporary. Even after we find ourselves back at our starting weights, we may continue abnormal eating habits for months or years.[157]

With cycles of weight loss and regain, "fat overshooting" often occurs. Fat overshooting is the tendency to, after losing weight, gain it all back... and then some, leaving us with slightly more fat with each cycle of weight loss and regain.[158, 159]

Biologists observe that the mechanisms behind fat overshooting seem to be related to the differences in fat and lean tissue lost during a diet, as well as the differences in the rate of fat and muscle regained following a diet. During any weight loss, humans shed pounds from a combination of both fat and lean tissue (muscles and organs). These losses result in a slightly lower metabolism, as well as an increased appetite. Weight gain follows.

Since our bodies can gain fat at a much faster rate than they can put on muscle tissue, when the pounds creep back on, we first refill our fat stores. But even when we have regained all the fat we lost, our amped-up appetite and dialed-back metabolism (encouraging us to eat more and burn less) don't return to normal until we have also replenished all of our muscle tissue. This means that we keep gaining fat during the extra time it takes to restore our lean tissue to the original amount.

Interestingly, the ratio of fat-to-muscle tissue lost during a diet impacts how likely a person is to be affected by fat overshooting, and by how much. If, as you lose weight, you lose less muscle mass, you are less likely to regain weight or excess fat.

People beginning a weight-loss diet who are lean to begin with unfortunately lose a greater percentage of muscle, and thus are more likely to regain excess fat while replacing that muscle. Meanwhile, people with higher body-fat percentages at the beginning of a weight-loss diet lose a lower percentage of muscle mass, and are less prone to significant fat overshooting.[160]

In other words, strength training can help you maintain muscle mass and keep your results. However, trying to shed weight from an already-lean body might backfire.

PERMA-DIETING
(AKA RESTRAINED EATING ALL THE TIME)

We just looked at the fallout that results from a quick rendezvous with a rapid weight-loss diet, and the aftermath that occurs if a diet dalliance lasts for a period of weeks or months. The greatest peril, however, isn't from this type of on-and-off dieting, but what happens when a woman *internalizes* the diet's messages and mission.

This is where it gets downright scary.

Perma-dieting, also called restrained eating, refers to LESS-minded eating that becomes just the way we eat. In other words, if we become restrained eaters, we don't think about being "on a diet" because we constantly have our internal surveillance systems governing our food choices and behaviors. We're always concerned with how much we're eating, and every day we eat every meal with our background program running, reminding us, *don't eat too much*. Restrained eaters might count calories over the long term, or just try to police their fullness and food choices to avoid taking in too much or eating "fattening" foods.

There's been a great deal of research on so-called perma-dieting.[161] However, it's not correlated with reduced BMIs, indicating that putting forth a constant effort to control eating often has no actual efficacy on eating less.[162, 163]

THE PSYCHOLOGICAL FALLOUT

Restrained eaters show psychological differences from unrestrained eaters, including heightened emotions and ambivalence about food. Having strong emotions about food isn't necessarily a detriment; however, it can make everyday food decisions more difficult. Having a lot of emotional baggage tied to food forces women to not only consider the nutrient content and taste of the foods they might eat, but also which emotions they want to experience or avoid. Such thought processes happen with every single food decision. All day long.

For example, imagine that your co-worker taps you on the shoulder to tell you there's a chocolate cake in the break room. If you're a restrained eater, this isn't a trivial matter. You might think, *Ooh, cake sounds absolutely wonderful. But is it worth the flood of guilt that follows? I want to have some, I really want to… but I shouldn't. Ah, look at Jane and Chris going in there, I bet they're going to get cake. Maybe I'll just go in and see the cake.* Internal conflict characterized the ambivalence. You want to move both toward and away from something at the same time.

This creates tension and psychological stress… and it goes on and on.

Conversely, unrestrained eaters might think, *Oh, cake? Sure, I'll have some, but if there's only one piece, go ahead and have it.* They don't typically have strong emotional drives involved in the decision whether to eat or pass on a single food. It's an easy call because it's no big deal either way.

Restrained eaters, however, have strong emotions on *both* sides of the equation, and it feels like the stakes are much higher. They powerfully want the food, possibly with an attention-grabbing focus that makes it hard to think of anything else. Yet, at the same time, the cake brings up strong emotions of guilt, sadness, and fear.

It's almost a lose-lose scenario, because if they have the thing they want that much, they also get a flood of bad feelings. If they pass on the thing they so badly want, they avoid the bad feelings, but it expends enormous willpower and involves possible deprivation. Perma-dieting creates this tug-of-war tension, robbing women of peace, making them feel powerless and trapped, and denying them the ability to just enjoy a simple piece of dessert without mind-exploding drama.

Living in this chronic dieting mindset also creates increased ambivalence about healthy foods.[164] While it's no surprise that people often have love-hate relationships with low-nutrition foods, researchers have found that, for restrained eaters, even healthy items like broccoli and carrots can simultaneously trigger intense positive and negative emotions.

This may be because "healthy foods" feel virtuous to eat, and yet symbolic of pleasure deprivation.

Healthy foods might bring back bad memories of past diets, or just not taste good to us. Georgie notes that many of her clients have developed mixed feelings about healthy foods as a result of years of chronic dieting.

After following a diet plan that included a lot of nonfat cottage cheese, for example, a woman might never want to see the stuff again, even if she liked it before she ate it 14 times a week for seven months. A woman with a disordered eating history might recall salad with nonfat French dressing as her repetitive, go-to, low-calorie lunch. But looking back, if the thought of the meal brings to mind the fear, insecurity, and depression she once felt, it will repulse her.

CUE CRAVINGS

Despite what you may have seen on social media, cravings are not a result of your body needing a specific nutrient. They're psychological phenomena—not physical—enhanced by deprivation and restriction.[165, 166] Restrained eaters feel lots of persistent cravings, whereas unrestrained eaters report very few. This isn't because restrained eaters consume fewer calories, but because of increased sensitivity to external food cues, such as sights and smells, particular times of day, or the influence of other people.[167]

In daily life, everyone encounters food cues, such as seeing a pizza commercial on television. We think, *mmm, that looks good.* What we do with that thought impacts whether that thought is fleeting, recurs, or hangs on as a strong, long-lasting craving.

According to elaborated intrusion theory, for a pizza-related thought to become a persistent craving, it must be sufficiently intrusive, attention-grabbing, and pleasant.[168] A tiny, far away photo of a food you aren't crazy about is unlikely to trigger a cascade of cravings. A full-color video advertisement with sound effects played on a big screen is far more intrusive and attention-grabbing. If that advertisement displays a food you really enjoy, it's an even stronger set-up for persistent cravings.

Here's how it works: As you're minding your own business, taking a breather on the chest-press machine at the gym, the giant television on the wall snags your senses. It's your favorite food in the world—pepperoni pizza, with its melted cheese being stretched across the screen. You can tell from the steam that it's piping hot, which, in the chilly weight room, looks delightful. The ad has your attention in a major way, but you don't (yet) have a craving.

Next, you proceed through a second phase of cognitive elaboration, creating in your mind vivid images or sensory experiences.

You imagine the taste of the pepperoni, the pizza's smells, and the warmth of holding a piece of it in your hands.

Cognitive elaboration can also include thinking about logistics, which might include where you could get it, when you could get it, and so forth.[169] You haven't had a pizza in several weeks since you cut back on carbs. You imagine that after work, you could stop at the pizza place on 7th Street on your way home, since it's only a block from your usual route. But the pepperoni pizza at Mario's is just a notch better, even though it would mean driving 15 extra minutes. *But pizza has lots of calories*, you think. You begin doing the math on how many calories you think are in a slice of pizza.

You officially have a craving.

The foodie idea or image grabbed your attention, was sufficiently pleasant, and you elaborated on it by imaging the sensory experience, and thinking about when and where you could get the food. Feeling restricted or deprived after trying to reduce your carb intake for a period of time only added fuel to the fire.

For restrained eaters, any image or suggestion of food is more attention-grabbing, as well as loaded with more intense positive emotions, making this whole cravings process more likely to occur.[170, 171] Our brains are primed to focus on food-related stimuli literally every waking minute, everywhere we go when we're trying to minimize our intake.

THE BEHAVIORAL FALLOUT

Restrained eaters also show some ironic behaviors: While they attempt to limit their caloric intake, they often eat more than people who aren't concerned with their weight do. They tend to eat slightly smaller meals but slightly more of them, negating their efforts to create an energy deficit.[172]

Restrained eaters also consume more high-calorie foods than unrestrained eaters do when they're feeling a strong emotion, have to do a task that uses some of their self-control, or are simply distracted.[173, 174, 175] When they drink alcohol, restrained eaters also eat more than unrestrained eaters do.[176, 177]

Regardless of whether a person is concerned with weight, scientists have consistently found that people consume more of a food when they believe it's healthy. For example, in a study in which people were asked to help themselves to as much trail mix as they wanted, they helped themselves to 50% more when it was labeled "fitness trail mix" as opposed to simply "trail mix."[178]

Compared with women who are unconcerned with dieting, restrained eaters seem to be even more susceptible to increasing their intake of food if a health claim is made about it, or it's marketed as a "fitness" food.[179, 180]

For example, in one study, researchers gave undergraduate students jellybeans, but labeled them as either "fruit chews" or "candy chews."[181] Students who weren't concerned with dieting ate almost the same amount no matter the food's label. Students who were restrained eaters consumed 71% more jellybeans when they were labeled "fruit chews" compared to when they were called "candy chews."

A later study found that female restrained eaters consumed 50% more chocolate chip cookies when they were labeled as low-calorie than when they were labeled as high-calorie or were served with no nutrition facts.[182]

These examples highlight how perma-dieting amplifies our reliance on and susceptibility to external food signals and marketing claims. Thinking that something is "healthy" blinds us to our internal experience of how the food tastes and whether we're still hungry. While our internal cues may nudge us to pass on food or conclude a meal, external food cues like smells, sights, and health claims almost universally invite us to increase our intake.

Restrained eaters also tend to eat significantly more than intended when experiencing strong emotions, positive or negative. In one study, when watching a comedy or horror film, restrained eaters ate significantly more than they did when they watched a neutral movie.[183] Many of our clients have also shared that they aren't only prone to overeat on bad days; they often find they lose their inhibitions on vacation or when celebrating a happy occasion.

These episodes of consuming more food than intended produce intense feelings of guilt. Counterintuitively, the feeling of having eaten too much or having consumed a "forbidden food" often leads restrained eaters to consume an even greater quantity of food.[184]

We fall victim to the sort of thinking that says, *I blew it, might as well finish the whole box.*

COGNITIVE RESTRAINT DOESN'T WORK

Restrained eaters use a very popular, albeit ineffective, weight-loss strategy: cognitive restraint. Cognitive restraint is defined as a conscious attempt to limit and monitor food intake. It's 100% a mental process; it's not a physical experience like feeling hunger and satiety.[185, 186]

Why does cognitive restraint so easily fail? Cognitive dietary restraint is limited in the same ways as are other cognitive processes, such as solving math problems or recalling information.

When we're distracted, threatened, or experiencing high levels of arousal or negative emotion, we have less ability to do a quick calculation or remember the Italian phrases we learned in school. The necessary parts of our brain are working on other things. Experts theorize that when a woman's brain is utilizing resources for another task, not enough resources are available for regulating her food intake, and so she fails to do so.[187]

It seems like using cognitive restraint to hold back our food intake over the long term may only be effective if or when we remove ourselves from all food temptation, avoid emotional arousal (both positive and negative), steer clear of alcohol, avoid misleading "healthy" food labels, and avoid all tasks requiring a modicum of effort.

You know, like work, raise kids, or manage a household.

Clearly, cognitively restraint—thinking our way through every food decision—doesn't pass the "real-world test" as a method we can use for lifelong weight management.

Despite great efforts to count, track, and manipulate food choices, most women don't successfully reduce their calories when they restrain their eating, and so they don't lose weight.[188, 189, 190, 191]

The more likely outcomes of perma-dieting include emotional eating, feeling more cravings, eating in response to those cravings, feeling high levels of guilt and negative emotions, and-binge eating, all of which increase the odds of gaining yet more weight.[192, 193, 194, 195, 196, 197]

In every way imaginable, it's a losing battle.

CHAPTER 5
A SHORTAGE OF PLEASURE

When women have trouble reaching their weight-loss goals, they usually have a few ideas about what shortages might be contributing. "Maybe I'm not eating enough protein," or "I need more support from my friends and family," some say. But there's one shortage that tends to go completely undetected by our clients, and warrants major emphasis here: *You aren't having enough fun, pleasure, and positive experiences in your life.*

Experiencing a drought of pleasure or joy in our lives is a lot like falling victim to a poisonous carbon monoxide gas leak. It's a silent killer; has neither an odor nor color to catch our attention. Yet, it can be fatal, depriving the body of the oxygen it needs to survive. Dwindling amounts of pleasure in our lives can similarly go unnoticed while causing us widespread and dire problems. Those problems can take the form of unhealthy eating or drinking habits, substance abuse, social isolation, or inactivity.

A lack of joyful experiences often commingles with depression in a chicken-or-egg relationship, in which neither clearly precedes or causes the other. For many women, depression makes pleasure feel inaccessible, yet not engaging in enjoyable activities or human connections can impede depression recovery.

In this chapter, we'll use the words pleasure, joy, and fun interchangeably. By pleasure, we're talking about positive emotions as well as the experiences, objects, and people that trigger them.

It's worth noting that the absence or rarity of pleasure doesn't necessarily mean the presence of suffering or sadness. It's okay for many of our daily hours to be emotionally neutral, but it's also one of the reasons we can slip into a shortage of pleasure without noticing it. Feeling intense pain gets our attention, but feeling neutral pretty much all the time is less noticeable. Yet, this can be how a lack of pleasure feels.

WHAT GETS IN THE WAY OF PURSUING REAL-LIFE PLEASURES?

We have an innate desire to pursue pleasure; we're hardwired to approach things that feel good and flee things that cause suffering. As babies, we turned our heads in the direction of music or sounds we liked, and stared at smiling faces. Once we could crawl, it was pandemonium! We were all over the place, looking for and getting into things we liked.

We were fun-hunting machines as kids. We loved our toys, our Play-Doh, and our board games; when the gym teacher said we could play with that giant parachute, it was the pinnacle of euphoria. When we pulled up to Sandy's birthday party and saw a piñata, we got excited and couldn't wait to swing at that paper donkey with everything we had.

Yet when we ask grown women what they regularly do just for fun, just for them, or what activities bring the most joy to their lives, something has clearly changed since childhood. There can be an extended silence while they dig in their minds to find… something. It's like they just stopped the fun hunt.

How does this shift happen? Most frequently, joy simply gets crowded out. When our lives become filled edge-to-edge with responsibilities, work, caring for others, and commuting, the things we do for enjoyment tend to get bumped from the agenda.

Moreover, society places shockingly little value in the pursuit of joy. Society encourages us to earn an income, pay our taxes, care for our families, and be rational, law-abiding citizens. But nobody will nudge us to make sure we get outside and enjoy the sunshine this weekend. We won't receive any reminders of our duty to laugh our butts off by April 15th. If we defy social values, corrections are in place; but if we deny ourselves pleasure, nobody comes knocking to help set us straight.

When it comes to leisure time, things are considerably worse for women than for men. It's not that women like having fun or free time less than their male counterparts do—quite the opposite, in fact. Women rate their leisure-time experiences as more highly enjoyable than men do.[198]

However, study after study shows that women simply have far fewer moments of leisure, largely as a result of spending greater amounts of time on unpaid work in the home and caring for children.[199, 200] Over the course of a week, the average U.S. man enjoys five hours and forty-four more minutes of leisure time than the average U.S. woman does.[201] While women are engaged in tasks or work, they multitask more often than men, a finding that's likely linked to the fact that women also report feeling greater time pressure.[202]

It's tough to enjoy yourself when you don't have much free time, and when you do have a few spare minutes, you feel like you need to hurry to get back to a task.

Researchers are quick to point out that not all leisure time is equally enjoyable. Since the 1960s, both men and women have had a decrease in the amount of their free time they spend doing things they find highly interesting and enjoyable.

Meanwhile, the percentage of their leisure time they spend in "neutral downtime" activities such as watching television has increased. That's even while reports of television enjoyment have declined. [203]

In his 2007 paper, *Are We Having More Fun Yet? Categorizing and Evaluating Changes in Time Allocation,* economist Alan Krueger hypothesizes that the shift from positive to neutral downtime may be due to people being so fatigued that they don't have the energy to do more engaging and positive things like socializing or entertaining. This is likely particularly true for women, who have increased their time and effort at work. The author also notes that "some people may be seduced by the ease of watching television into allocating their free time sub-optimally."[204] We might be too tired or we might just have fallen into a pattern in which we do the easiest thing instead of the thing we want and enjoy the most. Either way, we can do better.

CARING OR NEGLECTFUL?

Back in 1966, psychologist David Bakan published an essay titled *The Duality of Human Existence,* in which he described two ways of existing in the world: agency and communion.[205] We can think of these as personality traits. Self-improvement and asserting ourselves show agency, while we demonstrate communion through cooperative, caring orientation toward others. Agency and communion are central to understanding gender psychology, as men and traditionally masculine gender roles tend to be more agentic, while women and traditionally feminine gender roles tend to be more communal.[206]

While neither of these traits is positive or negative, there are downsides to what has become known in the research world as "unmitigated communion," or displaying 100% communion without any agency. Unmitigated communion takes caring for and being involved with others to the extreme... a focus only on others to the exclusion of one's self.

Many of us have toyed with unmitigated communion. When we do, we can find ourselves in positions that feel like our lives have little or no pleasure. We crossed the line into focusing on other people's problems and needs to the point of dismissing our own.

We introduce this concept here because unmitigated communion gives us a concrete, evidence-based example of why so many women have gotten to this mysterious place where there's no pleasure in their lives, and they're trying ineffectually to create it with snack foods and alcohol.

Unmitigated communion isn't the only reason people have shortages of joy and pleasure, but it's a pervasive one that we've observed in many of our clients. And since there's a scientific name for it, you can believe us when we say it's not just you who's experiencing it!

Here are some examples of behaviors and characteristics that are common in those with high levels of unmitigated communion:[207]

- Having imbalanced relationships—providing support to others without requesting or receiving support

- Fear and concern over what other people think

- Having intrusive thoughts about other people's prolems for days after those problems have been revealed

- Feeling responsible for fixing other people's problems

- Putting other people's needs above their own, even neglecting their health

- Always helping others, even when exhausted

- Being exploitable—letting others take advantage, having a hard time saying no

It can seem like this tendency to always put other people first would be a positive attribute. However, it's actually not something other people like or admire, and it can be harmful to those we care about. Unmitigated communion harms our relationships as well as harming us as individuals. It leads to self-neglect, psychological distress, and over-involvement with other people's problems.[208]

Self-neglect becomes an issue when even our basic and urgent needs take a back seat to every whim and desire of other people. We can't maintain our own health and wellness if we plan to do it after every other person's every desire is fulfilled. You'd never even take a shower if your plan was to make everyone in the universe comfortable and get them a cup of tea first.

The psychological burden of feeling responsible for fixing other people's problems is unfairly heavy, and this isn't the type of heavy lifting that makes you stronger… because you never get to come out from under it. Some experts believe that unmitigated communion explains why more women than men suffer from depression. [209]

Even worse, if we become too involved in other people's problems, we may drive friends and loved ones away. Being on the receiving end of someone else's unmitigated communion can trigger annoyance or a feeling of invaded privacy or being smothered. We might only be trying to help, but sometimes the most helpful thing to a relationship is to respect each others' boundaries and decisions.

Lastly, self-sacrificial giving often makes others feel guilty. They can see when we're neglecting ourselves to constantly care for them. Even if we never comment on it, our tired faces and exhausted demeanors speak volumes. They make people feel like a burden. The people we love want us to love ourselves, too.

WHAT HAPPENS WHEN WE
SHORT OURSELVES ON JOY?

Having a lower amount and variety of pleasurable activities has been linked with higher body weights and a greater likelihood of post-diet weight regain.[210] How does that work; does having fun somehow burn calories? Not quite. It's more like a shortage of enjoyment leads to increases in caloric intake. When fun experiences and pleasant sensations dwindle, fun food is generally first to fill the gap. And the foods we go to for fun are generally high-calorie, low-nutrition choices. Weight gain is a natural result.

Some of our clients tell us that food has become their go-to for a good time. Unfortunately, some feel like it's the only type of joy available to them; it's low-cost, quick, and won't inconvenience anyone else. Research shows that many people with chronic pain describe eating as "the only activity that continues to bring them regular and reliable pleasure," especially when their options for other types of recreation are limited or they spend much of their time alone.[211]

When energy needs are already met, this drive to eat for pleasure, called "hedonic eating," typically involves consuming high-fat and -sugar snack foods in large amounts. Eating foods rich in fat and sugar is a way to seek pleasure, relieve pain, and distract a person. It's easy to see how this pattern leads to the development of overlapping problems: When burnout, pain, or depression prevents someone from enjoying pleasurable activities on a regular basis, obesity often follows.

Other women fall into abusing drugs or alcohol to cope. Lacking pleasurable activities is a risk factor for initiating, escalating, and maintaining substance-use disorders.[212] Despite clever memes and jokes, "mommy wine culture" is a prime example. Not unlike the "Mother's Little Helper" epidemic of the 1960s in which women used Valium to cope with motherhood, the embossed "mommy juice" tumblers and "wine mommy" Facebook groups promote substance abuse over joy.[213] When a 2017 *JAMA Psychiatry* study compared drinking habits between 2001 and 2002 and 2012 and 2013, it found that high-risk drinking—consuming four or more servings of alcohol on at least one day each week—increased by 29.9%.[214]

It's clear that a life focused on work, providing, and achievement, yet devoid of laughter, rich relationships, and sensory pleasures causes dysfunction. We don't just "settle for it," we seek something to fill the void. In the maladaptive responses women adopt to cope with low-pleasure lives, that's actually very healthy: *Something in them is fighting back.*

Georgie often tells her clients who are recovering from binge eating disorder that the urges they have to binge are actually rooted in trying to take care of themselves. She explains, "The impulse to take something for yourself, in large quantity, is an indicator that you need something you aren't getting.

It's not a broken circuit; it's a signal from an important, healthy part of you, elbowing you to realize you're living a life that's LESS than it could be."

TOO MUCH GUILT TO ENJOY THE FLAVOR

It really is cruel, the way food guilt steals our enjoyment of taste. We look forward to that slice of creamy cheesecake or the perfect crunch of a salty potato chip. Anticipating enjoying our favorite foods can make us feel happy!

But then we see a headline at the grocery checkout on "How Sugar Poisons Your Brain," and our mood comes slumping back down. Womp womp. Then there's a woman on a magazine cover standing in one leg of her old blue jeans, thanks (supposedly) to cutting out carbs.

And we feel like we aren't supposed to have treats either. Instead of thinking about how killer a cheesecake is and how perfectly the flavors combine, we spend the time we're eating it admonishing ourselves that *we cannot do this again tomorrow.*

And then the cheesecake is gone, and *we didn't even enjoy it.*

Articles and advertising often use moral and religious ideas when talking about food and weight control.[215] Terms such as "sinfully delicious," "clean," and "guilt-free" implicate the moral superiority of particular foods, while wrapping others in shame. This leads to many of us feeling morally or ethically tainted when we consume a glazed donut, and prestigious or superior when we eat a sugar-free protein bar or low-calorie ice cream.

Many women wouldn't eat an ice cream cone in front of a doctor or a personal trainer, or perhaps in public at all. They feel better having it at home, where no one will see. Just one experience of someone giving you a disgraceful look in the coffee shop is enough to cause you to choose to take your next muffin and coffee to go. Maybe you'll just hide the paper bag in your jacket...

This sort of food shaming, and the resultant eater shaming, doesn't result in eating fewer unhealthy foods. It actually stokes our appetites; shame, guilt, and sadness increase our desire for food, total food intake, and sugar intake.[216, 217] Guilt results in us doing mental gymnastics to avoid feeling bad about what we've eaten or are about to eat. We tell ourselves things like, "It isn't my fault; Sarah ordered the French fries," or use other justifications that we "deserve it" because of other righteous acts we've done or promise to do tomorrow. "I'll put in extra time on the treadmill!"

But these tactics aren't effective, and the experience of eating cake, cookies, or candy remains one that, for many people, is more strongly associated with guilt than with celebration or pleasure. Loss of food pleasure isn't just unfortunate; it contributes to eating disorders, low psychological well-being and body satisfaction, as well as weight gain over time.[218, 219] Additionally, when the guilt from eating cookies is the reason women trudge into their workouts, they're going to miss out on the joy of movement as well. Food guilt that drives exercise penance is lose-lose.

Have you ever worried what onlookers would think of you based on the breakfast cereal you placed on the checkout conveyor? That's a perfect example of how food moralizing can make us feel that the totally logical act of eating something *that was designed to be eaten* is somehow wrong.

It's not in our heads. Other people can and will comment if they notice that what we're eating doesn't fit their opinion of "good."

"I can't believe you're eating that."

"Didn't you have enough already?"

"Are you sure you don't want the salad instead?"

Foods don't have the ability to alter our moral fiber or value. They're just combinations of molecules. And still, the idea of certain foods being shameful has sunken into our consciousness. When we hear another woman say she's been "good" or "bad," it's most often not a reflection of what she's said or done, but a commentary on what she's eaten. And we learned this from a world that equates eating foods with few nutrients and lots of calories with dishonor.

Oddly enough, we're also sandwiched between parallel universes, because the inverse also waves at us. It's the "good girls" who get the candy prize, the reward for excellent behavior. Take a second with that: Eating low-nutrition foods makes us feel like we're badly behaved, yet what do we tend to use for rewarding good behavior? The same low-nutrition foods.

So you're bad if you eat these foods. But if you're good, someone might give them to you as a reward. Is it any wonder we have confusing "it's complicated" relationships with food?

Using external rewards, such as food, money, or praise to motivate behavior has been widely discouraged by motivational experts for other reasons as well. If you give your child candy for doing homework each night, you're setting up a situation in which homework will potentially never get done if you eventually stop the candy bribe.

In such situations, external rewards tend to become the main reason for doing a task, so removal of the reward results in a failure to feel motivated to do the task. When there's an external reward we expect from doing a task, it minimizes the intrinsic benefits of completing it.[220] Intrinsic benefits (or rewards) are internal reasons we want to act, things like feelings of accomplishment, curiosity, a desire to learn, or the satisfaction of doing things that are in line with our values.

In short, we experience less pleasure from doing a task if we're just doing it for the cookie. Using food repeatedly as a reward can diminish enjoyment, persistence, and psychological well-being, moving us further from filling our lives with pleasure.[221]

THERE ARE NO POINTS FOR SUFFERING

As we explored in Chapter 2, the efficacy of a workout is often equated with how much it hurts. And as we now know, this is far from the truth. Yet outside of the weight room, it's not unusual to make things harder on ourselves in subtle ways… and for no good reason.

In some cases, we believe the hard way has benefits, such as making us tougher, or ensuring a better outcome. And this can be true: Taking the time to master a craft through diligent practice will yield more skill than hastily hacking it after watching a couple YouTube videos. Running uphill in your workouts is an appropriate way to trigger the adaptations you need to do well in an uphill race.

However, sometimes our minds trick us into believing that the hard way is the way we should do something. We sometimes choose inefficient or arduous methods of accomplishing tasks because we associate "doing it the easy way" with being lazy or dishonorable. This line of illogic can lead to not delegating tasks to others more apt for the job, refusing pain-relief medications, or, when lost, not asking for directions or turning on the GPS that's within arm's reach.

Asking for help or delegating is sometimes one of the biggest leaps forward in creating a sustainable healthy lifestyle. After frantically rushing home every day on her lunch break for years to let her dog outside, one of our clients finally hired a dog walker. What a difference it made for her in her ability to tolerate the workdays with less stress! Finally, she could have a real lunch break, tasting and enjoying her food, while the dog got a longer walk and was happier. She wondered why she spent so many days frantically rushed, choking down a sandwich in one hand while driving home for the dog walk.

Similarly, we health-minded women often consider hiring a trainer, trying a meal-kit delivery service, or subscribing to a fun-looking workout app. But then we think, *Nah, I can get by with my same workout routine. I can cut up my own onions and search for recipes. Why spend extra money?*

While it's all-around wise to not waste money on truly superfluous purchases, this tendency to dismiss help can be an indicator that we aren't assigning much value to making something more fun, varied, interesting, or engaging for ourselves. And sadly, this value system wrecks our results much of the time. When the cooking is too hard, the workouts are boring, and we get tired of the bland meals, we quit.

Behavioral experts have suggested that sometimes we choose difficulty or discomfort because it helps us feel more in control, and that by engaging in more effort or enduring more discomfort, we feel we've influenced the outcomes.[222]

Unfortunately, working harder or suffering more doesn't change the fact that many things remain out of our control. Staying up all night checking our email doesn't make the email we're waiting on arrive any faster; it just makes us feel terrible the next day. Worrying continuously about our loved ones, playing out various disastrous storylines in our minds, doesn't make anyone any safer... or you a better person. It's only the trap of LESS telling you, "Don't you dare be happy or relaxed!"

Worrying excessively and purposely trying to expect the worst in lieu of getting our hopes up are also forms of suffering with no benefits. We tend to brace for horrible things when we notice we're in a blissful moment. As Brene' Brown describes it, dress-rehearsing tragedy is one way we cut ourselves off from joy. In her words, "It's like we think, 'things are going too well... I'm too happy... something bad is sure to happen!' and so we don't allow ourselves to feel joy to the fullest."[223] The real fear, she explains, is that we'll lose joy or never experience it again.

We've seen clients experience this fear too. Often, when progress is coming along as desired, people get scared. *What if it just stops? What if I can't keep the weight off and these new clothes I bought won't fit?* They become so frightened at losing the current joy that they're hesitant to fully feel it.

Of course, we cannot avoid loss and difficulty in life. Bringing it on ourselves, however, doesn't make the blows easier to bear. We can't inoculate ourselves against future pain by adding suffering to whatever we're doing now. Allowing ourselves to enjoy this moment isn't going to bring a hex upon us. There are no points for suffering. Don't suffer just for the sake of it.

As you can see, the role of pleasure and enjoyment goes far beyond having a good time. It's not a superfluous detail in life; it's a crucial element in optimal mental and emotional health, relationships, and nutrition.

CHAPTER 6
NO REST FOR THE WEARY

Speaking of enjoyable things in life, when was the last time you reveled in rest? For many women, the answer is pretty fuzzy.

Sure, we understand that rest is important. And we fully intend to get it—once we hit our work deadlines, put the kids to bed, pay the bills, move the summer clothes into storage, clean out the garage, and get that gross goop cleaned off the refrigerator shelves. This sort of thinking, that rest will happen when *everything else is done,* fitting into the vacant space in our schedules, produces very under-rested people.

As we talked about in the last chapter, women have a serious shortage of free time for things like rest. And all signs point to them having even less time going forward. Recent data reveals that, year over year, women spend more time doing work around the house and caring for their children, regardless of whether they engage in paid labor.[224]

At the end of the day, this leaves women with an average of 20 minutes for pure relaxing,[225] 20 measly crumb-on-the-floor minutes. However, women don't even enjoy those minutes. In our experience with clients, it's not uncommon for women to say they're "bad at relaxing," and that the only time they stop and shut off their brains is during sleep. But, of course, they also have a hard time sleeping: Stress is the foremost cause of insomnia, and about half of all women say it's caused them to lie awake at night in the previous month.[226, 227]

More than a third of women get fewer than seven hours of sleep per night. And while the current recommendations urge all adults to snooze for seven to nine hours, experts believe that, for optimal health, women may actually need more sleep than their male counterparts do.[228, 229] The reason comes down to more than biology or the universe ganging up on women. Instead, experts suggest that women may need extra ZZZs because they're constantly multitasking and expending greater levels of mental energy than men are. (Take that as you will.)

While that's unfortunate on its own, what's even more troublesome is that we're often proud of how little rest we get. "Busy" is the new female status symbol, and we wear it daily, after first giving it a good polish, of course. Think about it: How many of us have bragged about how little sleep we've gotten? Maybe a friend says, "I'm exhausted; I only got six hours of sleep last night." And we chime in, "Well, I only got five!" Or when venting with our colleagues, we're quick to rattle off everything on our to-do lists, crushing everyone around us in a pile of responsibilities. (Both of us have done it!)

Why? Because our current overworked, overstressed culture falsely equates being tired, stressed, overwhelmed, or just plain busy with being important or mattering at all. Taking time for ourselves to relax or simply take a nap hardly fits into the societal expectation of the woman who climbs the career ladder, cares for her family, maintains an impeccable home, and generally gets an unfathomable number of things accomplished while having little to no personal needs.

As we've taken this image to heart, being exhausted and self-sacrificial has become part of the normative discontent shared by millions of women. It's not unusual anymore; it's expected. We expect it of ourselves.

NO REST, NO RESULTS

The irony is that being tired, stressed, overwhelmed, and busy achieves the opposite of what we hope—it makes us less productive and effective in everything we do. That's especially true when it comes to nurturing our health and well-being.

Optimal health involves not only taking on challenges, but also recovering from them. Exercise provides the easiest example: It's not *during* our workouts that we get stronger, faster, or healthier; it's between our workouts as our bodies recover. Our bodies are in a constant state of remodeling, sloughing off old, stress-wrecked cells and replacing them with new, spry ones.

Exercise—whether we're picking up heavy weights, going on a long run, or swimming laps—forces this process to go double-time. Working our muscles, connective tissues, and organs causes cells to drop off more quickly and in bigger numbers. To build muscle, endurance, cardiovascular fitness, or anything else, your body has to replace these cells. None of it happens without rest.

Whether or not we ever break a sweat, our bodies are still re-modeling and have to rest. Our brains have to recover from thinking, working, and worrying, and during sleep is when they consolidate memories and make room for new information.[230] Our metabolic systems have to recover from churning out energy and refill their fuel stores. Our bodies have to recover from simply being awake.

Without rest, nothing is able to fully repair. Instead, the daily damage accumulates, until everything's in disarray. High levels of the stress hormone cortisol contribute to excess weight gain, obesity, and greater levels of visceral fat, even in "normal-weight" women.[231, 232] By residing in and around the body's vital organs, visceral fat is the most deleterious form of fat in the human body.[233] Similarly, chronic sleep deprivation or routinely getting poor-quality sleep increases the risk of disorders including high blood pressure, cardiovascular disease, diabetes, depression, and obesity.[234]

The thing about rest is that even if you aren't intentional about it, you still end up taking it. It's a biological inevitability. Your brain just calls recess. You might check out in front of your phone or kill hours scrolling through social media instead of sleeping or engaging in an activity that would better help your mind and body recover from stressors. You might find yourself absent-mindedly eating handfuls of popcorn in the evening while not really watching the TV screen.

These patterns are like treading water: They keep you from drowning, but they never get you anywhere and definitely don't leave you rested.

BUSY, STRESSED, AND EATING (OR NOT EATING)

Shorting ourselves on rest hurts our nutritional habits from every angle. On a biological level, a lack of restorative rest—and the accompanying climb in physical and mental stress—increases the very real possibility that a lot of our eating will be stress-or emotion-induced.

Stress also reduces our brains' ability to make decisions, especially healthy ones or those that require prioritizing long-term rewards over short-term ones.[235] For example, walking away from fried foods because you want a healthy heart. When we're up against a work deadline, instead of fueling ourselves with a healthy meal, we guzzle a sugar-filled, blended coffee drink or raid the vending machine for something sweet... and then something salty.

In one American Psychological Association survey, almost half of women reported overeating or eating nutrient-poor foods out of stress. However, not only did the women report that their eating was ineffective at managing their stress levels, they said it made them disappointed in themselves, feel bad about their bodies, and deem themselves sluggish or lazy.[236]

That's not how we want you to feel about your body and yourself! A lack of rest can become a cascade of stress eating, followed by feeling disappointed in ourselves, and then emotionally eating to cope with those uncomfortable feelings! Where's the escape?

Even if you're diligently working to use hunger and fullness to guide your eating (so as not to emotionally eat!), being under-rested will monkey with those signals, making them less accurate and leading you to still overeat.

In fact, lack of sleep and increases in cortisol trigger a wide variety of hormonal changes throughout your body, including decreased levels of the "feel-full" hormone leptin and increased levels of the "hunger" hormone ghrelin.[237] Just thinking about a future stressful event can increase your levels of ghrelin and food intake, while a lack of ZZZs primes your brain with the same chemicals that are behind marijuana munchies.[238, 239]

On the opposite end of the spectrum, shorting yourself on rest can cause you to straight-up starve yourself. When you're overloaded, you might think you're too busy to eat, or you might be too stressed to even notice you're hungry. You might deny yourself the nutrients you need to thrive (or simply live), just so you can frantically work through never-ending lists of "just one more thing."

We've likely all done this to some extent. How many of us have missed a meal because we were too busy with something on our to-do lists? We're guessing... close to all of us. After all, research shows that more than half of young women say they *regularly* skip breakfast because they're too rushed, and that they tend to eat on the run. About a third say they're too busy to eat healthy foods, that healthy eating takes too much time, and that they have a hard time finding time to sit down to eat.[240]

Similarly, when parents don't have time to sit down with their families and eat a home-cooked meal, they usually turn to un-healthy alternatives: eating at work, eating in the car, ordering take-out, eating low-nutrient processed foods, skipping meals altogether, and often over-eating later.[241] Of course, women are also far more likely to turn to such strategies than men are.[242]

While it might seem obvious how some of these behaviors can backfire in the form of weight gain, a lot of women aren't aware how extensively deprivation of dedicated sit-down mealtimes af-fects the brain's ability to register, enjoy, and regulate food intake.

For example, when you eat a cereal bar as you click away on your work computer, you automatically split your attentional focus between work and food. And since work involves more mental effort than does chewing, chances are your brain isn't devoting much attention to your "lunch." As a result, you derive far less pleasure from your food, and have less stored memory of having eaten it.[243]

Since your distracted brain may not fully acknowledge all the calories you've consumed, chances are you'll be hungrier and eat more through the rest of the day than you would have if you'd just taken a break to eat your food sans distractions.[244]

MOVEMENT, REST, AND RECOVERY

As we mentioned in Chapter 3, exercise is one of the most effec-tive—yet least-used—antidepressants. It's also one of the healthi-est ways to combat stress. And, unfortunately for many women who are short on rest, exercise sounds like the least attractive stress-management technique possible. There's too much to do to spend time exercising!

Lack of time is a primary barrier to exercise participation; when women are stressed, they skip their workouts even if they know that moving will help them feel better.[245] Plus, when they're stressed out, fatigue is a given. Just the idea of physically exerting themselves is exhausting.

When women are low on rest and high on stress, they prioritize quick bandages over long-lasting solutions. They think, *What would I rather do? Collapse on the couch and scroll through Instagram? Or peel myself off the comfy, cozy couch, get dressed, fight traffic, and muster my way through a workout?*

The answer's obvious: Survey findings show that U.S. adults far prefer to manage their stress levels with sedentary activities such as watching TV or going online.[246] (Still, most people admit such distractions aren't really effective.) And getting to the gym feels like an unsurmountable hurdle. It often doesn't occur to women that doing a few push-ups, bodyweight squats, or stretches in the living room is an exercise option. *Ahem, absolutist thinking.*

However, as common as it is for a lack of rest to stand in the way of regular movement habits, rest shortages can just as easily reduce the benefits of the exercise in which we do engage. Rest (sleep as well as recovery days and workouts) is critical to the body's ability to adapt to the stressors of exercise. Yes, exercise is a stress to your body's physiological systems. It's when your body recovers from that stress that it replenishes its energy stores, lets hormones get back to baseline, repairs muscles, and increases bone mineral density.

Without purposefully engaging in quality rest through healthy sleep habits, active recovery workouts, meditation, and times of purposeful relaxation, it becomes harder for our bodies to positively adapt to exercise. Instead, they adapt with hormonal irregularities, reductions in immune-system function, burnout, and exercise-related aches, pains, and sidelining injuries.

Mental and emotional stresses also thwart our workout gains. Research from the Yale Stress Center shows that psychological stress can inhibit muscles' ability to recover from strenuous resistance exercise.[247] This may be in part because cortisol's a catabolic (muscle-degrading) hormone, blunting the effects of anabolic (muscle-building) hormones such as testosterone (yes, women have some T) and human growth hormone.

EMOTIONS, PLEASURE, AND WELLNESS

Rest is a powerful tool in helping us recover from emotional stressors, protect our mental health, and experience pleasure. Life is meant for us to enjoy and fill with meaningful experiences and connections. Shorting ourselves on rest, however, casts a busy, overburdened shadow over our entire existence.

When packing every moment with work, chores, house and family management, and other responsibilities or imagined responsibilities, it's easy to miss out on important moments with friends and family. And "me time" can seem like a wonderful, but sadly, mythological llamacorn. As we explored in the last chapter, enjoying such real-life pleasures is surprisingly fundamental to not only our mental and emotional health, but also our physical health.

Plus, when rest-deprived women do take the opportunity to engage in such experiences, they're often unable to fully enjoy them. They're unable to live mindfully. They might spend time with friends, but be too riddled with headaches to really hear the conversation. Maybe they get a massage, but they spend the entire hour on the table thinking through what they need to do when they get home. When performing fulfilling work through their careers or volunteerism, they might be too stressed to appreciate it.

The effects spiral. The lack of rest makes the nervous system more sensitive to stress, inhibiting the ability to sleep or otherwise rest. The stress and fatigue dull cognitive functioning, making everything feel extra difficult and taxing. This state pushes us toward unhealthy and ineffective coping strategies. Examples include emotional eating and inactivity, smoking, increased caffeine use, substance abuse, alcohol use, and television viewing[248] that leave us with lower levels of self-esteem and body love. The result: more stress, more ineffective coping mechanisms, and even less rest.

The cycle just keeps churning.

SELF-CARE, REALLY?

Today, more women are aware of self-care than ever before, and they see it as a welcome break from the tired, rest-restricted cycle. It's becoming part of our normal dialogue with friends and family, and something we prioritize. Some women block out "me time", work to get more sleep, and focus on not just pushing themselves in their workouts, but also fully recovering from those workouts. That's awesome.

But unfortunately, far too commonly, our culture's perception of what constitutes self-care is intimately wrapped in the same *go, go, go* attitude that's leaving us fried in the first place.

Examples are everywhere. lululemon sells an entire line of "self-care" branded face masks and under-eye creams.[249] Goat yoga is somehow a thing. On Facebook, juice-cleanse companies talk about self-care to push their products—products designed to help us deprive ourselves of food for extended periods of time.[250] Gratitude journals, sleep trackers, self-care subscription boxes, and countless other products convey that self-care is about buying and doing more stuff.[251]

In effect, "self-care" runs the risk of becoming something that drains women's pockets and crowds their schedules without filling them emotionally or providing any actual rest or relief. It can become one more thing on an already annoying to-do list. Sometimes, it's just another way of keeping up with the proverbial Joneses.

The other big problem with self-care is that many women don't actually pursue it as a way to benefit themselves, but to benefit others. After all, we're guessing that somewhere down the line, someone has told you that you can't really take care of others—your friends, partner, kids, or family—until you first take care of yourself. "An empty glass has nothing to give." "Put on your own oxygen mask before helping others."

Such statements are 100% true; you can't do much for anyone else if you're exhausted, beaten down, and broke. Frequently, they're exactly what sell women on self-care and trigger healthy behavior changes... in the short-term.

However, they're not successful in helping women maintain long-term health because, once again, they run on extrinsic motivators—such as helping or making others happy. Eventually, when the goings get tough, such as in times of stress, long work hours, or rest shortages, extrinsic motivation fails to effectively motivate. Women fall back into their frenetic pace, and don't stick with beneficial habits, even if they were only doing them in an attempt to be a better mother, friend, or partner.

What's more, this external focus also reinforces the idea that women earn value in how much they do for others, that the prime purpose of filling their tanks is to use them to fuel others. At its core, this goes against the entire idea and power of giving yourself MORE.

PART 2

THE POWER
OF GIVING YOURSELF MORE

CHAPTER 7
MORE, DEFINED

As we discussed in Part 1, living with shortages of body love, strengthening movement, emotional skills, healthy nutrition, everyday pleasures, and times of rest deprives women of everything they need to thrive. It propels weight gain, the inability to lose weight, reductions in overall health, unhappiness, and burnout.

Fortunately, we can refill those shortages to abundance while developing more skills to live happily and with confidence. We can quit the fruitless pursuits we've been taught, and end the efforts to hold back our borders, shrink, confine, and pursue LESS.

It starts now.

Breathe in deeply, letting your lungs fill up to their maximum. Relax your stomach; let it make room for the air, and feel it expand in space. Notice how the air surrounding your body accommodates your growing belly, comfortably and easily shifting aside for you to take in all of the air you need.

Then, let the warm air flow from your lungs. Just let go. You don't need to hold onto any of it because infinite air is all around you. When you need more, you can simply draw in another breath. Settle into this feeling of abundance. Find peace in the space and your body's place within it.

This is your first glimpse of MORE.

But MORE isn't just limited to our bodies. We can gain in our lives, too, appreciating life for the *experience* that it is, rather than how it's *assessed by others.* By becoming stronger, better nurtured, and more fulfilled in our physical, mental, and emotional needs, we gain a sense of pride and growth while naturally attaining our health, fitness, and body goals.

LET GO, GRAB WHAT FEELS RIGHT

Here's a message we insist on emphasizing: *Giving yourself MORE doesn't mean doing more.*

We think it's important to highlight this because, as you've already read, the wellness field largely equates self-care with an enormous list of to-dos. Many women feel like self-care is just one more job they have to do. Envisioning this extra layer of responsibility on top of paid work, cleaning, cooking, feeding their families, and caring for their friends only increases the already overbearing amount of pressure women feel.

Looking forward, if Part 3 encourages you to do things you haven't been doing, that's an invitation to first make room; explore what you might need to pull back from in order to allow those fulfilling habits to be part of your life. Many of our clients discover they've been doing too much of some things (like working, taking care of others, and judging, criticizing, and punishing themselves) and not enough of others (ahem, resting, reflecting, having fun, and enjoying the moment). Shifting this balance can add to your overall health and happiness without adding to your list or crowding your schedule.

Giving yourself MORE also doesn't come with a stipulation of somehow earning it. You're enough, right now. You don't need to wait until you achieve a work promotion, lose 10 pounds, or can do a chin-up to be more generous with yourself. It's not a purchase or reward; the MORE to which you're entitled is a gift. You're wonderful and worthy already, and you deserve more than what you've been taking.

We know, because it's not just you. As you read in Part 1, almost all of us have fallen victim to giving ourselves too little at different points in our lives. For many women, LESS has been a round-the-clock mode for decades.

MORE offers us a new perspective and way of life. That includes seeing more options and having the liberty to deliberately choose our responses, rather than feeling like we *have to* do this or that. We can respond to almost any scenario in dozens of ways, as long as we remember to look for them and see past our usual rote reactions.

There isn't just one way to get strong. There isn't just one way to think or act. There isn't just one way to eat healthfully. In the chapters that follow, you'll find a treasure trove of options that are yours to consider when you need a smile, have something to say, or crave comfort.

Life is a dressing room. Try on different options, and find those that feel the absolute best to you. Make those behaviors and attitudes yours, and don't hesitate to leave the others behind.

CHAPTER 8
WHERE ARE YOU IN NEED OF MORE?

To start to give yourself MORE, it can be helpful to first consider the areas of your life in which you're currently shorting yourself.

In this chapter, we'll help you do that by walking you through a simple self-assessment. In it, you'll first answer some big-picture questions about the life you're leading and the life you want.

Then, you'll dive into each of the six areas of MORE—body love, movement, emotion, eating, pleasure, and rest. You'll read through series of statements, answer "true" or "false" to each, and gain insight into unhelpful LESS-focused thought patterns and tendencies.

It's important to not just be honest, but also kind to yourself. In the pages that follow, it's possible you'll discover that you've been striving for LESS in several or even all of these areas! You may realize a lot of your day-to-day thoughts and actions have been cutting you down and keeping you from living a full life. In turn, you might feel frustrated or disappointed in yourself.

It's good to acknowledge those feelings; but please resist the urge to sink into self-blame or negativity. Instead, remember that to give yourself MORE, you first need to identify the ways in which you currently give yourself too little. So give yourself a pat on the back by choosing awareness. By simply taking this assessment, you're already on your path to a happier, healthier life.

SELF-ASSESSMENT

Imagine what your life will look like in 10 years if you start living with a MORE mentality. Describe the condition of your health, happiness, and relationships.

_____

_____

_____

_____

What about that future is specifically important to you, and why?

_____

_____

_____

_____

Now imagine what your life will look like in 10 years if you change nothing. Describe the condition of your health, happiness, and relationships.

_____

_____

_____

_____

LET'S TALK ABOUT YOUR BODY LOVE

For each statement, check "true" or "false."

	TRUE	FALSE
I'm preoccupied with a desire to be thinner.		
I'm afraid to gain even a little weight, even if it's from muscle.		
I would rather lose 10 pounds than win $100,000.		
I weigh myself almost every day.		
If I gain a pound, I worry I'll keep gaining.		
When I think about my body's appearance, I feel unpleasant emotions like anxiety or shame.		
I focus on what my body looks like more than on what it can do.		
My body shape or weight affects my self-worth.		
I regularly compare my body to those of other women.		
I check my body in the mirror several times per day to see how it looks.		
I feel bad about myself when I see #fitspo photos, even if I know they're likely edited.		
I think my stomach, thighs, or hips are too big.		
I avoid situations like shopping for clothes and going to the beach because of how my body looks.		
I think if I were five pounds lighter, my life would be significantly happier.		
My feelings toward my body are more negative than positive.		

If these statements hold true for you, chances are that you spend a lot of your time and energy worrying about the size of your body and trying to subtract from it.

It's also likely that many of the statements listed in this chapter's five other assessments (movement, emotions, food, pleasure, and rest), will resonate with you. After all, your relationship with your body is the foundation for how you treat it—whether that's with exercise, nutrition, sleep habits, and even how you express emotions and experience life's pleasures.

This is the spiral of LESS, and if you've been playing the game for years, we're sorry. It sucks, right? We also hope you can find some relief in knowing that there's another way to think about your body and exist in the world.

In Chapter 9, we'll help you lean into a positive, empowering relationship with your body, and teach you how to appreciate and take pride in your physical self. No more feeling like your body is a burden. You'll see what a growing, evolving gift it truly is, and learn how to establish and work toward goals that allow you to revel in that gift. Can those goals include weight loss? Yes, absolutely! "Weight-loss goals" is on the cover of this book, isn't it? If weight loss is a goal for you, you'll learn how to achieve that outcome without body criticism or negativity, or expending inordinate amounts of time and energy.

Just as a lack of body love has led you to give yourself LESS, falling in love with your body will trigger positive changes in all areas of your health and life.

Welcome to the spiral of MORE.

LET'S TALK ABOUT YOUR MOVEMENT

For each statement, check "true" or "false."

	TRUE	FALSE
Losing weight is my primary motivation to engage in physical activity.		
The more I eat, the more I feel I need to exercise.		
I get mad at myself when I have "off" days in the gym.		
I use mantras like "no pain, no gain" to push through hard workouts or motivate me to exercise.		
I often talk about needing to get back on track with my workouts.		
I keep an eye on fitness and calorie trackers.		
I usually have an all-or-nothing mentality about exercise.		
I feel bad about myself when I work out, getting frustrated with my physical limitations or appearance.		
If I don't feel wrecked after exercise or get sore, I question if I really got a good workout.		
It's fair to say I don't enjoy exercising.		
I don't feel like I belong in most fitness settings.		
I push through my workouts even when I'm sick or dealing with an injury.		
Throughout the day, I rarely take movement breaks.		
The weight room intimidates me.		
When I exercise, I tend to focus on my "trouble spots."		

In this section, the frequency with which you agree points to an increasingly rough relationship with physical activity. The good news is that if many of these statements are true for you, you have an incredible amount to gain by changing how you think about and approach movement.

Looking through how you responded to each statement, you may notice that when it comes to your workouts, you're pretty tough on and unforgiving of yourself. Or that you don't just *not* exercise, you actively *avoid* exercise. It's also possible you observe both tendencies. After all, if your workouts are a suck-fest, why would you want to stick with them? If exercise feels like pure punishment, you'll undoubtedly resist your body's inherent drive to move, bend, skip, stretch, and flex.

What's more, you may observe ways that your relationship with your body, nutrition habits, and rest influence your approach to exercise—for the negative.

All that ends in Chapter 10 when we dive into the nitty-gritty of both structured exercise and free-flowing movement. You'll learn how to repair your relationship with exercise, find ways to enjoy physical activity (we won't tell you to just "learn to like it"), and establish a lifelong movement habit that supports your body goals.

LET'S TALK ABOUT YOUR EMOTIONS

For each statement, check "true" or "false."

	TRUE	FALSE
I often check out in front of the TV or on social media.		
I sometimes have difficulty describing how I feel.		
I'm big into retail therapy.		
I avoid conflict and difficult discussions as much as humanly possible.		
When a negative thought comes up, I immediately try to think of something else.		
I eat when I'm anxious, sad, or frustrated.		
I usually try to distract myself when I feel angry or upset.		
When I feel overwhelmed, I want to eat.		
I need wine, chocolate, or comfort foods to deal with life.		
Others have told me I hide or suppress my feelings.		
When I'm feeling down, I fall short of my exercise intentions.		
When something upsetting comes up, I try very hard to stop thinking about it.		
Sometimes I can't handle the amount of stress, sadness, or frustration I feel.		
When I'm stressed or upset, I either sleep way too much or way too little.		
I won't do something if I think it will make me physically or emotionally uncomfortable.		

The more often you check "true," the more excited we are to help you build skills to process and handle a wide range of emotions in a healthy way.

By looking over these statements, maybe you notice you avoid negative emotions like potholes on the road, sure one of them is going to take you out.

You may also get a glimpse of how swerving around them can come with unintended consequences for your nutrition, exercise, financial, and sleep habits—and how all those can lead to difficulties losing weight or maintaining weight loss.

Maybe you eat out of stress or as a way to seek emotional comfort. Perhaps for you, sleep isn't about giving your body the rest it needs, but rather about avoiding stress or anxiety. If that's true, it's also likely that all of the avoidance is making you more stressed and anxious. Cue more eating, skipping the gym, and an increased risk of becoming dependent on substances like alcohol.

In Chapter 11, you'll learn that emotions—even negative ones—are anything but potholes. Rather, they're opportunities to grow and be more authentically you.

You'll get practice learning how to identify and express your emotions in healthy ways, without negative repercussions to your mental, emotional, or physical health and goals. Instead, your newfound emotional skills will help you excel in every area of your health.

LET'S TALK ABOUT YOUR FOOD

For each statement, check "true" or "false."

	TRUE	FALSE
Thinking about food can make it hard to concentrate on other things.		
My meals regularly contain zero fruits and vegetables.		
When I'm alone, I serve myself foods or portion sizes different from what I eat around others.		
I try to follow specific eating rules to influence my shape or weight.		
I get stressed or anxious about eating at restaurants or social events.		
I count my daily calories.		
I try to cut back on food to make up for overeating.		
In the last month, I've eaten to the point that I was uncomfortably full.		
I exercise so I can eat.		
In the last month, I've intentionally skipped a meal or tried intermittent fasting.		
I regularly avoid carbohydrates.		
I've eaten fast food in the last month.		
I have taken or am currently taking appetite suppressants or weight-loss supplements.		
I serve meals or foods to my family or friends that I don't eat myself.		
In the past, I've tried multiple diets and "cleanses."		

The number of items in this section that ring true for you reveals a lot about your relationship with food and eating. It's possible you're just now realizing how much of your mental real estate is currently being taken up by food, or how much you're focused on restricting certain foods, nutrients, or calories.

What's more, you may notice concrete ways in which your food-related thoughts and habits have hampered your health, fitness, body image, and happiness. Fortunately, each comes with an incredible opportunity to shift how you think about food and eating for nutritional success.

It's not a bad thing that you care about the quality or long-term effects of what you eat. We think it's fabulous that your nutrition is important to you!

In Chapter 12, we'll show you how to shift your focus to what you can add to your food life: more nutrition, more appetite satisfaction, and more clarity in understanding your body's signals so they no longer feel problematic. As a result, you and your body will work as a team; you'll cut down on food stress while getting more nutrition and appetite satisfaction for your calories, and you'll automatically gravitate toward healthier foods and portion sizes.

LET'S TALK ABOUT YOUR PLEASURE

For each statement, check "true" or "false."

	TRUE	FALSE
If I want to reward myself, it's always or almost always with food.		
My daily experiences tend to be more negative than positive.		
I don't have anyone in my life who understands me and with whom I'm deeply connected.		
I don't spend money on myself if I can avoid it.		
I rarely or never enjoy exercise.		
There's hardly any fun in my life.		
I feel selfish if I do something that's just for me.		
I can rarely make time for things I enjoy.		
Sometimes I finish eating something and then realize I barely tasted it.		
I don't really have any hobbies.		
Sometimes I feel resentment bubbling up at my spouse or kids because they have all the fun.		
I often get bored with my food, but still keep eating the same things.		
Sometimes I feel guilty for having fun.		
Food is the one joy I look forward to every day.		
I'm always on the prowl for "guilt-free" foods and desserts.		

If you agree with many of the above statements, we want to talk about the pleasure in your life!

By going through these statements, are you realizing you really don't have that much fun or pleasure in your days? Do you notice that food is your main source of pleasure, or that you're getting absolutely no enjoyment out of healthy activities?

When it comes to health, enjoyment is a crucial yet under-appreciated topic. Just as you need nutrients, activity, and water, optimal health calls for having a wide variety of pleasant experiences in your life, as well as the ability to savor them mindfully and without guilt.

In Chapter 13, you'll learn how to increase the amount of pleasure you get from the life you already have, while making room for new joys. You'll be empowered to savor edible treats without guilt or shame, or pass on them confidently and easily. You'll find out how much fun you can have while getting fitter, eating healthier, and feeling glad you're finally getting MORE.

LET'S TALK ABOUT YOUR REST

For each statement, check "true" or "false."

	TRUE	FALSE
I eat most of my meals while multitasking with work or chores.		
I pack way too many things into weekends and often end up exhausted by Sunday night.		
When I lie down at night, my mind keeps going.		
I'm a workaholic.		
When I'm on vacation, I tend to work a bit or keep up on my email.		
I often skip workouts because I just don't have the energy.		
If I can't get everything on my to-do list done, I feel like I've failed.		
When I'm tired, I just push through using things like caffeine, energy drinks, and sugar.		
On average, I sleep less than seven hours per night.		
30 minutes or more of "me time" typically happens less than once per week.		
I always get in my workouts, no matter how tired or sore I am. It's non-negotiable.		
I don't remember the last time I felt rested.		
When I get sick, I worry about everything I'm not getting done and everyone I'm disappointing.		
I'd love to eat home-cooked meals, but I just don't have the time to spend in the kitchen.		
I rarely sit still or relax. I'm go, go, go.		

Eeek! Are you seeing a "do everything and then some, rest when you're dead" trend emerging? Take notice, then take relief in the fact that you don't have to be so busy. Factoring more rest and recovery into your life can be an immensely pleasurable tool in reaching your health goals.

Based on the statements that are true for you, you may have an inkling that getting more sleep could be just the trick to having more energy to cook healthy, satisfying meals, or to exercise. Maybe you see that your workouts don't adapt to the needs of your body; you just cram them in because it's on your to-do list. You may realize you're just flat burned out.

As good as incorporating more rest in your life sounds, doing so isn't always easy, and it can be at odds with how we've long assessed our own value and worth. So, in Chapter 14, we'll dig into how to make peace with rest and recovery, and teach practical ways to be intentional about rest and recovery in your life.

The result: better health and more sustainable progress toward your physical goals.

PART 3

THE MORE METHOD:
HOW TO GIVE YOURSELF
EVERYTHING YOU NEED TO THRIVE
(AND HIT YOUR GOALS WHILE YOU'RE AT IT)

CHAPTER 9
BODY LOVE, AT LAST

In this chapter, we'll focus on giving our bodies more space, freedom, and love. And, as we discussed in Chapter 1, that won't mean forgoing all aesthetic or weight goals. Instead, we'll identify goals that are empowering to us. We'll practice celebrating our bodies while encouraging their growth.

Taking this approach allows us to make sustainable progress toward our goals in a way that feels good and is aligned with our values. However, because it goes against much of our experiences with our bodies, other women, and the world, embracing a MORE mentality as it relates to our bodies won't be like flipping a switch.

It will feel counterintuitive. You'll hear self-destructive thoughts threaten your newfound body love. That's part of the reason Chapter 15 is entirely devoted to troubleshooting and responding to forces that encourage you to shrink back!

Be gentle with yourself and when you find yourself struggling, focus on one thing: how amazing your body is… right now.

FALL INTO LOVE

Few women have stopped to really appreciate their bodies and everything they do—every second of every day. That changes right now, so get comfy and get ready for a little exercise.

Consider this: Your body is made up of 37.2 trillion individual cells.[252] Those cells form more than 200 bones and the more than 430 muscles that connect to and move your skeleton.[253] Every single movement you make—when you walk, give a hug, smell a flower, or belt out songs to Spotify—requires extensive chemical and electrical reactions, with a single nerve cell firing up to 1,000 impulses, or signals, every second,[254] to contract hundreds or thousands of muscle cells. Each of these muscle cells is about the diameter of a human hair. The contractile structures within them are as little as 1/26,000 the diameter of that same hair.[255]

While all of this is going on in your musculoskeletal system, smooth muscle cells in your digestive tract, respiratory system, reproductive organs, eyes, and skin operate constantly and involuntarily. The cardiac muscle keeps your heart (and everything else) beating along in rhythm.

Oxygen and carbon dioxide trade places, hormones communicate messages between organs, foods turn into your body's structural cells, chemical reactions create energy, tissues repair as you sleep, and experts routinely call the brain the "most complex object in the universe."[256]

The female body is extra special. It's the only body capable of giving life. It's the only body that can grow an embryo into a human being, and give that tiny person all the nutrients they need to thrive. And no matter how much you hate your periods, the fact that the female body can bleed for five days and not die is impressive.

When met with challenges in conceiving, carrying a pregnancy, or producing milk, many women report feeling like their bodies have let them down. If that's you, honor that experience and, as we'll explore shortly, know that it's possible to both value your body and feel disappointed in it.

Your individual body's awesomeness is in no way contingent on the desire or ability to conceive or breastfeed. While some women may actively choose to not procreate or breastfeed, others may not have that option available to them.

Suffice it to say that your body is cool. Like, really cool. Let that set in for a minute. Seriously, stop reading and consider everything you're fortunate enough for your body to allow you to do: walk, dance, have sex, jump, run, hug, literally climb mountains. It's often not unless we encounter injury, illness, or disability that we fully appreciate that these abilities are available to us; don't wait.

Now think about everything that's happening inside your body this very instant. Think about how awesome it is that you're able to look at some squiggles on a page, understand them as words, and then follow their instructions to just sit there and think about that awesomeness! (It's also pretty meta.)

So what's the point of all of this? It's that you have phenomenal reasons to be in awe of your body. It's a rock star. It's a freaking masterpiece. It's worth far more than just accepting. It's worth falling head-over-heels, prematurely-change-your-relationship-status-and-make-everything-weird in love with your body.

Loving our bodies is part of loving ourselves. And loving ourselves is the foundation of giving ourselves MORE. It allows us to better mentally and emotionally connect with ourselves. It makes us want to give our bodies all the nutrition they need to thrive. It drives us to soak up pleasures with all of our senses. Loving our bodies helps us build fulfilling habits around exercise that, instead of punishing our bodies, leads us to revel in them!

Still, loving our bodies isn't a fairytale scenario. Think about it like loving a romantic partner; we've had to learn the hard way that "happily ever after" doesn't exist—at least, not in the way cartoons taught us it did. Instead, after the carriage pulls away from the castle, at times we're frustrated with, disappointed in, or mad at our partners. We freak out over their clothes on the floor, cry over broken promises, and never understand how they walk around with tree trunks sprouting from between what we'd think would be two separate eyebrows. But here's the thing: We love them, regardless. In some ways, those blips make us love them even more. They allow us to see and fully appreciate the intricacies of the people in front of us.

Similarly, loving our bodies doesn't mean that at times we won't be frustrated with, disappointed in, or mad at them. Occasionally, our bodies will resist healthy change, tucker out when we want to keep going, and bloat with no regard as to what we were planning to wear. We'll have times when we eat so much it hurts. We'll mourn missed race PRs and see that the mirror doesn't always reflect our goals. And we'll love the quirky, complicated homes that our bodies are.

OWNING OUR PHYSICAL PRESENCE

Allowing our bodies to take up literal space can be a powerful way to express and grow body love.

For example, think back to Chapter 7 and how it felt to take in a full, deep breath, and know that you had all of the room you needed. How cool would it be to feel that way all the time? What if when talking to friends, family, or coworkers, you opened your chest and looked them in the eyes as opposed to curling your body forward and looking at the floor. What would happen if you entered spaces like gyms and fitness studios, fancy restaurants, and dance clubs with confidence?

Now imagine how it would feel to stay on the cement when passing people on the sidewalk, instead of letting them run you into the grass, ditch, or tree planter? How would it feel to not pretzel up like a contortionist on the train so everyone else would be more comfortable?

Note: We aren't advocating being rude. There's a difference between walking straight down the middle of the sidewalk so everyone has to move around you, and staying to the right (or left, depending on your country!) part of the path. Body love is about treating your body in a way that acknowledges that it merits the same space freedoms as anyone else's.

How we move in situations like these reflects how much room we believe our bodies deserve, and as cheesy as the term "power pose" is, a recent review of 55 studies shows that how we carry our physical bodies does in fact impact our sense of self-worth, confidence, and mood.[257] With practice, taking up the space we need can cause a ripple effect. We begin to more highly value ourselves, learn we belong anywhere we want to be, and enjoy a greater ability to approach all of our health habits in a more empowering way. We open ourselves up to MORE.

To get started, we encourage you to pick one experience in which you find yourself regularly trying to shrink or give others more space than you afford yourself. No, you don't have to invent the wheel here; if one of the previous examples resonates with you, go with it. Now, this week (or month, if the situation isn't very frequent), make a concerted effort to own your physical presence in that situation and space. Keep your head up, chest proud, and don't scrunch unless everyone else is scrunching, too. In and immediately after those moments, pay attention to what happened when you gave your body room to be. What did you feel?

Next week or month, try taking up space in another way. Again, it can be in a situation we've already mentioned. Keep identifying ways to show up in your body and make you feel worthy in the world around you.

ESCAPING THE COMPARISON
TRAP AND FINDING ABUNDANCE

As we explored in Chapter 1, your natural tendency to compare your body against those of other women is a major source of negative feelings. That's the case whether you're checking out the woman next to you in cycling class or photos in advertisements, movies, shows, and social media.

We aren't going to tell you to put on blinders and ignore every woman around you. *Threat alert, threat alert!* We also aren't going to urge you to rid all comparison from your life. Making social comparisons is part of human nature, and ditching it altogether is close to, if not entirely impossible.

What *are* we going to do? We're going to teach you how to practice seeing the women around you in a way that doesn't put you or them down. We'll help you admire others without envying them. It'll require embracing a spirit of abundance, rather than scarcity. This involves fully affirming that one woman's long legs or six pack doesn't make your body any less attractive, strong, capable, or worthy.

It also involves knowing that another woman's body shape or size doesn't make you any more attractive, strong, capable, or worthy.

There's enough love, value, and beauty to go around—no rationing necessary. It sounds simple, but it's a radical idea that requires *a lot* of intentional practice.

So, let's get practicing.

To ease into things, look at a single picture of a woman. It can be of you and your friends; it can be a post from someone you follow on social media; it can be a makeup ad torn from a magazine. Whatever works; the priority is picking one single image. Don't spend 10 minutes scrolling through photos and feeling bad about your body before we even get into this exercise, which is supposed to be all about *not* feeling bad about your body.

Once you have the picture, close your eyes and take five slow, deep breaths. With each inhale, repeat in your head, *I breathe in abundance*. With each exhale, repeat, *I let go of competition*.

Now open your eyes. Take a minute or two to notice the picture and the body form(s) it displays. You can set a watch if that's your kind of thing. Describe the shapes and textures you see. Maybe the woman's arms, legs, stomach, or back are slender, soft, rippled with muscles, curved, straight, or dimpled with cellulite. They are likely several of these things!

If you feel your mind start to wander toward self-criticism, we invite you to *not* get mad at yourself. That's not going to help anything! Instead, show yourself compassion. Something you might tell yourself:

"This image makes me feel bad about myself because I'm not as X, Y, or Z, and that's an understandable response given all of my past experiences. Plus, our minds naturally seek out comparisons that make us feel bad about ourselves. It's not a sign of weakness, but a part of being a human and a woman. However, her body doesn't affect the worth or beauty of my own body."

We encourage you to take this practice at your own pace. If this sounds like a nightmare, maybe now isn't the time. If you're feeling down or emotionally vulnerable, it can be beneficial to hold off until you're in a good place. This exercise isn't intended to make you feel horrible. It's designed to help you learn to observe women's bodies without getting down on yourself, and when you do get down on yourself, to learn to stop the spiral and get back to abundance.

Over time, and once you're comfortable giving it a go, you can try this exercise when you're out and about in three-dimensional life. We advise against creepy staring, but encourage you to get in the habit of appreciating the other women in your life rather than strictly focusing on images. After all, they're real.

> It's healthy to recognize that women don't necessarily wake up with push-up-style breasts and perfectly styled hair. Some of the women around you may have undergone weight-loss or other cosmetic procedures. And most women you see have put in some effort to look how they do. *Slimming, high-waist jeans, check!* That's okay! What every woman does with her body is her right.

When we pay more attention to women who fill our worlds rather than our feeds, we automatically calibrate our comparisons closer to reality. That way, when we do start to fall into comparisons, at least we're not comparing ourselves to things that are only achievable with strategic posing, lighting, and a lot of reshaping and retouching. In fact, research suggests that in-person comparisons are associated with fewer negative outcomes than are comparisons with social media and magazine images.[258]

What's true, no matter what you see: your body's value, strength, and beauty.

WORKING OUT OF LOVE: GOALS AND MOTIVATION

Truly loving your body radically alters the attitude with which we seek a physical goal. It allows us to work toward goals with an eagerness to connect with, grow, care for, and fall more in love with our bodies, rather than to correct, fix, or punish them.

SETTING HEALTHY GOALS

If establishing love-based goals is pivotal to giving yourself MORE, what are your goals? What about your body do you want to change? (Because, yes! You can totally love your body and want to change it!)

What about it do you want to stay the same? What qualities or abilities do you love and want to build upon?

In the following section, you'll learn how to establish motivating and empowering goals that nurture your physical, mental, and emotional health.

STEP 1:
DETERMINE WHAT GOALS REALLY MATTER TO YOU

Unfortunately, as we explored in Chapter 1, a lot of our body goals are actually someone else's—internalized over decades of conditioning. It can be incredibly powerful to straight-up ask yourself, "Is this something I want?" Although it's not easy to tease apart what we truly want from what we believe we're supposed to want, it's possible with introspection and practice.

Let's get to it! Go ahead and write down your current body goals. No censoring; as soon as something pops into your head, write it down!

_____

_____

_____

_____

_____

Now, pick one of those goals and consider the following questions. As you move through them, plug your answers into the following table. It doesn't matter which goal you select first—we're going to repeat this exercise for all of them. The table has room for five goals, but don't feel like you have to limit yourself. If you run over, grab a piece of paper and keep going.

	GOAL ONE	GOAL TWO	GOAL THREE	GOAL FOUR	GOAL FIVE
When do I remember first having this goal					
How will I feel when I achieve this goal?					
How will striving toward this goal affect my life?					
Is this goal—and the work involved in reaching it—in line with my values?					
Who in my life has suggested this goal—and why?					
At any point, have I said "should" about this goal?					

WHEN DO I REMEMBER FIRST HAVING THIS GOAL?

Maybe it's when a kid at school made fun of your body, or when you first noticed your mom dieting. Maybe you don't remember the first time the goal occurred to you, but you can't remember ever *not* having it. Whatever the case, seeing how this goal falls on a timeline can be helpful in determining its roots.

HOW WILL I FEEL WHEN I ACHIEVE THIS GOAL?

Achieving goals can make us feel capable, strong, talented, and tenacious—and that's great. However, many of us work toward goals believing their achievement will make us feel worthy, happier in all areas of our lives, or loved. None of these things are actually contingent upon performance!

You're a worthy human, irrespective of your performance. Losing 10 pounds will not make you a happier person. A "2" printed on the tag inside your jeans won't make you happy in your job. Having a six pack will not earn you love or allow you to better receive it.

HOW WILL STRIVING TOWARD THIS GOAL AFFECT MY LIFE?

Even if you think it would be awesome to run a marathon, it doesn't mean you want to run 40 or 50 miles per week to enter the race strong and finish injury-free. In some cases, the simple realization that you want the result but not what's involved in reaching it is reason enough to abandon or revise your goal.

However, just because you don't want to do something doesn't necessarily mean it isn't worth it—that's a call only you can make.

If you really, really, really want to run that marathon and have it as a bucket-list goal but don't exactly want to spend so much time training, consider how that training will affect your life. You'll obviously spend a good bit of time running, and it's likely you'll improve your blood pressure, aerobic capacity, and muscle strength and endurance in the process.

If you don't properly train, and even if you do, it's also possible you'll experience some sort of exercise-induced ache, pain, or injury. You'll likely have to rework your daily habits to make time for training. Maybe you'll have to exercise on your lunch breaks or devote Saturdays to long runs. You might need your partner to prepare dinner or put the kids to bed without you some nights.

That's a lot of possibilities—some more positive than others. When it comes to many goals, you might not really know how working toward them will affect your life. You might think you do, when in fact the work required is really significantly more or less.

Women often approach us with body composition goals that, once exploring, they realize are either unrealistic or unhealthy. A client might want to lose 20 pounds in two months. However, that's a rate of weight loss that would put her at great risk of not just rebounding, but also compromising her overall health. For example, losing weight that quickly might result in her losing half, if not more, of that weight from muscle.

Another client might want to get to a body-fat percentage of 12%, but be unaware that at that level, some women lose their periods—and not in a "yay, no more periods!" way. Instead, hormone levels can fluctuate to a degree that women's reproductive organs' regular functions cease. These hormonal changes can also lead to decreased bone mineral density and, even in young women, osteoporosis and frequent bone breaks.

On the flip side, many clients also approach us with goals they think will involve more work or be far harder than they actually will. They might think they need to deprive themselves of the foods they love and hit the gym seven days per week. Some think they have to push themselves through pain.

In the end, determining exactly what work's involved in reaching a given goal isn't always easy. They didn't teach this stuff in health class, and it can feel like everything you find online is conflicting. Educate yourself on your specific goal by turning to reputable sources (-.edu, -.gov, and -.org sites are good places to start, as are georgiefear.com and kaleishafetters.com) and working with qualified health professionals. Letters to look for: MD, DO, PhD, RD, CSSD, CSCS, DPT, PT, CPT. Those letters aren't the only making of a knowledgeable expert, but they're a good place to start.

IS THIS GOAL—AND THE WORK INVOLVED IN REACHING IT— IN LINE WITH MY VALUES?

If you value being in nature, hiking, exploring, and camping, a goal to build the strength and endurance to climb hills, scramble over rocks, and carry firewood is very much aligned with your values. However, if you value social time with friends and family, vowing to never eat out should be a hard pass. Make sure the changes you're considering fit with your current lifestyle, or at least a life that you can feel good about adopting.

Georgie learned this lesson through an unfortunate decision to try the oh-so-trendy hairstyle of side-swept bangs. The goal was to have more stylish hair than the daily braid or ponytail. The hard truth, however, was that her priorities will never include styling her hair with hot tools every morning. It was a long year of bobby-pinning.

Pursuing goals aligned with your values orients the motivation as internal, increasing its intrinsic nature. That explains why it's often easier to make large behavior changes for ethical, religious, or value-based reasons.

For example, when cutting down on or removing animal products from meals, ethical or identity-based reasons are often far more motivating over the long term compared with health-related ideals. The same goes for eating kosher, or halal, or biking to work.

WHO IN MY LIFE SUGGESTED THIS GOAL—AND WHY?

It's possible for people, even loved ones, to push goals as a result of their own body-image issues, insecurities, or weight stigmas. A mother might suggest that her daughter lose weight because she believes her friends will think less of her if she's overweight.

What's more, negative comments often serve as a way to make the commenter feel better about their own body. Again, since people tend to think in terms of relatives and social comparisons, deriding someone else's perceived flaws can be a way to temporarily boost their sense of self-worth.

However, just because someone proposes a goal doesn't mean it can't be your goal too. In fact, those who love and support us often suggest goals designed to give ourselves MORE. For example, a family member may want you to start a workout plan because you're more energetic and mentally healthy when regularly engaging in exercise. Maybe they want you to be around for a long time, and consider weight loss or changing your eating habits as a way to increase your quality and length of life.

Trusted friends and family members with whom you have deep, meaningful relationships can be important sounding boards in your life. These people often have insights into your nature and habits you aren't even aware of yourself. Take advantage of their presence to help you process your goals, unpack the motivations behind them, and think through how they might impact various aspects of your life.

AT ANY POINT, HAVE I SAID "SHOULD?"

Saying "should" is a pretty strong sign you feel something is being forced on you. It may be that the goal—or what you think must be done to reach it—is something you've internalized.

At the very least, it's likely you don't feel good about whatever it is you "should" do, and that, over the long term, your chances of sticking with it are minimal. "Shoulds" suggest that extrinsic rather than intrinsic motivation is behind your goal. And extrinsic motivation wears out fast.

STEP 2:
TURN LOSS INTO GAIN

After determining what goals truly matter to you, it can be good to also think through how we can reframe those goals to make them more internal or compatible with our values.

How can we reframe them to make them feel better to us, like they're helping us give ourselves more—more vitality, freedom, body love, pleasure, more of everything we value?

Let's look at all of your goals that seek LESS and examine how it would feel to rework them into goals for MORE. In the table on the following page, write all of your goals that concern loss or subtracting from your body.

Then, try to reword the goal in a way that focuses on the positive, and what you have to gain, rather than lose.

GOALS FOR **LESS**	REFRAMED FOR **MORE**	HOW DOES THIS REFRAME FEEL?

Lastly, write down how this mental reframe feels.

Does it feel more motivating?

Does letting go of your loss-focused goals make you uneasy?

There are no right or wrong answers here… just exploration.

If you're feeling stuck, take a look at this example for help. Don't worry; this can be pretty counterintuitive at first. Your answers don't have to look anything like these, and it's possible you'll have more or fewer loss-centric goals to work through.

GOALS FOR **LESS**	REFRAMED FOR **MORE**	HOW DOES THIS REFRAME FEEL?
Lose 20 pounds	Be able to wear those pants I love.	I'm digging it.
Burn at least 500 calories in every workout.	Move an hour during each workout.	Sounds like it will require a lot less tracking.
Get rid of my belly pooch.	Define my core.	Excited!
Cut calories.	Eat more fruits and veggies.	Good. I hate counting calories.
Make my arms less jiggly.	Perform a pull-up.	It would be awesome to do, but it's hard to imagine I'll ever be able to do a pull-up!

We find that for our clients and for ourselves, framing goals in terms of what we want to gain in our bodies and lives instead of what we want to subtract from them fosters healthier body images and relationships to both food and exercise.

In fact, research shows that weight-neutral approaches to behavioral change result in greater improvements in body-led eating (something we'll dive into in Chapter 12), physical activity, produce intake, cardiovascular health, self-esteem, and quality of life.[259]

STEP 3:
CONSIDER PROCESSES VERSUS OUTCOMES

To keep us motivated and prevent the frustration that comes with chasing big, pie-in-the-sky goals, you likely know it's helpful to break big goals into smaller ones. That's completely true, but it can also be helpful to tilt goals toward processes as opposed to outcomes.

Let's explain.

Process goals are goals over which we have control and are action oriented. If we give it an honest try, we're pretty much guaranteed to achieve the goal. Conversely, outcome goals are goals over which we have much less control and that are more focused on results. Even if we put in all the work, things might not pan out. Sometimes, reaching outcome goals doesn't just depend on what we do, but also what the people around us do.

Of course, as in all things "health," none of this is black and white; it's a million shades and hues of gray. The majority of goals fall somewhere in the middle, with many having both process- and outcome-related characteristics. This is especially true when it comes to exercise performance.

For example, deadlifting a certain number of pounds could be considered a process goal, but it also requires us to perform— and the reality is that we all have off days when, even if we put forth 100% of our max effort, we can't complete a lift we usually can. And while doing 10 consecutive push-ups per day could be considered a process goal, for someone who can currently perform one or two push-ups at a time, it's certainly an outcome goal.

We encourage women to think of goals as lying on a spectrum between pure process and outcome. Here's where some might end up:

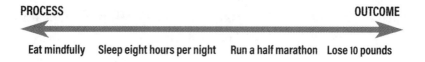

PROCESS   **OUTCOME**

Eat mindfully   Sleep eight hours per night   Run a half marathon   Lose 10 pounds

Where do your goals lie? Go ahead, write them below the line.

PROCESS   **OUTCOME**

It's okay for your goals to exist across this continuum, but we recommend that the bulk of yours tilt toward the process rather than outcome end. When our clients have an abundance of outcome-focused goals, we often find it's more productive to shift attention to process goals. Here, reframing can again be useful. So, if an outcome goal of yours is to build your glutes, a more process-related version could be to perform some form of hip thrust, deadlift, and squat three times per week.

However, even that goal has some outcome-related features, right? After all, achieving it isn't entirely under your control. What if you have a fever, are throwing up, or are sick with other symptoms that contraindicate exercise? When working toward our goals, it's important to treat ourselves with kindness, flexibility, and to remember that our foremost goal is to give our bodies what they need.

REINFORCEMENT AND KEEPING THE GOOD VIBES GOING

When working toward your goals with body love, it's vital to have an eagerness to celebrate it through positive reinforcement. Recognizing and applauding progress helps build self-efficacy, self-esteem, and confidence. It colors our relationships with healthy behaviors as affirmative and enjoyable.

In *The Power of Habit*, Charles Duhigg affirms that a leading reason people struggle to adopt new habits is because they don't adequately reward their efforts along the way.[260] This applause is called **positive reinforcement**. While we've all thrown around this term at one time or another, to actually give ourselves positive reinforcement, we have to fully understand it.

Positive reinforcement is the act of rewarding desired actions with something desirable. For example, when you hit a personal record in a workout, you might play your designated victory song, something you love and that makes you feel invincible. When you hit your fruit-and-veggie goals for an entire month, you might buy yourself something that's long been on your wish list.

The big idea is to reward the behavior with goodies!

GIVE YOURSELF CREDIT! Positive reinforcement can take the form of noticing your intrinsic rewards, like feelings of accomplishment and greater energy levels. Intrinsic rewards are things like feeling proud of yourself for that healthy meal, admiring your own persistence in figuring out that trail map, and appreciating how hard you worked to speak your feelings more openly. Every little choice to give yourself MORE deserves positive reinforcement.

Don't just stop with a pat on the back. Heap this positive reinforcement on yourself, roll around in it, and soak it up. Too often people discount their small wins rather than celebrate them; yet celebrating them is the most effective way to propel your momentum and consistency to keep on with your wins.

Negative reinforcement also refers to rewarding actions, but with it, instead of adding something, an unpleasant thing is taken away or stops. For example, if you perform all your planned workouts for the week, you might reward yourself by skipping dinner at your in-laws' house. If you drink a glass of water and discover your headache and sluggishness evaporate, that's also reinforcing. It makes us more likely to repeat and make that choice again.

These types of reinforcement are often confused with **positive punishment** and **negative punishment**. However, positive and negative punishment are all about decreasing actions by either subjecting you to something you hate or by taking away something you love. Either way, yuck.

For example, if you ditch a workout class at the last minute, you might reprimand yourself, force yourself to pick up a spider (we have no idea why we're using this as an example, but yeah...), or cancel your pleasurable weekly massage. If you eat something you regret, you might tell yourself all sorts of mean things.

Hopefully, from simply reading these examples, it's evident why reinforcement tends to be the most effective and healthy approach. Positive reinforcement is our favorite to use with our clients and ourselves because it focuses on our successes and encourages better mood states, which not only feel pleasant but are optimal for learning.[261]

Reinforcement keeps us focused on performing the actions that take us toward our goal, rather than on worries or dread about what might happen if we miss the mark. In contrast, punishment fosters negative mood states, anxiety, and possibly avoidance. (Here's a garbage receptable you can put those punishments in; you won't be needing them anymore.)

While you're reinforcing your desired behaviors, it's important to do so without creating a negative relationship with other things in your life. We aren't into framing exercise as a bad thing, so suggest you don't choose to skip a sprint workout as a negative reinforcement for hitting your vegetable nutrition goals! Cancelling a workout as a reward is similar to using exercise as punishment, and we want to keep movement associated with fun and good feelings.

This is another reason we advise against using food as a reward. Yes, food is delightful! And we encourage you to wholeheartedly savor it, but we don't want you to set up a transactional relationship in which food is a bribe to get you to do other things.

Food is not something you earn; it's your right as a living human being so you should be giving yourself enough of it—and making it tasty—every day.

List five desirable things or actions that can serve as positive reinforcement as you work toward your goals, whatever they may be. What would you love?

1. _____

2. _____

3. _____

4. _____

5. _____

All this begs one more question: What actions are you going to reward? First and foremost, lean toward process goals. Then you can sprinkle in some outcomes!

Filling out fitness trackers and food logs can be handy to gauge what you're doing from week to week and even year to year—and for some women, looking through them can impart a sense of pride and accomplishment.

That can be a form of positive reinforcement on its own. Seeing everything you've logged can alert you to the fact that you've done something awesome. It can also let you know it's time for a a more external reward. Get excited!

> If you're following a workout plan, tracking your workouts can be critical to making sure you get the greatest physical benefits from them and stay safe (no putting too much weight on the barbell!). This can be a logical place to look for positive habits or the accomplishment of goals.

Still, please don't become a slave to these trackers. We discourage tracking calories, macros, and mealtimes unless it's for a very short time to gain awareness about your eating habits.

If following and filling them out starts to feel like another "should," abandon ship!

This is where simply focusing on recognizing your healthy behaviors in the moment can be the way to go. And even if you track your workouts, don't rely on your tracker to notice success.

After you take a timeout for a mindful bite, give yourself a little nod. When you identify that you're stressed, anxious, bored, or sad, and respond in a way that meets your needs, be proud that you did.

Even with goals, it's the journey that matters most.

CHAPTER 10
FIND WHAT MOVES YOU

Can't seem to stick with your workout plans? Hate exercise? Always need to get "back on track?" Let's make one thing very clear: There is no track.

Go off-roading. Make your own path. Explore tons of different directions. Get a feel for the infinite number of ways to revel in and grow your ridiculously fabulous body's ability to bend, stretch, flex, carry, lift, and take in meaningful experiences.

That sounds pretty nice, right? Maybe even a little fairytale-ish? But how on Earth do you make it happen? Like you do with all things health: with practice.

You're about to learn how to change your relationship with exercise, move in ways that are both physically and mentally rewarding, and even start to enjoy your workouts. Then, you'll put it into practice—again and again and again. That doesn't mean it will all be arduous work, though. After all, the goal is to *enjoy* exercise! In time, your mental and physical skills will grow, and as they do, you'll notice your relationship with movement expanding even more.

WHAT DO YOU HAVE TO GAIN?

As women, most of our experiences with exercise have been focused on loss, subtracting, and fixing perceived faults.

We aren't interested in any of that. We're into a "gain" mentality, and believe it can be a powerful reframe in women's fitness and in your personal relationship with exercise. It's the antithesis of LESS. It goes against many of the factors that encourage us to hate exercise, actively avoid it, or be unable to stick with it for very long.

However, we're expanding our "gain" mentality beyond pure muscle size or pounds lifted, although those can be fun ways to gain, and we'll explore them later. There are an infinite number of ways we stand to gain from movement.

Here's a small selection:

- **Greater Energy:** Exercise expends energy, but it also develops it. There's a strong, consistent relationship between physical activity and increases in energy.[262] While researchers aren't sure of the exact mechanisms, the mental benefits of exercise may play a role.

- **Better Mental Health:** Endorphins are great, but exercise doesn't stop there. (Fun fact: Exercise also influences the body's endocannabinoid system, the same one that the THC in marijuana affects to get you high.[263]) By easing anxiety, depression, and negative mood states, as well as by improving self-esteem and cognitive function, exercise significantly improves mental and emotional health.[264] This is true both acutely (immediately after exercise) and chronically (over the course of your life).

- **A Longer, Happier Life:** Speaking of the long term, research shows that any exercise, for any duration and at any intensity, is associated with longer lifespans.[265] But what good are those if they aren't made of healthy, happy years? Fortunately, physical activity also significantly boosts quality of life.[266]

- **Career Success:** Research links regular movement to increased mental creativity,[267] time management skills, and work productivity.[268]

- **More Great Memories:** With more years—and more life quality—ahead of you, you'll have that many more memories worth treasuring. Luckily, exercise improves memory in people of all ages. Bonus: Studies have shown it improves memory not just in older adults,[269] but even in youngsters.[270]

We hope that as you read through this seriously abbreviated list—and maybe even brainstorm some things you have to gain in your personal life—you feel some of the relief that comes with focusing on gain over loss. You may notice that by exploring these possibilities, your focus on aesthetic goals softens. You may also discover that this approach to exercise is way more fun than your current one!

Another cool side effect is that when we focus on how exercise can expand what's possible for our bodies and futures, we automatically start to have greater appreciation for how other areas of our lives, such as rest and nutrition, can support our physical growth. Research shows that the more time people spend engaged in even light physical activity, the more likely they are to stick with their nutrition goals.[271]

GET YOURS: STRENGTH

Strength is one of our favorite gains. It's a gain that, apart from giving the middle finger to gender expectations (something we love to do), is consistently one of the most mentally transformative goals we see women pursue.

Strength training is perhaps the most common way to build physical strength. It's linked to increased mental resiliency, lower levels of anxiety, and improved body image and perceived physical appearance—no matter the actual aesthetic results.[272, 273, 274]

In one study, after women performed strength workouts twice per week for 12 weeks, they felt significantly better about their physical selves and had improved body images. Interestingly, this was despite the women *gaining* an average of a pound during the study. Note: Their body-fat percentages decreased, suggesting that the women's weight gain was from lean muscle rather than fat.[275]

Learning to take on and grow against physical resistance helps give us the confidence to work against resistance in other areas of our lives. "If I can do this, I can do anything," might be a cliché, but it can also be a pervasive mental experience during strength training. For instance, many of Aleisha's clients describe completing their first pull-up as one of the most empowering moments of their lives.

In everyday life, strength widens the number of things you can do in life, granted you want to do them. Greater strength might allow you to lift your own bag into an overhead compartment without incident, move furniture around your living room, easily tackle flights of stairs, climb on the kitchen counters to reach top cabinets, and play with your nieces and nephews without restrictions.

However, traditional strength training is not a requisite for building strength. The female body is capable of pursuing strength goals in an infinite number of ways. After all, in yoga, holding a handstand certainly counts as a feat of strength. Strength is what enables runners and cyclists to sprint toward the finish line. Boxing, rock climbing, Pilates, hiking, swimming… these all build strength.

If strength is a goal that perks up your ears, you'll want to build strength in a way that, similarly, keeps you having fun.

STOP THE PUNISHMENT

With a focus on using movement as a way to grow and nurture our bodies, exercise starts to become less like an act of punishment.

We're able to think of working out as something that's giving us more years, functional abilities, and quality of life. In turn, we start to become less worried about how many calories we burn. Maybe we throw our towel over the cardio machine's monitor because we really don't care what it says. (Those calorie counts are always wrong, anyway.)

You may have already started to think about how having a "gain mentality" would change your movement habits. You might have considered what forms of exercises you'd do and what you'd cut from your plan. Haven't thought about it? No worries, because we're going to focus on that throughout this section.

Digging into the activities and ways in which we exercise is critical to fostering a relationship with exercise that isn't about pain, punishment, or just pushing through, but about caring for and enjoying our physical selves.

LIKES AND DISLIKES

Having a healthy view of exercise as a whole doesn't mean we still aren't going to hate certain types of exercise. All of us have preferences, likes, and dislikes—and there will be some activities that won't feel good to you. No single exercise is mandatory, no matter how beneficial or popular it might be. There are thousands of ways to move, and even within a single sport, options abound. When moving for MORE, we want to fit exercise to our individual bodies, rather than cramming our bodies into exercises we think we "should" do.

Thinking through the following questions will help you identify your individual preferences about exercise and learn how to structure your workouts around greater enjoyment. The best forms of exercise are those you enjoy! It will also help you gain a sense of autonomy over your workouts, which is a crucial component of intrinsic motivation.

WHAT FORMS OF PHYSICAL ACTIVITY, SPECIFIC EXERCISES, OR WORKOUT SET-UPS DO YOU HATE? WHAT FORMS DO YOU LOVE?

Some women hate running. Is that you? Cool. You don't have to run. Maybe lifting, yoga, boxing, or rowing is more your style. But maybe you just aren't into running sprints. So how do you feel about steady-state jogging? What about treadmill versus outdoor running? Do you feel the same about hitting the pavement solo or with friends?

Other questions for reflection: Do you prefer regularly switching up workouts or having a lot of consistency in your routine? How do you feel about "can't stop, won't stop" circuits? Do you like to have plenty of rest between exercises so that you can dive into each one feeling fresh and ready to rock?

Think through your best and worst exercise memories and consider what factors made them so good or bad. If you don't have any great exercise memories, rest assured that's about to change.

WHAT ABOUT YOUR DISLIKES RUB YOU THE WRONG WAY?

You may not like certain forms or styles of exercise because you just don't. That's fair; but consider the possibility of your distaste being due to having always approached such workouts with a punishment mentality or without compassion. Maybe you've frequently pushed yourself to pain, sickness, or injury. Maybe you have existing health issues such as cranky joints or low blood pressure that make certain movements miserable, but you've always tried to "tough it out."

Another strong possibility is that you don't like a certain exercise because you don't think you're good at it. We all dislike things that make us feel like we should be donning a dunce cap!

WHAT ABOUT YOUR LIKES GETS YOU GROOVING?

The most likely scenario is that you think you're good at them. That's competence, and it's a big part of the intrinsic-motivation equation. We all have a natural desire to do things we believe we are competent in doing because it reinforces feelings of self-efficacy and confidence. *Yeah, we rock.*

It's also possible that when doing workouts you love, you tend to lose track of time. Your mind just shuts off and, at the end of the exercise, you're like, "Where did the time go?" Psychologists refer to this mental state as "flow," and believe it plays a large role in runner's highs—which, no, aren't limited to running.[276]

A central tenet of mental flow is that to experience it, we must have a nice balance between the perceived challenges of the task at hand and our own perceived skills. For something to get us flowing, it has to feel challenging yet doable.[277] If it's not challenging, we won't devote all of our attentional focus to it and our minds will wander. If it's too challenging, we'll just get frustrated. (Remember, we yearn to feel competent!)

It's important to focus on moving in ways that challenge us, but that we feel confident in our abilities to overcome. However, that doesn't just mean doing things we're already good at, but also approaching the things we aren't so great at with a growth rather than a fixed mindset. With a **growth mindset**, we view our qualities and abilities as mere starting points, and failure as an opportunity to expand them. With a **fixed mindset**, we treat our qualities and abilities as more set in stone. Tasks therefore become tests, with failure being an indicator of personal defects.

Fortunately, it's possible to build a growth mindset by paying attention to our thoughts and words, stopping ourselves when we sense our slippage into a fixed mindset, and trying to reframe things through the lens of growth. For instance, if we start telling ourselves, "I'm so bad at yoga," we'd pause, and switch it up: "I have relatively little experience with yoga, so of course it isn't going to be my strong suit. But a regular practice can improve my muscle flexibility, joint mobility, balance, and strength so that in time, I'll crush it."

It can also be helpful to calibrate the exercises we perform to levels that are more doable and closer to our perceived levels of competence. Going back to yoga, if we're just getting started with regular classes, of course we're not going to be able to do headstands and other gravity-defying poses. Instead, we focus on the fundamentals and mastering the poses that feel challenging, but also doable.

Plus, that's the only way the handstands will ever happen.

PLAY AROUND!

When pursuing fitness goals, it's critical to exercise in a way that's designed to help us reach them. But that doesn't mean all of our workouts need to revolve around those goals. Here's a novel idea: Integrate one pure "play day" into every week.

What's a play day? It's a "workout" in which you approach movement in the same way you did as a child: for pure fun and with no agenda. As a kid, maybe you loved swinging on swings or playing flashlight tag. We're willing to bet you'd still love them. It's amazing how good it can feel as an adult to just sit down and swing, to feel the wind on your face. And there's no reason you can't play flashlight tag now. Seriously, you and your friends could have a lot of fun with a game!

Adulthood is also an opportunity to explore new ways to play. Maybe you'll discover cross-country skiing, soccer, or dodgeball. Maybe you'll try fun-looking, level-appropriate exercises you see on Instagram. Maybe you'll climb on rock walls with the fervor you used to take on jungle gyms. Maybe you'll go to a trampoline park and just bounce.

Your choices are completely up to you, but don't put off play! Right now, we want you to devote one day per week to play. Move in ways that make you smile, laugh, and add deposits to your I-love-exercise memory bank.

As your balance grows, your relationship with exercise will become even more rewarding.

GET A FEEL FOR INTENSITY

If you've long placed a priority on wrecking yourself through your workouts, it can be difficult to know exactly how hard to push yourself. Exercise isn't supposed to be painful, but it isn't supposed to *always* feel like butterfly kisses, either. To optimally benefit from exercise, you do need to push yourself out of your comfort zone. How far? There's no single answer, but Aleisha likes to tell her clients, "When you finish a workout, your body deserves to feel better than it did when you started."

It's simple, but taking this message to heart can radically alter how you approach your exercise intensity and push your body. It also allows you to make more efficient gains—in all areas of your life. By focusing on how you feel, you're better able to ensure your body improved recovery, as well as consistency.

Consistency is vital to exercise gains, whether you're vying for increased strength, aerobic endurance, cardiovascular fitness, or mental health. If you're able to move well and often, rather than once a week and then limping around for the rest of it, you're going to reap greater gains. (That's true even if you spend the same total number of minutes exercising per week.) Plus, in fitness, physical gains don't actually happen during your workouts. They happen as you rest and recover.

Let's talk about some additional tools for calibrating your exercise intensity to your body's needs.

RATE OF PERCEIVED EXERTION (RPE)

On a scale from 0–10, how hard do you feel you're working? Consider 0 lying on the couch, and 10 working as hard as you imagine is physically possible. Moderate-intensity exercise is roughly anything between 3 and 6, and vigorous exercise is about 7 and up.

The U.S. Department of Health and Human Services recommends that adults get at least 150 to 300 minutes of moderate-intensity or 75 to 150 minutes of vigorous-intensity aerobic physical activity per week. Another option: Do an equivalent combination of moderate- and vigorous-intensity aerobic activity. The department also recommends for adults to also engage in total-body muscle-strengthening of moderate or higher intensity at least two days per week.[278]

THE TALK TEST

For being so low-tech, it's a surprisingly accurate way to gauge intensity. Here's how it works: If carrying on a conversation or singing along to Spotify is easy, your body's aerobic (low-intensity) system is primarily working. If, however, you can only get out a few words at a time, your anaerobic (high-intensity) system is running the show. In between, when you can get out a sentence or two at a time, you're pulling relatively equally from both systems and are in a moderate-intensity range.

FATIGUE VERSUS FAILURE

Here's the difference: When you hit muscular fatigue, your muscles burn, you're pushing it hard, and you might have one or two more reps or seconds left in the tank. Failure happens when your muscles actually give out or form falls apart.

But you've sworn off running on empty, right? Instead of pushing yourself to and right over the edge, exercising to muscular fatigue can still develop strength without compromising form and safety. It also reduces the risk of overreaching (aka overtraining).

Plus, research shows that in strength workouts, as long as you work to fatigue, you can effectively build muscle.[279] It doesn't matter if you lift a heavy weight for six or eight reps, or a light one for 12 or 15.

DELAYED ONSET MUSCLE SORENESS (DOMS)

Women love to use post-workout muscle soreness as an indicator of a workout's intensity and quality. The problem is that more soreness isn't better, and having a hard time lowering onto the toilet doesn't mean you got a good workout. Rather, being incredibly sore can be a pretty good sign that it was too intense for your body's current needs.

If a workout leaves you with serious aches or those aches last for more than two days, ease things up. No matter how fit you are, trying anything new will make you sore. (It doesn't mean you're out of shape or weak!) However, DOMS still shouldn't last into day three. If it does, you're in definite need of an extra recovery day or two.

RECOVERY DAYS

Some days, it's beneficial to move with the least intensity possible: cocooned in savasana, taking a gentle stretching class, foam rolling, or stretching. It can be incredibly powerful to devote entire workouts to recovery, and every body would likely enjoy at least one or two of these workouts each week.

We'll dive more into how to give yourself the rest and recovery you need in Chapter 14.

TAKING UP SPACE

For some women, gaining visual musculature or even overall body size is an outward expression of inner character: strong, capable, tough, persistent, limitless. Some women use strength training to build the size of a certain body part; to literally take up more space.

They decide that socially imposed goals of smallness are incongruent with their values and that what they really want is to become bigger. They want muscles big enough to break the patriarchy. This can transform their relationships with their bodies, but like all goals, this is individual. And, by the way, building size isn't a requisite for building strength.

Regardless of how you feel about pursuing size gains, affording your body physical space, in all settings, is important. For example, although female-only fitness studios, gyms, events, and classes can come with a sense of female camaraderie and reduce the risk of being mansplained to or sexualized by male gym goers, busting into male-dominated arenas can be an incredibly powerful way to take up space. It can also be a potential way to bond with other women who are claiming space in similar ways.

Still, taking up space in male-dominated arenas can be nerve-racking. Heck, even taking up space in female-centric exercise studios can be intimidating! That's especially true if you're prone to self-directed weight stigma or have long believed you don't belong in spaces with "fit people."

Listen, you belong anywhere you want to be.

FEELING AT HOME

Here, we'll explore actionable strategies for navigating possible gym anxieties. Each of them has helped our clients.

CHECK OUT THE CULTURE

As much work as we women have to do in taking up space, many gyms have work to do in welcoming us and our MORE. In some gyms, bulletin boards advertise fad diets and risky weight-loss tactics, and both male patrons and staff members (and even women!) can exhibit sexist attitudes.

We can't discount these as possibilities. And while it's valuable to assert ourselves in such situations, our physical and emotional safety is priority number-one.

Fortunately, increasingly more gyms and fitness studios are making efforts to foster environments in which everyone feels they belong. Some gyms have entire "experience" teams dedicated to fostering community and cultures that support every person who walks in the doors. Some staffs have posted "safe space" policies, stating how they value people of all gender identities, races, ethnicities, abilities, sexual orientations, and religions.

These policies, apart from providing a level of assurance, tend to attract gym community members who value and appreciate each others' differences.

Explore the different fitness cultures in your geographical area. Get a one-day or week-long pass so you can get a feel for things before committing. However, even if you've "committed," you're not required to just deal with whatever comes your way. If after joining a gym, you discover it has a less-than-welcoming culture or you experience discrimination or harassment of any kind, you can raise your concerns with management, or end your membership entirely.

Not that long ago, Aleisha quit her traditional gym and switched to one with a "safe space" policy and a radically different culture. Experiencing sexism is in no way a reflection on you, and can happen to anyone. Your response is the one thing over which you have control.

VISIT DURING OFF-PEAK HOURS

Even if you aren't intimidated by male-dense fitness spaces (or any fitness spaces, for that matter), hitting them up during off-peak hours can improve your overall exercise experience. After all, a packed gym can be overstimulating and, for a lot of women, can increase anxieties about being evaluated by others and the risk of performing upward social comparisons. Plus, crowded gyms make practical things like finding available equipment and having enough space way more complicated.

Most fitness studios are at their busiest immediately before and after normal work hours. Of course, those might be the only hours that you have available, and if that's the case, so be it. Just make sure that, when checking out gyms, you visit them during the hours you'll most frequently exercise. Ensure you're comfortable with the volume of people there at that time. If you aren't, keep looking.

BRING REINFORCEMENT

There's definite truth to the whole "strength in numbers" idea, and when working to get comfortable in new exercise settings, it can be helpful to bring someone along who supports you in your goals for MORE, or who also wants to learn how to take up space. Doing so can alleviate some of the perceived pressure to perform and help you more easily figure out things like machine settings and weight clips.

The goal here is to support each other, not become dependent on one another. Even if you love exercising with friends and have a lifelong fitness buddy, when that partner's sick, traveling, or just not able to make a workout date, we want you to feel comfortable exercising on your own. Hopefully, partner workouts help you feel more comfortable on your own as well. If you're not there yet, just keep reading.

WORK WITH A TRAINER

In-person trainers can take a similar role as workout partners, but they also come with the advantage of being able to teach you things, such as how to use different pieces of equipment, exercise form, and program design (how to set up your workouts to best fit your needs, goals, likes, and dislikes).

Some online trainers such as Aleisha prioritize teaching—you can expand your training knowledge and skills while having frequent online and video support. Still, an online trainer won't be there during every rep and set to help you with your form in real time. If you're new to exercise or suspect your form has a lot of room to grow, go with an in-person coach.

When choosing any trainer, look for certifications from an accredited organization such as the American Council on Exercise, National Academy of Sports Medicine, or National Strength and Conditioning Association. Ask potential trainers to share their certifications with you; anyone worth hiring will be happy to provide them, and be glad you asked.

Also, when talking with potential trainers, discuss your desire to improve your relationship with exercise and movement to ensure they're a good fit to help you in your journey for MORE.

CARVE OUT A CORNER

Sometimes, when easing into a gym setting, Aleisha's clients find it's helpful to claim a space and stay right there. That way, they don't have to constantly move around the gym floor. They might set up camp in a corner, along a wall, or around a weight bench.

If that sounds appealing, grab what you need, and take it to your spot of choice. Of course, it's important to still treat everyone else with the same respect you do yourself, so resist the urge to hoard four sets of dumbbells, a medicine ball, a stability ball, some resistance bands, and an ab roller.

When you're done with a piece of equipment, return it to its home, and if there's just one bench in the weight room, the bench definitely isn't the best spot to claim for a full hour. The same goes with squat and power racks, which are in-demand real estate.

Claiming a small space in this way can help you feel that wherever your body is in the gym, that's "your" space. As you get more comfortable, you can make conscious choices to move throughout the gym, explore new equipment, and begin to feel at home everywhere you want to be.

DON HEADPHONES

Similarly, wearing headphones can help gym-goers create a cocoon to block out the rest of the gym so they don't get caught up in what everyone else is doing and what they *might* be thinking.

If you want, you can certainly wear headphones during every workout. It's possible that soundtracking your workouts boosts your mood or keeps you "in the zone." Maybe you just don't like the music playing over the loudspeakers and want to block it out. However, if you're a permanent headphones-wearer, the goal is that eventually you don't *have* to wear them to feel comfortable in your surroundings.

PLAN AHEAD

To feel comfortable, it helps to feel confident. No matter your current skill or experience level, heading into any fitness environment with a plan is a simple, effective way to move with confidence. Think about it this way: How does it feel to enter a gym and have no idea what you're going to do, walking around aimless and unsure of how to proceed? Not great, right?

So let's try a different strategy; let's have a plan.

Following an exercise plan that fits your needs is a great first step, but it's not mandatory. Whether you have a plan or plan to play, before you even head to the gym, think through what you want to do when you get there. Consider what equipment you'll use, what spaces you'll visit, and in what order you'll do everything.

If you plan to do a new exercise, before you arrive at the gym is the optimal time to watch instructional videos and read form pointers. That way, you'll feel more confident as you get started. You also won't have to stop mid-workout to look up instructions on your phone, which can make anyone feel self-conscious.

INVEST IN COMMUNITY

Relatedness—a sense of belonging to a community that supports us—is a central component of intrinsic motivation and the ability to enjoy exercise. Connect with other women, and be open to men as potential allies. While some men won't welcome your presence as an equal, others will celebrate it.

For example, strength training and Brazilian jiu-jitsu are two areas that male coaches and practitioners are currently striving to popularize among women. In the case of strength training, men have often experienced many of the mental or everyday benefits, and want women to experience them as well. Meanwhile, Brazilian jiu-jitsu athletes highly value self-defense, and understand how important it can be for ensuring women's safety.

Some practical ways to find or build a fitness community:

- Talk to women at the gym: Some starters include complimenting a woman's strength or workout clothes, asking her where she got the hip-thrust pad she always brings to the gym, or requesting help with an exercise.

- Be open to allies: If a man engages with you in a friendly, non-creepy way, there's a potential to make a new friend or exercise buddy.

- Attend social events hosted at your gym: Give special notice to those aligned with your interests or passions.

- Join and participate in supportive online groups: The Give Yourself MORE Facebook community is one possibility, but it's far from the only one.

- Look into Meetups or active events near you: These are especially awesome if you're into niche activities like fencing and want to meet others who are too.

- Invite people to exercise with you: Maybe you could even create a group that participates in a different fitness activity every month or quarter.

- Every once in a while, take off those headphones: It'll let others know you might be up to talking.

- Join a team: For example, a friend from work might need another person to round out a Spartan or Ragnar team.

- Take group exercise classes: Actually talk to the other people in them!

- Look into group fitness programs or retreats: Make sure they're led by experts who inspire you and who have similar values.

BRINGING FORM AND FUNCTION TOGETHER

Do you have aesthetic goals for your body? It's natural to care what you look like and to use exercise as a way to affect your appearance. However, we encourage you to not hold a certain aesthetic as your only or main goal, which can negatively influence self-esteem and body image.[280, 281]

How do you balance aesthetic goals with functional ones? The first step is to make sure you actually have some goals that have nothing to do with how you look.

Next, pay attention to how your aesthetic goals make you feel, both now and throughout your fitness journey. Ensure you can pursue them in a healthy way, and consider if it's possible to reframe any "loss" goals into goals for gain.

How does it feel to break down big outcome goals into smaller processes? (Flip back to the last chapter to run your goals through some checks and balances.)

TRICKY PERFORMANCE GOALS

When you start to focus on your body's functionality and maybe ease off of aesthetic goals, it's natural to start to zone in on performance-based goals. You might want to complete a race under a certain time, deadlift double your body weight, do your first pistol squat, or perform pull-ups with ease.

Performance goals like these can be great, but for some women they can also become a surrogate for aesthetic goals. Instead of pushing and punishing themselves in the name of how they look, they start to do it in the name of accomplishing a particular fitness feat. They might get mad at themselves when they miss the mark.

Rather than viewing nutrition as something to support their fitness goals, they can become obsessed about perfecting their nutrition, calorie counts, meal timing, and macros, and get into a whole new array of (still not FDA-approved) supplements. Some women may exercise excessively, or resist ever taking a rest day.

When working toward performance-based goals, we encourage you to always treat yourself with compassion. Consider how you'll respond if you don't accomplish your goal, or don't accomplish it in the timeline you hope you will. What will happen when you have an "off day," and your numbers backslide?

While it's good to think through these questions, you probably aren't clairvoyant. So pay attention if you start to get harsh with yourself, beat yourself up, or get fixated on having to shave seconds off of every run or add pounds to the barbell every week. All are signals to reorient your focus toward *giving your body* MORE as opposed to simply *doing* more.

MOVEMENT VERSUS EXERCISE

We've talked a lot about exercise in terms of structured workout plans, classes, and gym settings. But, in reality, exercise is just *movement.* To nurture your body, gain strength, improve your mental health, and connect with your body, you don't have to follow a structured program. You totally can, and a well-designed program can help you move in a way that's most efficient in reaching your specific goals. But, nope, it's not required.

After all, people have been physically active long before the invention of structured exercise. And, honestly, humans are currently more sedentary than they've been at any other point in history. "Exercise" is just a modern-day solution to combat the lack of movement in our hour-to-hour, day-to-day lives.

Regardless of whether you decide to hit the gym, take exercise classes, or buy at-home equipment, move a little bit every day. You might be surprised how much even 10 minutes of intentional daily movement can impact your physical, mental, and emotional well-being. Go on walks, get up from your desk and stretch… take the stairs.

Let your body move. That's what it's here for!

CHAPTER 11
EMBRACING EMOTION

When we think of improving our health and loving what we see in the mirror, our first thoughts often concern what changes we'll need to make to our food and exercise behaviors. After all, most women are able to see what's holding back their progress—a few too many handfuls of popcorn here, too many skipped exercise sessions there. But what's *causing* those extra handfuls of popcorn or workout avoidance?

In most cases, emotions are a driving force.

In this chapter, we'll talk about how you can learn to give yourself MORE when it comes to your emotions. We'll show you new ways of thinking about and experiencing your feelings rather than hiding from them, feeling pushed around by them, or turning to food to cope with them.

As you read in Chapter 3, not everyone got a solid start in life by learning these adaptive emotional regulation skills. And societal expectations and companies seeking to turn a profit may have subtly cued you to stop using those skills, so you use their products to feel better.

The tools you'll find in this chapter are directions for identifying and meeting your emotional needs. We all have emotional needs—these tools literally apply to every human alive. Just as strength training builds our muscles and bone, the emotional skills training we teach improves mental health and interpersonal skills (the ability to comfortably and effectively interact with other people). As a bonus, this skill set is among the best techniques for preventing and treating disordered eating.

Our clients use these skills to reduce their frequency of emotional eating, binge eating, skipping workouts, or neglecting their self-care due to emotional difficulties. If you've been trying to part with maladaptive coping behaviors for a long time but haven't succeeded, this chapter might be the key to turning things around.

YOU HAVE TO SPEAK THE LANGUAGE

The ability to name and discern different emotions is the foundation for everything else that follows, so we'll start there.

If it's tough for you to name your emotions, you aren't alone. We wouldn't have included this part if a lot of women didn't need it. Alternatively, you might find that this part is easy. But a refresher and some quick brushing up won't hurt.

Alexithymia (Don't worry, it won't be on a spelling test!) is a term psychologists and researchers use to describe a difficulty or inability to identify and describe emotions. The roots of the word even mean "can't speak emotions."

This subclinical phenomenon is common in women with high levels of emotional eating, overweight and obesity, anorexia, bulimia, binge eating disorder, and other forms of disordered eating.[282, 283, 284, 285, 286] It's also linked to other physical health problems such as gestational diabetes.[287]

When we begin talking about emotions with our clients, we often start by developing an emotional vocabulary, and then practice looking inward to review emotional states throughout the day.

This foundation is essential in exploring how to handle emotions in ways that serve our actual emotional needs while promoting healthier relationships with food and exercise.

IDENTIFYING EMOTIONS IN THE WILD

When someone asks, "How are you?" do you naturally respond, "Fine! How are you?" or "I'm good, thanks," even if you aren't feeling good at all? This habit is almost universal.

But why? You might simply be trying to be agreeable, or you might not know how to actually figure out what you're feeling.

This week, practice answering that question, "How are you?" Instead of using the usual cookie-cutter response, find a more accurate word for how you feel.

At least once (if not two or three times) each day, ask yourself how you're feeling and write down a word. You can do it in a journal or notebook, on your phone, or in a document on your computer. Do your best to keep this practice going for seven days.

You can use multiple words. After all, we're often experiencing a mix of different feelings at once. If you can't seem to notice any emotions, remember that not all are strong—they can be so gentle you barely feel them. Feel around until you get a hint of something, even a trace of an emotion, and write it down. You can't do this wrong. There are no wrong emotions to feel!

This practice often resembles learning to identify trees. At first, you might only know two types of trees: leafy (deciduous) trees and needley ones (conifers). As you get more familiar with looking at trees, you can discern more varieties. Maybe you learn to tell an oak from a maple and recognize a pine versus a fir.

Georgie often tells people that until about the age of 29, she had two feelings. They were "good" and "bad." And that was about it.

Clients often respond with a resounding "me too!" or as one woman identified her two emotional channels, "neutral and pissed off." In the following exercise, we're going to build our emotional vocabulary as well as our ability to tell these emotions from each other, because we have a lot more than just two feelings going on!

We'll start with five basic emotions, and with each, a list of related, more specific words you can try out as well. If a word isn't listed, it's still totally okay to use. Flex your vocabulary!

For this exercise, we're only going to ask that you don't use the words "good," "bad," "fine," or "stressed," because they're so general. However, you absolutely have a green light to use the phrase "pissed off."

Your log of emotional check-ins can help you notice patterns that impact your eating and exercise habits. Plus, if you realize a particular feeling causes you to seek food when you aren't hungry or to overeat, you can be extra careful when you notice that feeling popping up on your radar.

ANGER

Feeling anger is a natural response when someone has intentionally hurt us or someone we care about. We often get angry when we feel powerless or controlled, are treated unfairly, or witness something that goes against our values.

Anger can be a healthy emotion when it moves us to take productive actions to improve something or to defend ourselves. It can be unhealthy if it looms prominently in our everyday lives or is out of proportion with the causative event.

Anger can also be harmful if we channel it into violence, self-harm, or hurtful words.

Anger-related emotion words you might use:

> *annoyed, antagonized, bitter, chafed, displeased, enraged,*
> *exasperated, furious, fuming, hateful, heated, incensed,*
> *indignant, inflamed, infuriated, ill-tempered, irate, irritable,*
> *irritated, maddened, offended, outraged, provoked, raging,*
> *resentful, riled, sore, storming, uptight, wrathful*

FEAR

We feel fearful when we anticipate something negative happening, or are aware of danger. Both physical and emotional threats can elicit fear. We can experience conditioned fear that we associate with places or things, such as airplanes or spiders, or even anticipatory fear of a threat that isn't present but might one day happen. In balance, fear is a normal, healthy response that acts to keep us safe and prevent us from danger.

If we're fearful all the time, or fear is interfering with us doing things we want to do, speaking to a therapist or counselor can help recalibrate and reorganize our triggers so we can feel better. But if fear doesn't control us, we have no reason to... well, be afraid.

Fear-related emotion words you might use:

> *afraid, agitated, anxious, disturbed, intimidated, frightened,*
> *hesitant, jittery, nervous, panicky, scared, shaky, shy, skittish,*
> *tense, timid, uneasy, worried*

HAPPINESS

Feeling happy is something we all enjoy. It's a pleasant emotion that arises when we're safe, fortunate, comfortable, or experiencing a sense of well-being. We all derive happiness from different things.

We might feel happy when gardening, doing yoga, painting our nails, or whooping a son in basketball. Excessive happiness isn't typically a problem; however, trying to feel happy all the time can be. Like other emotions, happiness is felt intensely at times, while it fades or is completely absent at other times. This is completely normal and healthy.

When you're happy, enjoy it, but don't feel like you have to be happy every day. It's not realistic, and might worry the people around you.

Happiness-related emotion words you might use:

> *blessed, blissful, blithe, cheerful, content, delighted, ecstatic, elated, glad, gleeful, gratified, jolly, joyful, jubilant, merry, overjoyed, peaceful, playful, pleasant, pleased, thrilled, tick-led, upbeat*

SADNESS

Feeling sad occurs when we lose something or someone important to us, are disappointed, or feel helpless. We might notice this feeling when in physical pain or emotional anguish. Sadness is an emotion everyone feels at times, and can be valuable in showing us who and what really matters to us. When they share it, sadness can bring people closer together.

Feelings of sadness that are overwhelming and don't go away can be a sign of depression. Talking to a professional is always a good idea if you have concerns about the prominence of sadness in your life.

Sadness-related emotion words you might use:

> *bitter, blue, cheerless, dejected, despairing, dismal, down, gloomy, grief-stricken, heartbroken, heavy-hearted, hurting, melancholy, mournful, somber, sorrowful, sorry, troubled, tearful, wistful*

GUILT OR SHAME

These are painful emotions, resulting from self-blame and failure to meet personal standards. Guilt applies when we feel negatively about a specific action we've taken. Shame is more encompassing, and includes when we feel like our self-esteem and self-worth are low. Embarrassment has also been called a mild form of shame.

Guilt can be a productive and healthy emotion; after all, having standards and striving to meet them is part of a fulfilling life. Guilt can serve to catch our awareness and guide us to avoid repeating the same action in the future.

However, both guilt and shame can become burdensome if we have unattainable standards, blame ourselves for things that aren't our fault, or blame ourselves for things we cannot change.

Guilt- and shame-related emotion words you might use:

> *abashed, apologetic, bashful, contrite, distraught, distressed, embarrassed, guilty, hesitant, humiliated, mortified, regretful, repentant, shy, sorry*

LET IT OUT

As we explored in Chapter 3, suppressing emotions is detrimental to our relationships, our mental health, and our physical health. Once we have some practice sensing our emotions, we hopefully become more aware of them, at least some of the time.

Next, we can explore what to do with them. Expressing ourselves is a healthy way of moving through an emotion, making it feel lighter and less burdensome. As a replacement for maladaptive emotional regulation strategies, it gives us something to do with uncomfortable feelings... other than eat them. Expressing doesn't fix our problems, but it can help us sort through our feelings and be less overwhelmed by them.

Additionally, sharing our feelings brings people closer, and going to people instead of food isn't just a way to reduce unnecessary calories, it also provides more relief.

INTERNAL COMMUNICATION

Expressing emotion is good for us even if it doesn't involve another person. It helps us understand and explore what we feel.

Getting our bodies moving can be incredibly effective for processing and expressing emotions; this has been found to be particularly relevant for people who have trouble regulating their emotions.[288] Even if we don't yet have the ability to put our feelings into words, breaking a sweat can allow our bodies to say what words can't. Also, exercising in a natural environment may have even more emotional restorative power than doing activity indoors, so head outside if you can.[289]

Artistic expression has long been used in therapy to help people access emotions they otherwise can't. However, studies indicate that making art is good for everybody, reducing stress hormone levels, decreasing anxiety, and producing feelings of relaxation.[290] Coloring, drawing, writing, and even just tracing shapes all produce positive moods in healthy adults, according to research.[291, 292, 293]

COMMUNICATING WITH OTHERS

If you live alone on a deserted island, you could argue that learning to express emotions to others isn't that imperative. However, if your life contains other human beings, being able to express yourself is the foundation of communicating with them and forming bonds of friendship, love, and teamwork.

If you can't express your emotions, you're powerless when it comes to changing the things that bother you, expressing your desires, and improving relationships over time.

For example, when a group of researchers studied what happened between people in close or romantic relationships when they suppressed or expressed their emotions on a regular basis, they found:

"...when individuals were more emotionally expressive during daily interactions, they experienced interpersonal benefits such as greater acceptance from others, greater relatedness and relationship satisfaction, and less distancing by others. Greater emotional expression in daily life also predicted increases in self-esteem and relationship satisfaction across time." [294]

A relationship in which one or both people don't share their feelings rarely achieves a level of satisfying closeness. And if you can't express your emotions well, you risk alienating other people, offending them, or blowing up randomly and making everyone wary of you. And, of course, the suppress-and-explode rollercoaster is torture for the person stuck riding it: you.

Healthy expression can be described as *effective communication, to the right person, at the right time, with the right intensity.*

Communicating effectively hinges on having adequate self-awareness and words, which is what we worked on in the prior exercise. If you use words that are general—saying "I'm stressed" without further elaboration—you haven't communicated in a definitive way what's going on or what you want or need. That's why we like specifics for labeling feelings. Specifics allow you to better communicate the situation at hand, your needs within it, and how to best meet those needs.

Being a little braver and a little more honest than the average person is the other thing we need for communicating effectively. It's hard for many of us to say when we're disappointed, ashamed, or sad. It's tempting to fake it, smile, and pretend we're great. But when it comes to communicating, we don't have to be superhuman or completely dauntless to do much better than the average person! Simply saying we're "glad to see" someone instead of falsely saying we're feeling "fine" already puts us ahead of the curve.

THE RIGHT PERSON

With your close friends and loved ones, you can be fully honest. If your day has been brutally hard, then say it. They won't love you less; in fact, they will have the opportunity to know you *as you are in this moment* and a chance to respond. If you don't let people in, they can't help you by listening, commiserating, or inviting you on a walk to cool down and chat it out.

On that note, the people closest to you are almost always the people with whom you should openly communicate your emotions. People you've recently met or those with whom you have professional relationships may not be the right people to tell everything; in these instances, we recommend honesty, but staying out of the details. "It's been a hard day, but it's getting better, thanks," will do for the dentist. You can admit to colleagues you're "eager to hear their thoughts on the project," but might want to leave out that you've been up since 2 a.m. shaking with anxiety over what they'll say.

Lastly, if you have feelings about someone's words or actions and can discuss them with that person; do it. If people make you happy, let them know. If someone makes you feel embarrassed or threatened, they deserve to know that too. That way they can apologize and consider changing their ways (or not, proving to you that they really are an ass).

As a general rule, friendships can tolerate more emotional vulnerability and truth as they grow over time. Look for reciprocity in relationships, and hopefully you'll find others communicating their feelings to you as well. Notice if people don't ever share their feelings, or worse, if they twist what you've said into being a personal attack.

Luckily, that doesn't happen often, but narcissistic or overly defensive people can turn any emotion into anger or even a fight. It's not your job to change people; just recognize these aren't the right people with whom to work on deep communication.

THE RIGHT TIME

The ideal time to express yourself is broad and forgiving, but make sure to avoid the "wrong time." Obviously, when you're at a funeral or another serious occasion, expressing happiness or laughter (even if something really great is going on in your life) would be insensitive to those grieving around you.

Depending on the type of job you have and the culture of your workplace, it may also be disadvantageous to discuss certain topics or feelings when you're at work.

Choosing the right time includes noticing if your audience is already dealing with their own difficult emotions, and if they are, picking a different time. Unleashing your unhappiness over the division of household labor to a spouse who broke his ankle that morning is bad timing any way you slice it. He's probably already seriously upset, and really isn't in the condition to clean the baseboards anyway, so wait until a more neutral time.

THE RIGHT INTENSITY

Most of the time, expressing our feelings isn't going to be a dramatic affair because we won't be weeping with joy or seething with fury. Most days, our state is more low-key—we feel moderately happy, excited, bored, down, annoyed with traffic, and so on. The extreme highs and lows are less frequent.

Extreme highs aren't problematic, assuming we don't do irrationally irresponsible things in moments of glee. But those extreme lows can be tough to handle. When we feel intense anger, frustration, or terror, we can easily say things that are hurtful or vindictive—even if we don't intend to.

Georgie recounts that after she progressed past her "two emotions only" phase and worked to recognize more of her feelings, there was a period during which she got... snappy. As she describes it, her old pattern of permanently agreeable repression was so ingrained she didn't notice an emotion until it reached an 8 or 9 on a 10-point scale of intensity. And at that point, she just kind of blurted it out without thoughtful wording.

Day to day, she was continuing to repress the normal small things she felt, appearing calm on the surface but allowing small annoyances to build and intensify. Then, maybe the 157th time her husband's natural walking pace left her trailing 10 feet back, she suddenly snapped at him, saying he should walk by himself from now on if he was going to leave her behind. And because she had said absolutely nothing until this point, despite the dozens of walks they'd taken together, this was understandably a complete shock to him.

This sort of disproportionate, snapping response to a small thing isn't abnormal for someone who isn't regularly communicating the little emotions. On a day-to-day basis, simple expressions like, "Can you wait up a second for me, honey?" or "I'm lonely when you work late, can we try to have dinner together tomorrow?" prevent the passive-aggressive tension from building. Georgie learned, as she now coaches her clients, "If you want something, ask for it.

If you want something to change, bring it up when it's small. Don't expect people to read your mind or just know what you want."

Letting people know we appreciate them or feel happy comes easily for many of us, but voicing our less-than-positive emotions is worth practicing. We recommend doing it when issues are small and you're more composed. That way, you don't surprise people out of the blue. (Note: Surprised people get defensive.) This way, you don't have to suffer through your own mounting displeasure. Life's just better when you don't get so upset.

This is the last point worth making on expressing emotions with the right intensity: Sometimes your emotions will be intense, negative, and sudden, with no lead-up at all. Once in a while, life serves up a big sudden whack of "job termination," "lawsuit filed against me," or "loved one victimized in a violent crime." Such things bring fierce emotions. In these moments, it's often beneficial to let the emotion have some time to de-escalate in intensity before communicating it to others, especially to those outside your closest inner circle.

It's in these intense emotional states that you're most vulnerable to doing things you later regret and can only partially patch up with an apology. For example, when you're quaking with anger, it's easy to get overly aggressive. Likewise, when wronged, it can be tempting to act immediately to save face or get other people on your side. But again, in this moment you're not going to be your best self.

It's often best to sleep on things before opening your mouth or putting your thoughts in an email, text message, or social media post. You'll be more rational, eloquent, and productive if you give it at least a night.

WORRIED ABOUT COMPLAINING?

Wanting to avoid being perceived as a complainer can make you reluctant to express how you feel when you aren't thrilled with something. If you identify with that, pat yourself on the back for

187

being a considerate person. You don't want to upset people or be unpleasant company, and that's kind of you. However, being someone who *never ever* speaks up is a detriment, and possibly prevents you from initiating improvements in the world.

When we think of what sort of talk constitutes complaining, the most repellent kind is repetitive, associated with no productive action, includes no admittance of a personal causative role, and is figuratively barking up the wrong tree. But even if you say things that fit into that pattern from time to time, it's unlikely that people will label you a complainer unless that's the theme of your typical conversations.

In terms of repetition, everyone complains sometimes; complainers are people who complain all the time. If you also tend to comment on things you appreciate or admire, people won't be turned off when your honest opinion isn't rosy. And what about productive action and ownership? If you do something about the things that displease you, it makes you someone who's improving the world, and people are more likely to admire you than call you a complainer.

As far as barking up the wrong tree goes, remember that if you want something to change, you have to let the person *who can change it* know.

We encourage you to practice using the tips in this section. If you have a close, trusting relationship but have tended to not always share how you feel, this is a perfect place to give yourself more freedom of expression. Try talking about your day, but instead of just giving a play-by-play of events, include how you felt.

HANDLING FEELINGS LIKE A PRO

The ability to recognize emotions and deal with them, as we just covered, is a characteristic of a healthy relationship with them.

However, just as suppressing feelings or ignoring them causes problems, paying too much attention to them also isn't ideal. If we hold our emotions too closely, we can get tangled up in them. That can prevent us from living our lives.

Think of suppression being on one end of a continuum. If we're in suppression mode, we deny our emotions are even there and look the other way. Suppression might sound like, *"Sad? I'm not sad, I'm fine."*

On the other end of the spectrum, we find overidentification. In this mode, we imbue feelings with so much importance and meaning that it starts to cause problems. Those problems can include emotional overwhelm and losing sight of the people and activities in our lives. We can feel like our emotions make up who we are, and lose sight of the fact that we're women who have emotions, but *we're not those emotions.*

Overidentified thinking might sound like, "Of course I'm sad. I'm always sad. Sadness is my life." When we overidentify with a particular feeling, we can end up paying so much attention to it that we block out feelings that may be pleasant, enjoyable, or beneficial to process.

Neither of these extremes is a healthy way to live. In the middle is where we find balance. We want to be able to acknowledge our emotions, but also know they don't make up our identities or run our lives.

Here are some reminders that will help you stay anchored to the middle ground:

- Feelings are things that come and go. They're not permanent.
- We can have different emotions at once. Wonderful times can have moments of worry mixed in, and difficult days can have spots of humor or calm.

- We have feelings, but we're not our feelings.
- We can observe our feelings impartially without judging them.

REAPPRAISAL

If you've ever had a piece of jewelry or a painting appraised, you took it to someone who told you how valuable it was. To reappraise something simply means to redo the valuation process. You might take your grandmother's antique silver to an expert for reappraisal. The value might have been $225 in 1970, but today, the value is likely to have changed.

Cognitive reappraisal is a process we can use to change the way a situation or stimulus makes us feel emotionally. In other words, we decide ourselves that we want to change the emotional value of something, and we can! Conveniently, we don't need an expert for this kind of reappraisal.

Let's say you're watching a movie, and there's a scene that involves one of the characters getting attacked and injured. Watching the scene, you feel panicky and scared, thinking about what that character is going through. But if you're getting too upset by the scene, you might tell yourself, "It's not real. That's all fake blood, and they're actors." And that makes you feel less freaked out.

That's reappraisal.

Now, reappraisal doesn't mean telling yourself a situation is fake when it's actually occurring in real life. But there are many ways we can look at situations to either reduce the negative feelings or enhance the positive feelings they elicit within us.

On the following page are some of the common tactics our clients use to successfully reappraise situations.[295]

- Thinking of lessons that can or will be learned from an experience, skills that may be strengthened, or relationships that will be stronger for having gone through something together

- Seeing how things aren't that bad, might not be as severe as they seem, could be worse, or can be handled

- Focusing on how things will improve in time

- Noting how someone has others to help deal with a situation, or possesses personal resources to cope with it

- Coming up with a detailed plan for how to proceed with solving the problem

- Acceptance of the situation as no one's fault, a part of life, or something that many people have gone and will go through

Cognitive reappraisal has widely established benefits. It helps us respond more healthily to life stressors.[296] Reappraisal is also less cognitively draining than suppressing our feelings is.[297] People who use reappraisal are less distressed by upsetting situations and less prone to seek avoidance.[298] Reappraisal also doesn't increase desire to binge, whereas suppression does.[299]

If this type of thinking doesn't come naturally to you, that's okay! You can pick it up quickly. In an experiment conducted in the U.K., it took just three sessions of reappraisal practice over a one-week period for people to be able to rapidly perform it on their own. Two weeks after the training sessions, people reported more habitual use of reappraisal in their lives compared to control participants who didn't receive the training.

At the two-week follow-up, experimenters showed the participants film clips designed to elicit negative emotions. (The clips contained footage of violence, injuries, and infections.) Viewers ranked how they felt on an 11-point scale with one representing "extremely negative" and 11 indicating "extremely positive." Those who received no training averaged 3.48 on this scale, indicating they were significantly more upset than participants who had received the reappraisal training two weeks earlier and reported an average of 6.53. Without being given any instruction to reappraise at the follow-up, the subjects had done it automatically.[300]

This is really positive, since practicing something just three times over the course of a week seems like a bargain to gain something as wonderful as a reduced proneness to negative feelings.

You can also leverage cognitive reappraisal to directly help with your behavior-change goals. Thinking about the positive long-term health impacts of frequently eating healthy foods has been shown to increase people's desire for those foods.[301]

Cognitive reappraisal is also an effective way to reduce the desirability of craved foods, especially for people who rank highly in eating restraint.[302]

We've used reappraisal techniques to help our clients feel more positive about heading to bed on time, drinking water, and working out. Reappraisal techniques can also help with persisting through a binge urge without giving in, or doing physical therapy exercises as prescribed.

Practice reappraising things this week. When upsetting conditions pop up, review the previous bulleted list and select at least one thought that helps you feel better about the situation. You might also try focusing on the long-term positive outcomes of executing a behavior pattern you're trying to form, and thinking about how important those benefits are to you.

TAKING ACTION

Action orientation is another asset of which you can give yourself MORE. Being action-oriented is a trait that leads people to take more concrete steps toward their goals, and remain in touch with their motivations amid difficult conditions.[303, 304] Action-oriented people enjoy higher levels of goal attainment as well as mental and physical well-being.

In contrast, people who are state-oriented—the opposite of action-oriented—have a greater tendency to get bogged down by their feelings, ruminate on negative emotions, and have lower levels of function in the face of stress.

Thankfully, levels of action orientation tend to increase with age, so we're all on the right track as a default. Experts believe this happens because, as we age, we gain experiences of overcoming challenges and setbacks, and have more willingness to do what worked before.

We also enjoy more freedom as we get older, which fosters self-reliance and the pursuit of our own goals and desires. Each year (on average) we get better at knowing what's important to us and making it happen rather than just wishing for it. We also become less distracted by worries or task-irrelevant thoughts. This not only helps us more effectively attain what we want; it's like a non-drug antidepressant. Getting up and taking action makes us feel better.

It's also possible to practice and develop this trait, and we encourage it. We don't want to wait on Mother Nature to slowly cultivate this trait in us. We're going to be action-oriented at becoming action-oriented.

For starters, let's not take just any old action. Some are more likely to improve the situation than others are. If we feel lonely, for example, calling a friend or going to a social event has a high probability of helping. However, watching TV until 2 a.m. or eating a quart of ice cream is not likely to help reduce loneliness.

When we don't have the ability to specify the emotions we feel or don't have a habit of tuning in and examining them, it's easy to pick ineffective actions just to do something. It's also easy to do nothing because we just freeze.

But we've already warmed up for this in the "identifying emotions" section, so we have a head start at labeling what we're feeling. Next, we'll lay out some potential action plans for the most common emotional situations.

Here's a short list of common emotional states our clients report as challenges to their health and weight-loss behaviors, and three actions for each that you can prod yourself to take instead of hitting the couch or turning to food, alcohol, or the TV. These are not meant as fixes, and there's no guarantee your emotions will change. But taking some action frequently helps, and you might as well take one that's likely to be productive rather than harmful.

- **Sad or Lonely:** 1) Talk to or call someone. 2) Write a letter or an email. 3) Read, listen to music, or journal.

- **Frustrated:** 1) Adjust your expectations to make them more realistic. 2) Take a break from the frustrating task or person. 3) Draw in 10 deep breaths, exhaling slowly after each one.

- **Tired:** 1) Slow down your pace (instead of quitting/stopping). 2) Take a nap or lie down somewhere quiet for 10 minutes. 3) Plan to head to bed early, or go directly to bed.

- **Overworked:** 1) Make the time to do something you enjoy. That may mean saying no, or drawing a boundary. 2) Leave nonessential chores until tomorrow. 3) Plan a break, like a day off or a vacation, marking it on your calendar.

- **Angry:** 1) Physically move yourself away from the thing angering you so you can cool off. 2) Seek to understand by asking questions and listening. 3) Calmly communicate how you feel and what you want.

- **Overwhelmed:** 1) Get organized. This might mean making a list, or scheduling specific tasks on your calendar. 2) Hire a pro to help, delegate tasks to others, or cancel nonessential things. 3) Approach one thing on the list at a time, leaving the rest of it for another time. Just focus on one thing.

For other stressful situations and feelings that arise, put on your problem-solving hat and think *What action can I take?* If you feel like a deer in headlights stunned into a frozen state, start with just moving your body... literally. Physical exercise is one of the most powerful ways to improve your emotional state in a short period of time. A single session of aerobic or strength exercise of any intensity reduces anxiety and depression. It all helps.[305]

Note: If you choose a high-intensity activity, immediately afterward you may feel signs of physical stress such as an elevated heart rate. Soon, though, your stress response will lessen to a point that it's even lower than it was before you broke a sweat, and you'll feel better.

ACCEPTANCE

You've probably heard the age-old advice about accepting the things we cannot change, and being courageous enough to change the things we can. And yes, knowing the difference between those two is advantageous.

However, feelings don't fall solidly into one camp or the other. Taking an action-oriented approach to a distressing situation won't mean the actions will fix the problem every time. You can't forcefully un-depress yourself, just as you can't *make* yourself happy, no matter how much effort you expend. You may also have discovered that controlling other people's emotional states is the epitome of frustration.

We can influence our emotional states, but not completely control them. In fact, trying to control them is the root of much suffering. We can influence our emotional states with the skills in this chapter, regular exercise, a nutritious diet, and adequate sleep. However, we can't tell our emotions when to come and go, and we don't get to select which emotions we feel and pass on experiencing others. We get the mixed platter of feelings.

Here, acceptance is a capacity that benefits us. If we can accept that all feelings will happen to us at some point, and that they won't harm us or last forever, we feel less distressed in painful moments. We're more able to give grief and loss the time and space they need. We can accept very low times along with the very happy times as part of being fully alive, and still take action. Acceptance isn't passivity or apathy. In fact, acceptance helps us struggle and flail less so we can act more effectively.

Acceptance can be one of the best weight-loss tools you'll ever discover. Here's how: Most of us operate under the assumption that we have to feel like doing something to do it. We don't go to the gym on days we're stressed, we don't cook dinner for ourselves when we're tired, and we wait for the day we have totally free time and a great night's sleep to take a walk.

By accepting that you can act in line with your goals no matter what emotions are along for the ride, you can fire up your inner Nike ad and *Just Do It.*

No matter what emotions are coming and going on a given day, do things to care for your body. Sure, it's lovely to be full of energy, but you can go for a jog even if you're sleepy. You can cook a healthy dinner even when you're upset. You can buy groceries even if you feel anxious. Air conditioning broken at the gym? You can accept that it's going to be a hot, sweaty workout, and go anyway. You can go get your flu shot even though you're preoccupied with other things. Your actions don't require a particular emotional condition.

It's freeing to know that you can feel what you feel and go about your plans all the same.

And of course, doing things that are in line with your goals reliably improves mood and overall well-being, whereas stalling and procrastinating reliably make you feel worse.

This week, if you have healthy meals and exercise sessions planned, practice doing them no matter how you feel—because that *will* help you feel better.

RECOGNIZING AND REPLACING SELF-DEFEATING BELIEFS

In Chapter 3, we explored how self-defeating core beliefs can cause negative feelings and prevent success in reaching our goals. For example, if we're looking at everything through the lens of perfectionism or operating with a rigid definition of how everything should be, we'll be frustrated and disheartened a majority of the time.

In this section, we'll talk about recognizing our self-defeating beliefs and replacing them with those that contribute to our health, happiness, and success.

The trickiest thing about self-defeating beliefs is that they're typically subconscious and more emotional than cognitive. Few women would shoot up their hands up and say "Yes, I have double standards!" or "Absolutely, my appearance and achievements are the reason I'm valuable." We most likely instantly disagree with these statements. But feelings can run deep beneath our awareness, and it's typical to hold fears and assumptions that govern our emotions and reduce our well-being without realizing it.

See if you notice any of these flags in your behavior or thinking.

FLAG: USING A LOT OF "SHOULD" STATEMENTS IN THOUGHTS AND SPEECH

The word "should" pops up with surprising frequency in our speech and thoughts. However, the whole idea that there's a reference for what a person should do, say, feel, eat, or wear is flawed. Using "shoulds" tries to corral our behavior into a narrow lane when, really, we have the freedom to make infinite choices. Self-defeating "shoulds" can sometimes sound like: "Women my size shouldn't wear shorts. She should be more grateful. I shouldn't order the steak. He should treat me better. I should be stronger. I should eat more green things."

That said, the choices we make come with certain outcomes, and the word "should" can be used to communicate a cause-and-effect relationship. This use of the word "should" isn't necessarily self-limiting as long as it's accurate.

For example: "If you want to avoid a speeding ticket, you should obey the posted speed limits. You should buy tomatoes if you want to make a tomato salad." Those are definitely accurate, and aren't based on restricting possibilities based on the opinions of others. But when "should" is applied to behavior, exercise, or eating, it's usually not true in any concrete sense; it's just a judgment.

When you hear the word "should" in your own language or thoughts, do a double check and ask yourself, "Says who?" and "Why?" This allows you to make sure you aren't falling into a completely baseless shame-trap of what's acceptable to wear, say, eat, do, or feel.

There are very few standards governing these choices: There's no *Book of Should;* you get to choose how you live your life. When you burn that imaginary book, you're left with greater freedom to explore an endless array of possible choices and select what you truly want to do.

Speaking of wanting to do something, that's our favorite way to upgrade should-laden thinking: Try to replace every "I should…" in your mind with "I want to…" and see what happens. You might realize you don't actually want to whatever it is, in which case, you have good reason to consider not doing it.

It's also much more effective motivation to say, "It would be advantageous to…" instead of "I should…" because it brings to mind the actual reasons we might do something, which are far more enticing than a baseless rule.

Being told we should do something, even through internal thought, is about as inspiring a rationale as "because I said so," which is to say… not very inspiring.

FLAG: INCONSISTENCY MAKES US WORRY

As human beings, we're going to experience ups and downs in our moods, abilities, productivity, and behaviors. They'll rise and fall on a daily or hourly basis. Why? Because we aren't robots. Yet, the self-defeating belief that we should be the same (or better) every single day persists for many women. This leads to fear that something is wrong if on a certain day we feel less capable, get less done, make more errors, or have less patience. Anxiety can well up as we think we're going downhill and that it represents a worsening trend that will only continue.

We have the option to replace this type of self-defeating belief with one that expects variation. With this more realistic belief, we can cut ourselves some slack. A day when we feel less chipper and grouchier is normal, and we'll likely feel better the next day. A day when we can't lift our usual weight at the gym is no reason to reconsider the training program; we're simply having a less-strong day.

Consider this helpful replacement belief:

> *Everybody's energy level, mood, and abilities vary from day to day. That includes mine. This isn't necessarily a problem.*

FLAG: HAVING DOUBLE STANDARDS (ONE FOR US, ONE FOR EVERYBODY ELSE)

Many of us hold ourselves to higher performance and appearance standards than those we use for other people. It can feel as though our high standards for ourselves lead us to achieve more and try harder, but the self-defeating belief that we need to perform to a higher standard does little more than increase pressure and anxiety.

Replacing double standards by treating ourselves as gently and flexibly as we do other people can bring about massive relief. For example, we might be hesitant to stay home from work when we're sick, concerned that our boss and coworkers will question our work ethic. However, we're unlikely to make such harsh judgments about our officemate's character if she has the flu and doesn't come in to work.

We can also hold our own bodies and appearances to standards vastly different from the ones we apply to others. Many women who feel concerned or displeased with their body shape would tell another woman with a similar figure that she looks great.

We can replace self-defeating beliefs based on double standards by applying to ourselves the same kindness, compassion, and appreciation we afford others.

We can remind ourselves:

We accept and love other people even though they aren't perfect.
Being extra-demanding of ourselves is uncalled for.

FLAG: NEEDING APPROVAL
(THE SLIGHTEST CRITICISM HURTS TO THE CORE)

This type of self-defeating belief makes trouble for us when we encounter criticism. If we believe that everyone must like us or we can't be happy, or that if someone doesn't enjoy our work, it must be terrible, we'll feel desperate to try to please everyone, even if it means losing sight of our own opinions and goals.

In nutrition and fitness, there are a lot of conflicting opinions. It's safe to say that whatever workout style we choose and whatever type of food pattern we enjoy is going to get a thumbs-down from someone. Even experts rarely agree.

If we need constant approval, we'll also feel personally hurt when people don't love our writing, our cooking, or our parenting choices. The reality is, many people may like us, admire what we do, and agree with us, but not everyone will. And that's okay.

We can reshape these self-defeating beliefs by remembering:

Approval from every person on the planet is not necessary
for us to feel good about our work and ourselves. Nothing
has ever made everybody happy.

FLAG: THINKING OR SAYING "THAT'S JUST HOW WE ARE"

Self-defeating beliefs about ourselves and other people can take the form of a fixed mindset. When we have a fixed mindset, we believe our traits and skills are "the way we are" and that other people also have unchanging characteristics and abilities as well. This limits us in major ways, chiefly because it prevents us from working toward improvements. Believing "I'm bad at math" makes students feel less confident in mathematics, and they underperform compared to students of equal ability who aren't held back by that belief.

If we have the belief that we're quitters or losers, or that we have no self-control, it will cause us to bail on projects... or never even start. We also might be held back from trying activities when we think we're a bad dancer, bad cook, bad at sticking to a diet, or generally unable. In truth, none of those characteristics is fixed, and we can improve any of them with the right type of practice. Most of our traits and abilities are not set in stone; we can improve at almost anything with practice and work.

Similarly, it's a disadvantage to our relationships if we sell other people short by assuming they can never change. Of course, some people retain the same abilities and impairments their entire lives, but many people change and improve throughout the course of their lives. If we maintain a fixed mindset about others and they let us down, we might just write them off. Then we lose out on seeing them change over time, working on some of their shortcomings, and regaining our trust.

We encourage you to replace fixed-mindset beliefs with growth-mindset beliefs such as:

> *I can practice and improve almost all my abilities and skills, if I'm willing to work hard. And even the willingness to work hard is something I can create.*

FLAG: CRAVING CERTAINTY AND CONTROL

Planning things in detail, excessively worrying, and hating unknowns is rooted in being comfortable only if we have 100% control over everything. It can make us think, *I can't leave this up to chance; I have to know for certain* or *I can't risk failure.* Unfortunately, this type of belief can lead to self-sabotage, because we have no chance of failing if we don't start.

Self-sabotage can take the form of not studying for a test so we don't have to risk trying our hardest and potentially still not doing well, not training properly for a race so we have an excuse if we don't finish, or doing things that undermine budding romatic relationships so we don't get dumped. Many people end up sabotaging weight-loss attempts in this way by buying tempting foods they know they have a tendency to overeat, then overeating them with a sense of proving to themselves, *See, I knew I couldn't last on that diet!*

Perfectionism can also lead to distress in cases where certainty is just not available. For example, maybe we can't get the results of a medical test for a few days. The belief that we can't function if there's uncertainty means we won't function for a few days!

Perfectionsim can also lead to desperately trying to control every detail of a situation like a vacation, and stressing out when the taxi is three minutes late or the plane is boarding at gate 34C instead of 18D. It can lead to other people feeling like we're micromanaging them. They can become unwilling to work or share experiences with us.

Life doesn't let us line up things exactly as we want them to happen. Sometimes we have to put control in other people's hands, or allow them to run their own affairs. We can cause ourselves greater stress trying to prevent any little problem than we would by dealing with things as they happened.

It's often the most helpful approach to do our best and accept that, beyond that, the outcome isn't up to us.

We can remind ourselves:

I cannot have complete certainty right now, and I'll be okay.
I want to take reasonable precautions and put forth my best effort, but if unforeseen things happen, I'll deal with them then.

FLAG: OUR SELF-ESTEEM IS ACHIEVEMENT-BASED

We all like to feel accomplished and look proudly on what we've created or done. However, that can become self-defeating if it's a prerequisite for feeling good about ourselves or we can't rest. Achieving things and making progress is a healthy source of positive emotions when it's not the only pillar of a person's self-esteem.

Common thoughts that reveal achievement-based self-esteem:

> *If I haven't done enough today, I can't go home.*
> *I can't rest unless I get everything done.*
> *Today was a total waste; I got nothing done.*

These thoughts rob us from enjoying processes and activities, company, nature, and the pleasure of just being. There is absolutely nothing wrong with getting stuff done, but we can upgrade self-defeating beliefs in this area to beliefs like:

> *I'm awesome not just because of what I do, but because of who I am. Some of the most enjoyable, meaningful things in life aren't my achievements, but experiences and the people I share them with.*

CHAPTER 12
FILLING AND FUELING UP

While food isn't the best tool for meeting your emotional needs, it's the perfect solution for fueling your body and giving you the nutrients you need to thrive. In this chapter, we explore how to stop aiming for LESS and choose MORE when it comes to food.

We're not going to give you a line of pseudoscience that you have to eat more to get out of "starvation mode," because that's just not true. We'll encourage you to identify the areas of your food life in which something is currently lacking, and to start seeking MORE. Most commonly, our clients have been shorting themselves on food enjoyment, while dietary restrictions have also whittled their food freedom down to an unsustainable level. We're bringing that freedom back.

We'll also talk about specific nutrients that are too low in many women's diets. Giving yourself more in this case can help prevent disease, make you more satisfied, boost your energy levels, and improve your recovery from exercise and stress.

As you read in Chapter 4, dieting and perma-dieting cause a cascade of problems, psychologically, behaviorally, and physically. They're ineffective at producing weight loss and cause food guilt and cravings. We'll show you how to feed yourself the right amount for your goals *without* depending on draining cognitive control. If you want to, you can lose weight (minus all the head games and negative feelings).

MINDFULNESS

Low-calorie diets used to be the way professionals treated patients who wanted to lose excess weight, but that's increasingly changing. Recognizing the dismal success rate of this clinical strategy, leading health professionals are now teaching behavioral and mindset changes as a more effective way to help people improve their long-term nutrition.[306] It might be a new way for you to approach your food intake, and it's wonderful to experience if the old ways haven't been working for you.

Mindfulness interventions have been found to be effective in improving mental health and eating behaviors.[307] You may feel inclined to dismiss such interventions as ones that won't meaningfully change your food intake, but that would be a shame. Where and how we place our attention directly changes how the brain functions in that moment. And as you know, your brain is calling all the shots here, so changing how it works at mealtimes is pivotal to improving food choices.

A 2019 study published in the *International Journal of Obesity* that had participants serve themselves food under three separate conditions explored how focusing on different aspects of a meal just before eating changes activation of various areas of the brain.[308] When people were asked to focus on the *pleasure* of the lunch they were about to eat, brain scans determined that regions of the brain involved with taste processing were activated. When asked to focus their mindset on the *fullness* they would feel as a result of eating the food, activity levels increased in reward-processing centers of the brain.

In the last condition, when participants were instructed to focus their mindsets on the *health* benefits of the food served at lunch, the researchers noted enhanced activity in the left prefrontal cortex. This area of the brain is part of the self-control network, the part that helps with rational decisions and keeps impulses in check.

Not only were the brain activity patterns different with a health-focused mindset, but participants also served themselves smaller portions after they adopted the health-focused mindset than when they focused on pleasure, fullness, or in the control condition when they could think about anything they chose. It seems that thinking about food in a health context is one way to automatically make healthier decisions around portions.

There are many types of mindfulness interventions, some of which are specifically focused on mindful *eating*, while others provide instruction on practicing mindfulness away from the table. Some mindfulness exercises call for participants to set aside practice time in a quiet location, similar to how we'd try a sitting meditation. Other formats teach mindfulness by increasing attention to sensations we experience while doing familiar activities like walking, showering, or doing the dishes.

The varied ways we can learn and cultivate mindfulness all carry similar benefits. Improved responsiveness to internal signals is a common outcome of mindfulness training. This, in turn, decreases cue-oriented eating—called external eating—such as getting pizza because you smelled it or eating simply because others are. Mindfulness training also helps with untangling internal signals such as emotions and hunger, which are often confusingly hard to differentiate for women with eating struggles.

Giving more mindful attention to food is also effective in reducing cravings.[309] Mindfulness interventions are useful for helping people reduce binge eating and emotional eating, lose weight, and maintain weight loss.[310] They are accessible to anyone, and can be used in tandem with other forms of counseling or psychotherapy. Classes and groups on mindfulness are available in most cities, and there are excellent books, audio recordings, and videos on the Internet that can help.

MINDFUL BITES

To benefit from mindfulness, you don't have to devote entire meals to long, involved mental exercises. Mindfulness works best when it's short, simple, and doable. That way, you'll actually give it a shot—all you need is three minutes to rock these mindful bites!

The best time to try this exercise is when you aren't in a rush. It's also a good idea not to have distractions battling for your attention, so turn off the TV, close the computer, and set aside your phone to give this a try. The key here is using all five senses, and for a moment not to focus on your worries, plans, or the other things going on around you. You can have all that stuff back soon.

- **Sight:** Notice the colors, shapes, sizes, and details on your plate. Is it pretty?

- **Touch:** How does it feel to pierce the food with a fork, scoop it up with a spoon, or grab it with your hands? Notice how it feels against your lips and mouth as you chew. It might be soft, crunchy, chewy, scratchy, smooth, dry, or creamy. Maybe, as with granola and milk, there's a pleasant contrast between textures. Try to feel the food as you move it around your mouth before you swallow it. There's a lot of sensitivity in our mouths! If you want to, take a couple more bites, focusing on the touch sensations before going to the next step.

- **Smell:** Pause for a second and inhale, trying to notice what your food smells like. If you have different foods on your plate, maybe try to see if they smell differently from each other. Notice how, when you eat, your senses of smell and taste are linked, and that you're smelling food in your mouth while you're tasting it. The oral and nasal cavities are connected.

- **Taste:** How would you describe this meal if you were a food critic working for a gourmet magazine? Is it salty, spicy, briny, meaty, sweet? If there are different ingredients, see if you taste each of them, such as the corn, the cumin, the beef, and the beans in a bite of chili. Eat a bite, thinking about all the tastes you notice. Again, this is typically a pleasant set of stimuli, so take a few bites with your full attention.

- **Hear:** Eating fills your head with a fair amount of sounds. The crunch of lettuce or carrots sounds different than the crunch of a potato chip or pretzel. What sound is this food making?

Those few bites are really all it takes to engage in mindfulness. You just did a meditation; you didn't have to set aside 20 minutes or sit in the lotus position. Congrats on taking a break to tune into yourself and your experience. Was it nice to take a break from the thinking/planning/worrying/fixing you do the rest of your day? We hope so.

If you believe the aromas and flavors of your food aren't all that important or worthy of your time and attention, remember that mindfulness isn't limited to eating. The ability to place your attention where you choose is powerful.

Noticing the crunch of your cornflakes or the symphony of your sandwich might seem tangential to your goals, but it builds toward skillfully recognizing your emotions, your appetite, and your satisfaction cues. These elements are directly important to your mental and physical health.

Besides, we like to keep things lighthearted. Spending a few moments feeling, tasting, and, yes, listening to food is a pleasant break from lives dominated by more serious activities.

NUTRIENTS

The foods we eat aren't just sources of calories (energy); they also contain nutrients such as vitamins and minerals, essential fatty acids, and protein. Some of the nutrients we need are used for structure. We literally build our bones, muscles, blood cells, organs, and teeth from molecules found in food, and we remodel and replace them on a continual basis. We can't use any old bricks to build this palace; we need the right ones in the right variety.

We need iron molecules to build the oxygen-carrying protein hemoglobin, which is contained in every red blood cell. We can't use nitrogen or sodium; it *has* to be iron. If we don't take in enough iron from our food, we can't get it anywhere else and without it, we won't make enough hemoglobin. When that happens, oxygen transport is reduced, leading to a host of problems including headaches, extreme fatigue, heart palpitations, mouth sores, and dizziness.

Even if we eat plenty overall, if our diets fall short of any one nutrient, some of the body systems have to limp along rather than run optimally.

Other essential nutrients are required for the chemical reactions that occur in our bodies. Essential nutrients are those the body can't synthesize on its own; therefore, we must consume them through our diets. Our bodies need vitamins and minerals for functions like turning food into energy, transmitting signals within the nervous system, dividing cells, maintaining proper blood pH balance, growing hair and fingernails, fighting off infections, and allowing muscles to contract and relax. Without essential nutrients, we literally die.

Maybe you haven't died, per se. But there's a good chance your energy levels, immunity, sleep quality, exercise tolerance, and mood will improve if you give yourself more of these essential nutrients. You might also reduce your risk of chronic disease by boosting the nutrient content of your diet, giving you more days of life to look forward to.

We're going to help you do it.

Scientists have recently discovered thousands of nonessential nutrients from the plant kingdom, and they identify more of these phytochemicals (plant chemicals) every year. Health research shows that while we don't die from a deficiency without them, they impact the long-term susceptibility to chronic disease. Higher intakes of phytochemicals are associated with lower risk of cancer, heart disease, diabetes, less systemic inflammation, and better brain health.[311, 312, 313]

You may have heard of polyphenols, lutein, anthocyanins, resveratrol, or lycopene. Or you may have seen the umbrella term "antioxidants" used to highlight the beneficial phytochemicals in a particular fruit or vegetable. And because we don't just want you to survive but also thrive and live your best possible life, giving yourself MORE when it comes to food includes these nonessential nutrients as well.

You may not know there are nutrients that can make it easier to manage body weight. In particular, consuming higher amounts of protein and fiber are well-established for aiding weight loss, as well as keeping weight off.[314, 315, 316]

This is due to several factors. First, protein and fiber are highly satiating, so even without counting calories, a woman who eats more protein and fiber tends to eat less. Second, both protein and fiber contribute to keeping blood sugar stable and moderating insulin levels. This means steadier energy, and a protective effect against weight gain. Third, fiber decreases the absorption of calories in the gut and feeds beneficial bacterial populations.

High-fiber diets promote a diverse gut biome and a prevalence of bacterial species that offer additional protection against weight gain.[317, 318]

Supplements are a common way to try to increase nutrient intake. In the case of protein, it appears that supplements such as protein powders, shakes, or bars produce the same beneficial results as dietary protein in foods like chicken, beef, or tofu. However, whole foods are superior when it comes to getting enough fiber, vitamins, minerals, and phytochemicals, and are our first choice. In all cases, whole foods pack nutrients, and supplements are rarely necessary.

If you have a deficiency of a specific nutrient, speak with your doctor or a registered dietitian about what food and supplement options will be useful to you.

GIVE YOURSELF MORE NUTRIENTS

Increasing your intake of essential vitamins and minerals, phytochemicals, protein, and fiber might sound like a complicated undertaking, but it doesn't have to be. Even though there are dozens of compounds that fall into these categories, the behaviors we need to adopt are simple.

1. Eat a large quantity and wide variety of fresh fruits and vegetables.

2. Include a protein source in each meal, which can be animal- or plant-based—it's totally up to you.

3. Eat a wide variety of foods, choosing mostly whole, unprocessed forms (unprocessed foods include whole grains, beans, nuts, seeds, dairy products, fresh meats, and produce).

Wasn't that simple? You don't need to memorize which foods have vitamin A or follow exact recipes to make certain you get enough selenium; those three principles are really all you need.

Here's why: Fresh fruits and vegetables are powerhouses of vitamins, minerals, and fiber. If you eat two servings of combined fruits and vegetables with each meal, and enjoy different colors in your rotation, you'll meet your needs for most vitamins and minerals, while also taking in a wide assortment of disease-fighting phytochemicals and weight-managing fiber.

Protein-rich foods such as meat, beans, nuts and seeds, soy, and dairy provide a complementary set of nutrients to those found in produce, plus they help satisfy appetite and provide the amino acids needed for body repair and maintenance. There's ample room for individuality in choosing a healthy diet, so feel free to choose a meat-free, grain-free, or eat-everything approach.

Choosing the most unprocessed forms of available food is a simple way to select a menu that naturally contains higher amounts of fiber, vitamins, and minerals than a diet made of primarily processed foods. Processed foods are fine to include in lesser amounts. (Some of them are super convenient and tasty!). But because processing removes vitamins, minerals, fiber, and phytochemicals, processed foods don't do much to help us reach our nutrient intake goals.

Giving ourselves more nutrients often isn't an issue of learning more, but an issue of more consistently taking action to prioritize nutrition. It's common to choose processed foods out of convenience because you haven't taken the time to buy and prepare whole foods. You might settle into a pattern of heating up frozen meals for lunch instead of packing leftovers or making a sandwich because it's easier and requires less thinking. Think about your own food patterns and determine where it's feasible to give yourself more nutrients.

You will have to invest a few more minutes in shopping, preparing, and bringing food with you to nurture your health. We think you're worth it.

LET YOUR BODY DO THE MATH

If in Chapter 4, you read about restrained eaters with a sense of creeping terror, we promise, it's going to be okay. You may have thought, "Oh crap, that's me." You're not alone, and we can help.

The answer, thankfully, isn't that you have to quit trying to attain a healthy weight. You absolutely can pursue weight loss if that's what you want for your body. By eliminating the underlying premise of restricted eating, you can avoid the dysfunction that occurs in restrained eaters, and the resulting overeating, binge eating, stress, and guilt. Throw out the cognitive restraint and you get to skip the problems.

Cognitive restraint is brain-centered; it's a resource-intensive process of thinking about food intake and planning how to limit it. The alternative to cognitive restraint involves learning body-led actions. With some practice, you'll find that feeling for the right amount of food is far more accurate and effective for weight management. And it's tremendously better for your mental health!

Switching from cognitive restraint to body-led eating involves learning some new tools, and setting aside others. The tools you'll be setting aside are calorie-counting apps and tabulations of how many points or grams you have available for the day. The dashboard of controls you'll be using to steer you in body-led eating are much simpler; your two main controls are your senses of hunger and satiety.

If you haven't tuned into these for a long time, or wonder if your switches are perpetually jammed in either the "on" or "off" position, don't worry! We've been helping women straighten these out for years.

The main challenges that most of us encounter with learning to use HUNGER as a guide are:

1. Differentiating physical hunger from the psychological desire for food

2. Maintaining a neutral or positive emotional state when hunger is felt

The main challenges most of us encounter with learning to use SATIETY as a guide are:

1. Sensing its subtle signals amid other more attention-grabbing stimuli

2. Differentiating physical satiety from the psychological desire to eat more or less—we'll cover these in more detail in the next section

HUNGER: WHAT IT IS, WHAT IT ISN'T, AND HOW MUCH IS A GOOD IDEA

Ask 10 people what hunger feels like and you'll get 10 different answers. The definition we like to use is an "empty-hollow sensation in the upper abdomen." Of course, no one says that when we ask what hunger feels like, but we're happy when our clients indicate anything relating to the stomach.

Sometimes women say they feel hunger in their head, mouth, or throat, or that their limbs and bodies feel overall weak or tired. These physical sensations can occur at the same time as hunger, but they're not hunger. Sensations felt elsewhere in the body are often thirst, imagining the taste of food, or experiencing a craving, low blood sugar, waning energy, or simply a headache.

It's worth noting all the things going on in your body and mind. But for the sake of using hunger as a guide to how much to eat, we want to stick with the abdomen- or belly-centered hunger as the truest guide.

Where in the body the sensation is felt is one of the key clues that helps distinguish hunger from desire. We feel desire as an *emotion of wanting*. Our desire for food usually goes hand-in-hand with hunger, but it can also occur in the absence of hunger.

As we learned in Chapter 4, cravings are initiated by external signals, and are psychological in nature. They're not a reliable way to make your food decisions or regulate your food intake for the best results. If you notice you're having strong desires for food when you're not physically hungry, that's good information to pick up on. Tuning into your emotional state can help you decode what's going on and then decide what you want to do. (Review Chapter 11 for techniques on naming emotions, and ways to de-escalate them through communicating, reappraisal, taking action, and practicing acceptance.)

Often our desires for food are rooted in emotions we're experiencing. It's also possible we're just plain looking for pleasure in our lives! In the next chapter, we'll give you lots of ideas for sourcing the joy and positive emotions you crave.

Here's one reason body-led eating frees up so much brain power: You don't need to monitor all these factors. You don't need to keep constant tabs on your energy, throat, mouth sensations, head, belly, and desire. You don't have to think back over how many calories you already ate, how long ago that was, and how "good" you want to be today. You can forget what workout you did (or didn't do), and disregard what time of day or night it happens to be.

All you need to do is notice when belly-centered hunger gets your attention, and consider that your trustworthy signal to eat. You don't have to keep a vigilant watch out for it, it will find you! You can engage yourself in other meaningful things like fun activities, meaningful work, or perhaps working on the book you've always wanted to write. You can be present in your life, and know when it's time to eat.

USING BODY SIGNALS
TO STEER TOWARD YOUR GOALS

It can be fabulous to use hunger as your cue to eat and to build a healthy relationship with food, recover from disordered eating, and support overall mental wellness. It's a healthy approach to teach children too, and it's a valuable skill for them to be able to sense hunger and verbalize that. Hungry right now? Then it's a perfect time to eat!

Practicing eating in response to hunger has even more benefits: It blocks the cycle of eating to cope with or avoid things, and is at odds with eating to entertain ourselves or alleviate boredom. This conflict can open our eyes to our patterns of using food for non-nutritive purposes. It also invites us to seek other ways of processing our feelings, finding joy, and experiencing pleasure. We become stronger and more capable by giving ourselves more than food.

For weight loss, hunger is a fabulous and healthy compass. However, this outcome requires responding to the information in a slightly different way. As a default, if we go along with them, hunger signals generally lead us to maintain a stable weight. Our bodies are great at fine-tuning the signals to ensure we take in about the same amount of energy we expend.

However, if we want to create an energy deficit to decrease weight over time, we do that by aiming to eat 30 to 60 minutes *after* we get a clear hunger signal. That waiting period before each time we eat is enough of a window to enable gradual weight loss. It's also a perfect guide to make sure we don't cut the food intake back too much.

If you've ever done a strict diet in which your food intake was greatly reduced, you probably felt several hours of hunger during the day. That's too much of a caloric deficit. This may seem like a fair price to pay for fast weight loss, but it's typically too demanding and unpleasant to be done for months or years at a time. And if you want to lose a significant amount of weight, you'll need to be able to stick to your plan for months or years.

Plus, maintenance is forever.

Worse yet, caloric reductions of that magnitude are likely to trigger binge eating, food obsession, poor sleep, and nutrient deficiencies. A half- to one-hour window of hunger before meals tends to feel much more doable, and is effective as a target to ensure gradual weight loss without those unpleasant side effects. Other than a consideration of the clock, there's no counting!

However, by this point in the book, you might already be leaning away from goals of pure weight loss and toward goals that focus on gains. Here's a table with some guidance on how to use your hunger signals to help steer toward whichever goals you have for your body. Working with a coach is the best way to personalize your hunger-timing strategy, but these starting points work for most people.

PRIMARY GOAL	TIMING	NOTES AND EXCEPTIONS
Healthy relationship with food	Practice eating within 0 to 60 minutes of feeling hungry, focusing on responding to your body's physical needs with food, and most of the time attending to your emotional needs in other ways.	During initial recovery from disordered eating, it may help to eat on a planned schedule, regardless of hunger. See a professional for personalized help.
Muscle or weight gain	Try to eat within 30 minutes of first feeling hunger. Avoid long stretches of hunger.	Evaluate your progress after two weeks to see if you need to shorten that time frame, or integrate protein-rich liquids, which are less filling than foods are. If you have a low appetite, you may need to eat even before you're hungry to see upward progress on the scale. Make small changes to avoid rapid weight gain, which is a sign of gaining more fat than lean muscle.
Endurance training or performance	Wait until hungry to eat, but try to eat within 30 minutes of first feeling hunger. Aim to maintain a steady bodyweight for maximum performance and adaptation to training. A steady bodyweight means you're just replacing all the fuel used in training.	Take in some recovery fuel after hard or long workouts (anything intense or more than 90 minutes in duration), regardless of hunger, which aerobic training sessions often suppresses.
Weight maintenance	Wait until hungry to eat, but experiment with reducing time spent feeling hunger to your preference.	If you lost weight by aiming for 30 to 60 minutes of hunger before eating, you might maintain by aiming for 15 to 30 minutes of hunger. You might simply need to ensure that you're physically hungry before eating. Regularly eating in the absence of hunger tends to produce weight regain, so try to use hunger to guide your eating.

Hunger strikes different emotional chords in different women. Many of us feel worried when we get hungry, irritable, panicky, or scared. Some women have a sense of urgency when they first notice hunger, and are prone to stop whatever they're doing to eat. Right. Now.

Other women don't have emotions arise when they feel hunger, and are content to work through it or keep hiking until they find a nicer spot to sit and enjoy lunch. Your emotions around hunger have likely been shaped by your history, but you retain the ability to shift them. The reappraisal techniques introduced in Chapter 11 are perfectly suited to growing this ability.

Consider the following examples of how to reappraise hunger into something that's no longer emotionally negative:

- Learning to feel hungry, just like I am right now, is part of learning how to eat an appropriate amount for my body. It will set me free from ever dieting again.

  Technique: thinking of lessons that can or will be learned from an experience or skills that may be strengthened

- This feeling of being hungry isn't outright pain; when I broke my leg, now THAT was serious pain! I can handle this; it's pretty mild, and I know it's only for 30 minutes.

  Technique: seeing how things aren't that bad, might not be as severe as they seem, could be worse, or can be handled

- After I've felt hungry for 30 minutes a handful of times, it'll get much easier. It's toughest now because it's totally new.

  Technique: focusing on how things will improve in time

- I've done a lot of hard things in my life, and have shown I'm tough, determined, and willing to work to reach my goals. I can handle feeling hungry for a while if that's the hard work I need to do for this goal.

  Technique: noting how you have the personal resources to cope with this problem

- Once I notice I'm definitely hungry, I'll start that 20-minute video I set aside earlier to distract myself. Then, I'll walk to the farthest lunchroom and start heating up my food in the microwave. That's enough to kill the 30 minutes easily!

  Technique: coming up with a detailed plan for how to proceed with solving the problem

- If thousands of people have learned to be okay with feeling hunger, I can too. It's just a body sensation after all, and I don't get upset at having to pee or feeling tired in the evening. It's part of how my body works.

  Technique: acceptance of the situation as a part of life, or something that many people go through

You don't *have* to let your hunger determine when you eat your meals. Many women don't have the liberty in their schedules to wait until they're hungry to have lunch or dinner.

Instead, you might consider hunger feedback on the previous meal. You might notice your usual breakfast results in feeling hunger four hours later. If that's when you want to eat, perfect! If it's too early, and you end up being hungry for longer than you want, you can add something to your breakfast to help it hold you over for a bit longer.

However, if you're not feeling belly-centered hunger when it fits your schedule to eat, you can use that info to pare back your previous meals. As you practice this habit, you'll get good at sensing how full to get at breakfast to make it to lunch, and how full to get at lunch to make it to dinner. If you have snacks between meals, size and time them so you're hungry for them, just like for your meals.

Give yourself time to practice and approach each meal like a new training session, a new opportunity to build a skill. If you rarely or never feel hunger before eating, moving up to successfully noticing it one or two times in several days is progress! Don't feel like you have to hit every single meal perfectly right off the starting line... or ever, for that matter.

SATIETY: WHAT IT IS, WHAT IT ISN'T, AND HOW MUCH IS A GOOD IDEA

Satiety, the body's other food control signal, tells us when to stop eating. Unfortunately, many people have stopped looking for this signal as soon as they begin dieting, letting the rules of a diet tell them how much they're allowed to eat. Stopping before reaching physical satiety is a common practice on a diet, especially when following plans that include small, frequent meals. You never feel all that hungry, but you also never feel fully satisfied!

Perma-dieting can also lead to overriding satisfaction signals when we go "off" the diet or are otherwise distracted from using our cognitive controls to determine portion size. Once we start using our thinky brain with all its judgments and plans to decide how much to eat, we easily ignore those body-led sensations.

We experience physical satiation through abdominal sensations and nervous system responses. It's a combined stomach and whole-body experience. Think of the last time you ate until you were comfortably fed—not overfull, but had enough to feel content.

You could probably feel the presence of food in your stomach, but there wasn't any pain or unpleasant pressure. Throughout your body, you might have noticed a mild relaxation, a loosening of your goal-directed drive to eat, and perhaps a small sigh coming from your mouth.

If you continue to eat, however, the pressure in your abdomen increases, and the relaxation can turn into a numbed or drowsy feeling. Eventually, continued eating produces stomach pain and discomfort. The goal is to stop at the early signs of satiety, when you feel comfortably relaxed, and before you start to feel anything unpleasant.

Sensing satisfaction is in many ways similar to noticing hunger; however, one key difference is that satiety is like hunger's quieter, soft-spoken cousin. It won't necessarily get your attention, especially if you're busy. You know how easy it is to continue eating past satisfaction while you chat and laugh with friends, realizing too late, "Oof, I'm stuffed!"

What happens when you're at that point of "I'm miserably full, but I can't stop eating"? You should know that, yes, you can. You always can. We might not want to, and that's worth looking into, but you can always stop. Nobody has taken control of your limbs and lips.

To notice the physical sensations of satiety, you need to check in with yourself. You don't need constant vigilance, but an awareness of the state of your body requires an inward glance from time to time. It can be a split-second check, just as the occasional glimpse of your rear-view mirror while driving gives you an awareness of the locations of cars around you. Your inward glances in this case are to check in with your stomach and body so you're conscious of your progress in approaching satiety.

One of the challenges of doing these internal checks is that we're often surrounded by attention-grabbing excitement. The music. The friends. The kids. The thoughts whirling about in our minds about how we'll get everything done that afternoon. The phone screen or email inbox in front of us.

It's effortless to allow ourselves to be swept along in the distractions and never tune into our developing satisfaction. Luckily, those split-second checks don't mean you have to give up paying attention to other things. You just need to flick your awareness back inside every few minutes, a habit that forms with time. Logically, reducing distractions helps with building awareness of satiety. It's also helpful to slow down the eating pace so the food you've eaten has time to trigger all the signals that add up to satiety.

DIVISION OF RESPONSIBILITY

While we encourage letting your body tell you how much to eat— as opposed to trying to think or rationalize your way through it—using your smarts is highly encouraged when it comes to selecting which foods to eat. The human brain developed for learning and assessment. It's evolved into an excellent tool for decision-making through its ability to integrate complex information, remember experiences from the past, and make predictions about the future.

Cognitively trying to limit food intake backfires; however, your cognitive abilities are still of good use. Analytical tendencies can be an asset, enabling you to problem-solve in challenging situations, like "How will I get some protein when I'm on a seven-hour flight?" and "What can I make for breakfast that's healthy but portable?" Using your knowledge of nutrition is necessary for selecting a diet that's balanced and provides health and weight-management benefits.

Still, resist the urge to get too much in your head. When in doubt, refer to the three fundamentals listed earlier in this chapter: Eat lots of fruits and vegetables, get protein at every meal, and fill up on whole foods.

In this way, our recommendations differ from some interpretations of a concept known as intuitive eating. Intuitive eating is sometimes presented as eating whatever you want, whenever you want it, essentially following your impulses with zero restraint or questioning from your logical mind. If you have a hard time swallowing this strategy as one that leads to a healthy body, we understand.

After all, eating exclusively based on impulses would lead most of us to consume more highly palatable foods like chips, ice cream, chocolate, and pizza than is ideal for health. Many of us would similarly eat fewer vegetables if we hadn't acquired the knowledge that these foods are high in nutrients, decrease our risk for chronic disease, and are a handy way to get full while managing our weight. We heartily agree with the intuitive eating principle that no foods are bad. However, we value scientific evidence and cannot ignore decades of research that have clarified which foods are healthiest to eat in large quantities and which are healthiest in small quantities.

GIVE YOURSELF MORE FLEXIBILITY

The amount of food we need fluctuates from day to day. We burn more calories some days and fewer on others, thanks to inconsistencies in the amount of activity we engage in, the temperature of our environments, and the metabolic changes that occur throughout our menstrual cycles. Additionally, fighting an infection or healing from an injury can mean we need extra fuel for cell division and repair, while having a gastrointestinal illness often calls for eating less than usual and sticking with easy-to-digest (aka low-fiber) foods.

Using your hunger and satisfaction cues naturally accommodates for these day-to-day adjustments. It also continually corrects and rebalances to keep your weight more or less stable. If you overeat for a day or a week, your hunger signals are less strong for a period of time. If you under-eat drastically on a day you do a five-hour bike ride, your appetite will roar the following day to bring you closer to a calorically balanced state. Losing weight is still possible with a gradual caloric deficit, but your body will fight hard if you try to sustain a large caloric deficit of 1,000 or more calories per day.

Everyone notices when their appetite is higher. Shaking our heads, we say, "I'm a bottomless pit today!" But very few women notice the times when appetite corrects in the other direction.

That's why athletes who become injured and gym-goers who abandon their fitness plans often gain weight. They eat the same amount they'd been eating, not noticing that their body isn't actually asking for as much food.

If we pay closer attention, we can feel how appetite dials up when we start becoming more active and can follow it to eat a bit more. We can also feel it dial back when activity level decreases. We can stay in balance.

Remember, hunger is the louder, more obvious signal, while satisfaction is the soft-spoken one. Noticing the times your satiety comes earlier will make you a real pro.

Giving yourself more flexibility also extends into an all-important topic many diets fail to address: mistakes. They're going to happen to everyone, and that includes you. There will be times when you do something like eat a brownie mid-afternoon despite being 0% hungry, thinking it would be a fun pick-me-up. And you might feel bad about it afterward, especially if the brownie wasn't all that awesome and you realize you were just procrastinating on work, which unfortunately you still have to do.

Giving yourself flexibility means the occasional slip-up isn't a disaster, and you don't have to see it that way. In fact, it's much better for your mental and physical health if you make exceptions from time to time, whether that means eating when you aren't hungry, having a low-nutrition meal, or choosing to eat more than you need to be satisfied.

The ability to make these exceptions allows you to handle unfortunate or difficult circumstances. It fosters within you trust that you'll survive and can still fit into your pants the following day, even if you ate Hawaiian pizza for dinner. One higher-calorie, low-nutrition meal doesn't ruin anything.

We are what we repeatedly do. If *most of the time* you eat healthfully and in the appropriate amounts, you'll be unharmed by the occasional deviation.

THE WISE-PARENT APPROACH

In an ideal world, we could follow our hunger signals every day, and that would forever prevent us from over- and under-eating. Cue the happy orchestra music!

But that's not reality. Some days, emotions get in the way of feeling hunger. Having an illness or infection can make your appetite completely disappear too. During periods of high stress, you may also find your hunger signals masked, and you don't really feel hungry even if you wait and wait and wait.

If intense emotions, stress, or illness leave you with no appetite, you don't have to force yourself to eat if you really don't want to. The human body is resilient and can get through a few extra hours without food. But if you skip meal after meal, sooner or later you're going to feel some unpleasant side effects of not eating.

Our advice is to use what we call the Wise-Parent Approach. This is the logical, loving attitude you'd imagine a loving guardian using with a child. If a child is sick or stressed out, she may say she isn't hungry and not eat much. And a wise parent would probably not sweat it if the kid didn't want a meal, but after 12 hours, it's a good idea to encourage the child to eat *something*. After all, bodies need energy and nutrients even when sick and stressed. Having nutritious foods at mealtimes is a smart idea.

Stress and emotions can also make our desire for food kick into high gear, like nothing will satisfy us. Grieving people have been known to eat and eat in efforts to ease pain. Being sad or irritated at the injury or illness we're dealing with, plus the boredom of being cooped up indoors, can also make eating twice as much food as usual seem appealing. It can also make hyper-palatable processed foods even more alluring. Suddenly, cake for breakfast and potato chips for lunch seems like a fine idea.

The Wise-Parent Approach can also help in these circumstances. Just because you feel like eating plate after plate of food doesn't mean your body actually needs that much food, and that frequently leads to stomach discomfort and unwanted weight gain. And getting some protein, vegetables, and healthy carbs will help a body persist through the difficulty, whatever it is. You can always have some chips with the meal or cookies after, but try to stick to about one plateful of food, not several.

To summarize the Wise-Parent Approach: If illness or emotions make your appetite disappear, eat a plateful of nourishing food three times per day anyway. Let the details go. If illness or emotions make you want nothing but junk food or desire far more food than usual, do the same thing. Eat a plateful of nourishing food three times a day anyway. You can always add some treats, but don't skip the healthy food.

Especially when you're going through a rough time, it's an important act of self-love to make sure your nutritional needs are fully covered.

TEMPTATION TO GET "BACK ON TRACK"

If food restriction or dieting has given you a feeling of control in the past, it's going to cross your mind again when things in your life feel out of control. But you don't have to bite just because you spot the bait.

You can interpret the sudden, shiny allure of going back to low-carb diets or calorie counting as a sign that right now you crave certainty and control. You can notice you might be struggling a bit with life's challenges. That's a normal way to feel at times. You can remind yourself of good nutrition habits—such as adequate nutrients, eating with mindfulness, and following your body's cues for hunger and satiety to avoid eating too much or too little—instead of jumping into a fad diet.

Imagine future-you, tempted to do a juice cleanse or elimination diet just to "get back on track," but choosing instead to realign your eating with healthy nutrition principles. You'd ask yourself:

- Am I eating lots of fresh fruits and vegetables (most days)?
- Am I including a protein source in each meal (most of the time)?
- Am I eating whole, unprocessed foods (most of the time)?
- Am I waiting until I'm hungry to eat and stopping when I'm satisfied (most of the time)?

If any of your answers are "no," you've identified a nutrition direction in which to take steps. Improving your eating behaviors to align more closely with these four goals can help you feel positive and accomplished. You can proudly sidestep the trap of trying yet another fad diet that only leads to binge eating or emotional distress.

For more extensive reading on how to use your body signals and other habits to lose weight without counting calories or following rigid rules, check out Georgie's book *Lean Habits for Lifelong Weight Loss.*

CHAPTER 13
WELL PLEASED

Women often assume that adopting healthy habits means a *reduction* in immediate gratification and pleasure. The presumption that weight loss or getting fit equates to low levels of enjoyment is rooted in four (false) oversimplifications.

1. Pleasurable food is universally high in calories.

2. We can't eat foods high in calories and lose weight, taking pleasurable food off the menu.

3. Food is the main source of pleasure available to us, so getting fewer kicks from our taste buds means less pleasure in general.

4. Exercise or working out is anti-fun, pretty much only used as punishment for eating lots of fun things.

We're glad to announce that in the following pages, we'll smash each of these false beliefs. We'll explore how to gain more pleasure and enjoyment in your daily life as part of your "get fitter and leaner" strategy. Joy, after all, has no calories, and laughter and smiles never made anyone overweight.

GOOD NEWS #1: FOOD PLEASURE ISN'T MATCHED WITH CALORIC INTAKE

Deliciousness comes in many forms. While most of us enjoy the taste of some lower-nutrition foods like chocolate chip cookies, potato chips, or craft beer, it would be a shame to think of food pleasure in that narrow sense, linked only to desserts, fried snacks, or alcoholic beverages.

Many delicious foods are rich in calories and low in nutrients, but not all delicious foods are rich in calories. A fresh juicy peach, just-baked crusty bread, a steaming lobster tail, or the perfect grilled sandwich can also be highly pleasurable to eat. Emphasizing the pleasure of healthy eating can be equally or even more effective in motivating change than focusing on the health benefits of wholesome foods.[319, 320]

Georgie finds that people who "don't like vegetables" typically just don't know how to season them! Nobody likes plain boiled green beans, people!

Herbs, spices, and seasonings go a long way toward making simple, unprocessed foods like vegetables, beans, and grains mouthwatering. Take some extra time in the spice aisle at the supermarket and try some pre-blended spice mixes to give your food more zing. Some of the most popular ones to try are Greek, Italian, Tex-Mex, and barbecue rubs. Also, don't be afraid to put seasonings made for meat or popcorn on your veggies or potatoes! Yum!

Specialty olive oil and vinegars (usually you have to hit up a specialty or online store for these) are also a flavorful treat we love drizzling on salads and roasted veggies.

Regardless of what food we're consuming, mindfulness has a powerful ability to increase food enjoyment. It doesn't matter if you're crunching on pork rinds or biting into an autumn apple; if you pay zero attention to what you're chewing because you're pecking away at your keyboard while fixated on the report you're writing, you won't be getting the maximum amount of enjoyment from your food. Enhancing enjoyment of your food might not actually mean changing what you eat as much as training yourself to mindfully experience its pleasantness in a more complete way.

The opposite effect holds true as well. Inattention, food stress, and guilt can sour the taste of even the most delightful food. You can eat 10 of your favorite chocolate bars in the name of "treating yourself" or "rewarding yourself," but if you're swamped with guilt and shame, distracted by the movie you're watching, or berating yourself as you unwrap each one and bite into it, pleasure is likely to be the least prominent thing you feel.

Assuming that an increased caloric intake will produce more pleasure is as erroneous and unhelpful as assuming that a decrease in caloric intake automatically leads to decreased food pleasure. It's not true! In fact, actual enjoyment of a food decreases when the portion size becomes too large, a phenomenon known as taste fatigue (AKA sensory-specific satiety).[321]

You may have had this experience when you ordered a large portion of pizza or French fries. At first, it tastes awesome. However, as you keep eating, the taste of the food isn't as great, and the last few lukewarm bites are scarcely as delightful as the first few mouthfuls. For any given food, enjoyment can vary based on whether you're hungry or satiated. When you're hungry, food is far more pleasurable.

Furthermore, taste and the ability to quell hunger aren't the only ways food can bring pleasure. The foods we purchase, eat, prepare, and share can powerfully reinforce our values. We can make a meal that feels like a step closer to the healthy people we want to be, producing positive feelings that go deeper than the taste of the food.

Cooking and eating are often part of sharing time with people we care about, and making food to share—regardless of what it is or how it ends up tasting—can be a source of positive feelings for both the giver and the recipient.

This sort of food-derived pleasure has been called Epicurean pleasure by some researchers, and is defined as "enduring pleasure derived from the aesthetic appreciation of the sensory and symbolic value of the food." As noted by researchers, "Epicurean eating tendencies are associated with a preference for smaller food portions and higher wellbeing, and not associated with higher BMI."[322]

In short, taking pleasure in your food is good for you. And you can give yourself more of it.

GOOD NEWS #2: YOU ABSOLUTELY CAN EAT HIGH-CALORIE FOODS AND LOSE WEIGHT

Since chocolate, cookies, and wine are super pleasurable for many women, we never ban these or any other beloved treat foods, even for our weight-loss clients.

Instead, we help each person clarify the personal criteria for which low-nutrition foods are "worth it" versus "not worth it," and develop the skill of saying "yes" or "no, thanks" to any edible treat. This approach allows us to moderate the amount of these foods, rather than being forced to swear them off or left to eat them uncontrollably.

DETERMINE YOUR "WORTH IT" CRITERIA

Think back over your life experiences, and all the times you've eaten high-calorie, low-nutrition treats. Desserts, fried foods, and alcohol are the broad categories.

We're guessing that some treats were amazing (highly pleasurable), some were just okay (less pleasurable), and some were probably actually bad (not pleasurable).

FOODS

What specific high-calorie, low-nutrition foods do you consistently find highly pleasurable? Examples might be your preferred type of candy, favorite fried food, or a specific kind of pie.

_____

_____

_____

_____

What high-calorie, low-nutrition foods do you find only somewhat pleasurable or not pleasurable at all? Examples might be things that always disappoint you, like a type of cookie you never really like, but will still eat if it's around or store-bought versions of foods that never seem to be as good as homemade.

_____

_____

_____

_____

SETTINGS

What settings allow you the most enjoyable treat experience? Think about the place, time of day, and company you're with. You might prefer having something at a restaurant, alone at a coffee shop on a weekend, or at home with your family around the table.

_____

_____

_____

_____

What settings lead to less-pleasant experiences? Again, think of the place, time of day and company. You might have found that eating workplace treats at your desk is a lackluster experience since you're always distracted by job stress, or maybe you know people whose comments reduce the pleasure of enjoying dessert in their company. Write your thoughts below.

_____

_____

_____

_____

REASONS FOR DIGGING IN

You may not have thought much about your reasons for saying yes to a cupcake or glass of wine, other than "I wanted it," which is a perfectly valid reason. However, you may be able to see patterns in which lines of reasoning lead to more or less pleasurable treat experiences.

Commonly, people find that eating a treat is less enjoyable when it's a reaction to a social or emotional situation, such as appeasing someone who's urging you to eat another slice of pie, or pounding beers to avoid a negative feeling.

Remember, there's no right or wrong; we just want to pare out the less-awesome experiences and keep the top-tier special food treat experiences in your life.

Circle any of the following ideas that seem like good reasons to have a low-nutrition food, and that you'll feel good about later.

Put a line through any reasons you think are likely to be less pleasant, or even regrettable.

Because it was a special occasion

Because someone made it for me

Because I was angry, sad, or stressed

Because I wanted to share the experience with someone

Because someone I love wanted me to eat it

Because I was being "peer pressured"

Because it was free

Because I thought it would be delicious

Because I wanted to feel better

Because I wanted to try it

Because I had already eaten too much

Because I wanted a distraction

Because I was bored

FREQUENCY OF EDIBLE TREATS

The degree of pleasure we get from a given eating experience is impacted by how often we have edible treats. If we have carrot cake with every meal for a week, the 21st piece of cake isn't going to be as pleasurable as the first piece was. You don't have to write anything for this; just bear it in mind when you consider a given treat and whether it's worth it (highly pleasurable) or not (pass on it).

If you've been having a particular treat frequently—or a lot of sweets, fried foods, and alcoholic beverages recently—it might not be as special to indulge in yet again. You might enjoy the splurges more if you include more time between your edible treats.

To keep the amazing experiences and pass on so-so things that just add calories without being special, consider saying yes to only the treat experiences that fall on your first list for *food* and *setting*, and for a *reason* you circled. It's likely to be a wise choice to decline treats that fall on your second lists for *food* and *setting*, or if you notice you're considering them for one of the *reasons* you crossed out.

With time, you'll get accustomed to thinking about pleasure and worth-it-ness when making decisions about food treats, and this thinking is far more helpful than plotting how many calories or points the food contains, or whether you've been "good" or "bad" that day. The real question is whether this treat is actually going to contribute pleasure to your life. Hold those treats accountable.

GOOD NEWS #3: FOOD IS ONE OF MANY SOURCES OF PLEASURE

As our clients work to moderate the number of treats they eat and drink, we like to talk about what we call *real-life treats*. These are all the enjoyable things in life that aren't edible. Real-life treats include activities like petting your cat, letting the sun hit your face, sharing a hug or kiss, smelling a pleasant aroma, or having a fun time dancing. Real-life treats come in so many forms, and a whole lot of them are free.

Enjoying abundant real-life treats on a daily basis is important, but many of us find they get pushed aside as we focus on all of our tasks and responsibilities. However, especially if we've been getting most or all of our pleasure from food and drink, it's a powerful change to purposely seek more real-life treats, experiencing as many and much of them as we can manage. You can't overdo it. Go all in.

Our clients often notice how much easier it becomes to consume fewer sugary desserts, impulsive handfuls of chips, or second glasses of wine when they load up on real-life treats at the same time. Doing so can show just how much of your sweet tooth was actually a broader desire for enjoyment.

WHAT BRINGS YOU PLEASURE, OTHER THAN EATING TASTY FOOD?

The answer to this question is different for every person. You might love a scented bubble bath, while your best friend dislikes them and would be much happier shoe shopping. Georgie finds a ton of joy in cross-country skiing and riding her bike, while Aleisha loves bouldering and throwing on the potter's wheel for her real-life treats.

This is about finding *your* sources of joy, not someone else's. You might not know what brings you joy just yet, and that's okay. Research has given us some ideas of handy places to look.

One of the first things many women think of is buying themselves something. And we agree, getting yourself a present can be really lovely and is a totally fine way to enjoy a treat. (We're big fans of buying ourselves flowers, for the record.)

But you don't have to open your wallet to enjoy positive emotions. Researchers have proposed that experiences can bring us even more pleasure than purchasing material goods can.[323] Experts believe this is because experiences:

1. Enrich our relationships with other people more than material goods do

2. Contribute to our identity more than the things we own do

3. Are readily enjoyed without comparing them to what other people have

So let's talk experiences!

First up, the outside one. After all, being in nature makes us happier![324] For many people, it can feel great to take in nature, whether it's an ocean view or mountain hike. Natural smells and sounds like freshly cut grass or singing birds can be delightful, nostalgic, and calming. And warm sunbeams are just the best.

Engaging in outdoor physical activity can be a great way to feel joy,[325] and just living in a greener neighborhood is linked to lower chronic stress.[326] While walking in natural settings may be more restorative than walking in residential areas, heading for a walk around the neighborhood is still better for mental well-being than not walking at all.[327]

Also, don't forget nature's gift of animals. Even if you don't always feel like a people-person, you might really enjoy playing with a cat or dog, petting a horse, or visiting a zoo—which conveniently also hits the experience category.

There are so many more: conversations with our loved ones and friends, creative expression, enjoying music, reading, playing games, traveling, or taking in entertainment can all help us meet our daily needs for novelty and pleasure.

There's also more to filling your life with joy than doing things that *immediately* feel easy and pleasant. Eating a tasty dessert is obviously pleasurable in an immediate sense (and it's pretty easy), yet it lacks a sense of lasting meaning. Surprisingly, things that *feel like work* can be sources of even greater joy than the superficial gratification we get from sugar, nicotine, or drugs—as long as we derive a sense of meaning and purpose from it.[328]

In that sense, helping another person, volunteering, working on your fitness, or practicing a skill you want to develop can be highly pleasurable.

SHOULD I EAT THAT TREAT?

#GiveYourselfMore   GiveYourselfMore.net

START HERE.

Is it one of your favorite, top-tier tasty things?

YES

NO

Do you have time and space to enjoy it mindfully?

Pass! You can do so much better.

If you can, save it for later to enjoy with your next meal or when you won't have to scarf it

YES   NO

Have you had a lot of food treats lately?

Hm. You might need more real-life treats! How about booking a massage or hanging out with a friend?

Go ahead and savor it, baby!

YES

NO   YES

YES

We won't tell if you don't. But if you're numbed up, be careful not to bite your cheek!

NO

Did the dentist tell you not to eat for the next hour?

NO

Would you be eating it out of anger, sadness or procrastination?

We're going to add a list on the following page. Think of it as a menu of sorts, a selection of joyful things you can experience in a day. And for the next week, we invite you to keep track and see how many of these you can rack up if you put your mind to it.

Post the list somewhere you'll see it often, and check away at it throughout the week. (You have permission to copy or rip out the page if you want to.)

REAL-LIFE TREATS	MON	TUE	WED	THU	FRI	SAT	SUN
Music, art, dance, crafts							
Outdoors, gardening, hiking							
Romance							
Alone time, meditation, naps							
Comedy, laughter							
Socializing with friends, family							
Meaningful purchases							
Bath, massage, grooming							
Movement, running, exercise							
Shows, movies, reading							
Experiences with animals							
Museums, fairs, plays, markets							
Journaling, writing letters							
Sports, puzzles, games							
Helping others, volunteering							

When you've completed the log, ask yourself the following:

- How many total real-life treats did I enjoy?

- Did the patterns vary considerably from day to day, or were they fairly consistent?

- If I had any binges or overate on low-nutrition foods, was it on days that were high or low in real-life treats?

As you contemplate these questions, you might notice some interesting things about real-life treats:

- Thinking of something as a treat changes how you experience it. You may have walked the dog every day as a "chore," but if you think, Hey I can check off outdoor activity and petting my furry buddy for a few minutes afterward, two treats! you may become aware of everyday experiences' potential to bring pleasant emotions into your days.

- While you're focused on getting more real-life treats, you're distracted from some unhelpful but routine food patterns, like grabbing a handful of almonds when what you really need is a laugh.

- Small pleasures are often more accessible than we think. Many of us fall into the trap of thinking that we can't have fun because we don't have the available money or hours to get weekly massages or take cruises to Tahiti. But plenty of the activities on our real-life-treats tracker are free or come with nominal costs.

- It's easy to fall into a rut, having the same one or two types of real-life treats day after day. If you notice this in yourself, it might be worth trying out some new pleasant activities next week. There's no need to push something on yourself that doesn't sound fun. Hopefully this section has given you some ideas.

Next, set a goal. We encourage you to try to increase the overall total or variety of real-life treats you enjoy next week. Give yourself MORE!

GOOD NEWS #4: MOVEMENT CAN BE A TOTAL BLAST

As we touched on in Chapter 2, most women at one point or another have had a pretty awful experience with exercise. It may have been in grade-school gym class, as you winced, lungs burning, while being forced by a whistle-yielding teacher to run a mile. Or it could have been later in your life that you first had unpleasant experiences exercising. Perhaps you signed up for an outdoor bootcamp class, only to have your body crumble into a sweaty, aching heap after far too many triceps dips on a park bench. *This sucks. I never want to do this again.*

After experiences like these, many women adopt the idea that they don't like exercising or that they don't like moving at all. They believe exercise has to hurt, make them sweaty and overheated, or be a social comparison trap where they always come up short. Or slow. Or uncoordinated. Or all of the above… and more. It's completely natural to form opinions based on our experiences!

But look: Exercise doesn't have to be a bummer. In fact, you can completely ignore the word "exercise" if you'd like, because it tends to bring up ideas of structured goal-oriented workouts. You might prefer to think simply of how fun it can be to *move your body.*

Movement can be a ton of fun! When your favorite song starts playing and you get the urge to sway and dance to it, that's movement, naturally occurring in you not because you forced it, but because it's something humans do.

And we like it, as long as we don't ruin the experience by making it painful or otherwise unpleasant.

Going too hard is one of the most common ways women unwittingly reduce the amount of fun they have moving their bodies. If that's true for you, it's not your fault. After all, you've heard the jocks say, "go hard or go home," right? Wrong. You'll have a lot more fun if you approach activity with the idea that you should feel better after doing it than you did before you started. You should feel energized and happy, not wiped out, trembling, and nauseated.

Having some challenge to the physical activity you choose can make it more engaging. As with anyting, if it's too easy you might get bored. But there's no need to push into pain, make your body ache for days, or flirt with injury. Go as hard as you want as long as it stays fun. (Flip back to Chapter 10 if you need a refresher on finding the exercise-intensity sweet spot.)

There are also countless options when it comes to getting moving, and you don't have to love them all. Most people *don't* love them all! As we've said before, it just takes finding one or a few activities you enjoy to build a physically active life. To find your best fit, consider the following questions:

ARE YOU AN INDOOR OR OUTDOOR GIRL?

If you like to work out indoors, you can explore exercising in your home or at a commercial facility. You don't have to bear the summer heat or winter chill, ever. You can shimmy your way through Zumba, challenge your legs to an indoor cycling workout, take a yoga class, play squash or racquetball, follow online yoga or strength training videos, walk through a shopping mall, try pole dancing, learn to use an indoor rowing machine, use machines or free weights in a gym, try rock climbing on an indoor wall, take a dance class at a studio, or learn to dance via YouTube. You can practice samba in your own kitchen, giggle at yourself, and entertain your dog all at the same time.

Or, if you're more into time outdoors, consider walking, hiking, jogging, running, roller skating, downhill or cross-country skiing, riding a bike, or watersports like kayaking or stand-up paddle boarding. You can also get your hands in the dirt and move your body gardening, raking leaves, transplanting bushes, or spreading mulch. It all counts.

DON'T BE AFRAID TO LAUGH!

Go ahead and bust out in giggles as you fall over in yoga class, or laugh about how funny you feel trying to swing a kettlebell.

Research shows that humor increases attention, reduces anxiety, makes participation more fun, and increases motivation to keep at it.[350] Laughter stimulates body systems that reduce levels of stress hormones, such as cortisol and epinephrine, and activates the dopaminergic reward system in our brains.

Taking yourself too seriously can put a damper on the fun, and can make activity less like play and more like a chore.

DO YOU CRAVE SOCIAL OR ALONE TIME?

Getting to meet new friends or visit with those you already love can completely change any given workout. Most cities have walking, running, and biking groups you can join to meet up with other people and talk while you enjoy getting your blood pumping. Commercial gyms, recreation centers, and parks all commonly host classes, ranging from swim lessons to acrobatics. Showing up for a class at the same time and day of the week, you're bound to get to know the familiar faces and gain a sense of camaraderie.

If you prefer being a solo act, you might love walking, running, biking, or hiking on your own. Just be sure to take safety precautions, such as letting someone know where you'll be and bringing a phone with you. At-home workouts are another option:

From exercise equipment to on-demand streaming workout apps, there are more ways than ever to break a sweat in your living room.

Even if there are other people working out around you, it doesn't have to feel that way. For example, swimming often feels solitary (thanks to the sound-dampening effects of water). And, on dry land, headphones can take you to your own little world.

WHAT ARE SOME OF YOUR NON-EXERCISE HOBBIES?

Physical activity often overlaps with other hobbies and interests, such as animals, camping, gardening, or volunteerism. Things you may not do "for exercise" still have mental and physical benefits.

For example, if you love training your dog to run agility courses, practicing with him might seem focused on Fido, but you'll be hustling and moving around quite a bit too. If you own large animals like horses, caring for them will ensure a certain amount of daily activity as well.

Beautifying your home garden is another project that can keep you active while investing in other real-life treats. Watering, planting, digging, weeding, and raking ensure that you'll have plenty of variety and always something to do.

Camping is a great way to spend quality time with people you love (aren't the conversations around a fire always the best?) and to see new places. Your foray into the wilderness can be a way to get moving, especially if you carry your own gear. Pitching tents, gathering firewood, and searching for the perfect marshmallow roasting stick will all have you up and around.

The sense of satisfaction that comes from helping others or being part of positive social change can make exercise feel doubly good. You might register for a walk, bike ride, or run that benefits a charity, or join an Earth Day cleanup along a local running path or shoreline. These activities get your body moving, but they also do something more by helping you express your values as you make a difference.

CHAPTER 14
GET SOME REST

We've said it before and we'll say it again: *Giving yourself MORE does not mean doing more.* Often, it involves the opposite—taking a break, resting, and learning to stop seeking value in busyness. And, fortunately, you don't have to be busy, stressed, or run down to be important. You're important for one simple reason: You exist.

We believe that taking that truth to heart has major implications for how you care for yourself and react to your need for rest. If you didn't have to "do it all" to matter in your own eyes, you'd stop devoting your time, energy, and money to things that drain you or just aren't important to you. Instead, you'd give them to things that fill you up. Rather than adding to your to-do list, they would add to your quality of life, happiness, and fulfillment.

So what would you ditch from your to-do list, and how would you learn to say no to them? How would you integrate rest into your life—and how the heck would you finally switch off your brain?

Don't worry about it. We're going to help you bring clarity to these questions so you can build a strategy around self-care and rest that best serves your physical, mental, and emotional needs. You'll learn how to recognize the signs of needing more rest before you hit the proverbial wall and face total burnout or over-training syndrome.

We want to help you put an end to passing out in front of the TV, staggering along with your umpteenth coffee in hand, or spending your days at such a frenetic pace that you can't even enjoy them. We'll teach you how to approach rest and recovery with intentionality and purpose. To feel refreshed and recharged, you need to plan, prioritize, and allow yourself to fully sink into it.

Take a deep breath, and get ready to chillax.

EASING INTO REST

It can feel great to relax, but at first, it mostly just feels really uncomfortable. After all, dedicating ourselves to rest doesn't jive with our idealization of the do-it-all-and-then-some woman who can't stop, won't stop. Taking time for rest can feel like an affront to productivity or achievement. *If I take a break, there's no way I'll get to everything I need to do!* Such trains of thought are incredibly common.

Similarly, if much of your identity has been wrapped up in achievement and you identify as a multitasking expert, you probably feel like taking a break is taking a break from yourself, like it isn't "you." You might feel like you're falling behind everyone else. *I'm resting while other women are accomplishing things! This is so lazy of me.* Also, you might feel bored. *What do I do with myself if I'm not running around?*

If that sounds irritatingly familiar, take comfort in the fact that resting can be one of the best ways to improve your energy, mental focus, decision-making abilities, efficiency, and overall productivity.[329, 330] One awesome real-life example: In 2019, when employees at Microsoft Japan cut their traditional five-day workweek down to four days, their productivity increased by an average of 40%![331] That's despite working fewer hours per week. It's all about quality over quantity.

Think about it: How much of your workdays do you spend staring at a screen, your brain so tapped out that you can't seem to make headway on anything? Maybe you constantly toggle back and forth between computer tabs, emails, projects, giving half-assed distracted energy toward all your work. Think how much more productive you'd be if you used your full ass!

You're allowed to get things done while you rest—within reason, of course. For example, enjoying crafts, knitting, puzzles, painting, pottery, cooking, yoga, tai chi, and practicing other gentle skills can all be incredibly relaxing, while also leaving you with a sense of accomplishment. Some of them even yield tangible results you can point to and say, "Look what I did!"

> The key to relaxing through activity is to choose things that are challenging but doable, tapping into your brain's love of mastery, and helping you achieve a state of mental flow.

When performance anxiety starts to creep up, remind yourself that refilling your tank allows you to be present in your own life. Taking advantage of self-caring rest gives you more energy to climb the corporate ladder, be active in your communities, play with your kids, and engage in meaningful conversations with friends without that glazed-over look in your eyes.

Of course, we encourage you to value rest for much more than its ability to increase your output. Remember how, back in Chapter 6, we warned that pursuing self-care solely as a way to serve others keeps us only concerned with ourselves insofar as it benefits others? That still holds true: You deserve rest and recovery, regardless of how much more efficient or helpful it might make you. However, if you really struggle with the idea of giving yourself more rest, keeping this productivity payoff in mind can help take the edge off, so that when trying to relax, you can actually relax. Baby steps.

A NEW TYPE OF SELF-CARE

True self-care hinges on seeking it for your own benefit. For that reason, we encourage women to define self-care as something apart from what the weight-loss and beauty fields pass off under the guise of "wellness."

Popular culture equates self-care with bubble baths, ice cream, and face masks. These can feel good, and that's okay. If you want to, you can include these in your personal brand of self-care.

However, do they really help you better care for and fill yourself up? The totality of self-care isn't about adding to a to-do list, covering up difficult emotions with indulgences, or eliminating under-eye circles (that you could address more effectively with some sleep).

So let's redefine self-care: *The process of identifying and meeting our individual physical, mental, and emotional needs.*

You worked on this a lot in Chapter 11 as it pertains to emotions—learning how to identify, express, and handle them in healthful ways that allow you to truly meet your needs, rather than flail through counterproductive strategies. We invite you to approach self-care and rest in the same manner.

GO AHEAD, BE SELFISH

You're your own and first responsibility. That might sound selfish to you. And you'd be right; it's selfish.

But here's something you might not have thought of: There's nothing wrong with—sometimes—prioritizing yourself and your needs above others. Isolated moments of selfishness can help you find balance. In Chapter 5, we explored how unmitigated communion, focusing solely on others, can steal your joy. Selfishness is your mitigator. Think of selfishness and communion as two kids playing on a teeter-totter. Sometimes you need teeter to selfish so you can totter to communion.

Also, by selfish, we don't mean being a jerk or not treating others with respect. But what's wrong with respecting yourself as you would anyone else? With valuing yourself the same as you value the woman sitting next to you? Your children? Your family? Your colleagues? Your clients? What's wrong with acknowledging that, as a human being, you deserve the same care they do? Nothing.

And, as a result of bringing yourself up to parity with the rest of humankind, a lot of wonderful things would happen, many of them automatically guiding you toward more rest.

If you treated yourself with that level of care, one of the first things you'd probably notice is that your to-do list would shorten and "no" would become a much larger part of your vocabulary.

You wouldn't feel guilted into doing things that really aren't important to you... and maybe that you even resent. You wouldn't feel like you had to be the head coordinator for your colleague's going-away party, or that you had to hemorrhage money on yet another baby shower for someone you barely know.

If and when your boss tried to pile more work onto your already overbooked workload, you'd be able to say, "I don't have the bandwidth to do this by _____, but can get it to you by _____."

Similarly, if you were invited to an event that conflicted with whatever you'd rather be doing, even if it was nothing at all, you'd be able to decide, "Nope, not going." You'd buy store-bought cookies for the bake sale instead of making them from scratch.

The words would roll off your tongue, "Thanks, but I'll pass." "I need to protect my energy." "I can't afford it." Or even, get this, "I don't want to."

> In Chapter 7, we noted that making room for fulfilling habits often involves pulling back from less-helpful ones. Right now, you're making room!

And all of it would be okay. You wouldn't feel like you needed to say "I'm sorry" for any of it. Because, you know what? You wouldn't be sorry and would have no reason to be. Why should you be sorry for not spending your hard-earned time, energy, and money doing things you don't want to do with people you don't even like? Why should you be sorry for respecting yourself?

You shouldn't.

Notice how thinking through these scenarios makes you feel. Are your shoulders, jaws, or breath relaxing? Are you getting nervous? Maybe you simultaneously feel senses of both relief and *I don't know if I can really do that*. Whatever you're feeling, know that it's valid, and we're not going to leave you to wade through it on your own.

Throughout this chapter, we'll help you grow your self-care in a way that respects yourself without compromising your respect for anyone else.

FINDING BALANCE

Most of us don't give much thought to rest until we're already teetering on burnout, anxiety attacks, stress eating, and decision paralysis. So when we start to evaluate our current balance between stressors (even good ones!) and rest, we tend to find that things are pretty skewed.

This section is all about identifying the concrete ways in which we can gain equilibrium.

WHAT'S RESTFUL TO YOU?

There are certain foundations to biological rest. We all need sleep to recover from daily wear and tear. We need food to afford our bodies the building blocks they need for cellular energy and repair. (Yes, food's critical to rest and recovery. You know the sympathetic fight-or-flight nervous system? The parasympathetic rest-and-digest nervous system is what brings us back to baseline.)

Meanwhile, gentle movement guides blood, oxygen, and nutrients to the heart, brain, and muscles for cellular remodeling. Practicing acceptance, as opposed to fighting our emotions, protects us from spending needless, ineffective energy and stressing ourselves out. Enjoying real-life treats can certainly provide opportunities for rest!

Still, every woman relaxes or finds energy in her own individual way. Fortunately, when it comes to rest and recharging, there's no shortage of options.

Here's a much-abbreviated list:

reading, being in nature, alone time, sleeping without an alarm, listening to music, doing nothing at all, walking, stretching, taking a bath or shower, meditating, napping, coloring in adult coloring books

It's likely that, to you, some of these ideas sound fabulous—and others make you squirm. Let's identify your favorite ways to rest. Take a few minutes on the following page to write down any activities or anti-activities that feel good to you and would help you more fully enjoy everything else you do.

Note: List them regardless of how often you engage in them. Even if you've never tried them, but might like to, write them down!

_____

_____

_____

_____

WHAT DRAINS YOU?

Now, we're going to repeat the brainstorm, but instead of focusing on things that recharge you, we'll focus on those that drain you. You get two more minutes to write down everything that drains you—everything that annoys you, that you dread… even hate and that keeps you from doing things you actually enjoy or find fulfilling. The ideas will likely come to you quickly, and in big numbers.

However, we're going to challenge you to not write down "work." If that's what you were going to write, instead, ask yourself what it is about your work situation that sucks the life out of you. Because, sorry to break it to you, you're not going to get out of work. Plus, ideally, work would add to your life, not just in terms of money, but also personal fulfillment.

> Speaking of personal fulfillment, please know that working a lot doesn't always equate to living with LESS. Being passionately involved in work you love can be a wonderful gift. Whether your work-life balance is healthful or harmful depends not just on how many hours you spend on the clock, but also on the motives driving you to put in those hours.[351]

If your work drains you and keeps you riddled with the "Sunday scaries," what's the real issue? Is it working weird hours that throw off your sleep schedule or keep you checking your email on holidays? Is it having a boss who doesn't appreciate you? Or devoting time and energy to a job you don't believe matters in the world?

Other common energy-sucks that might warrant a spot on your list: toxic relationships, lack of sleep, trying to keep up with others on social media, irregular sleep, negative self-talk, too much "on" time around others, paying ridiculous credit-card interest, multitasking, and hyper-focusing on negative emotions.

Ready? You're up!

_____

_____

_____

_____

RECALIBRATING

So, what do you do with these lists? You start making room for the things on rest-and-recover list by ditching those on the drained-and-stressed one.

Pick one item on your "this bites" list. If you walked away from it right now, how much more time, energy, and money would you have to devote to your restful pursuits? Would walking away from this draining activity automatically draw you closer to rest and recovery?

For example, whether we're introverts or extroverts comes down to where we find energy. Introverts replenish energy largely through alone time. And even though they might enjoy time with others, too much of it can leave them feeling zapped. Fortunately, by scaling back slightly on people time, introverts automatically get more restful alone time in return. It sounds simple enough, so why aren't the introverts among us doing it?

To explain, let's play out what that would look like. Pick one of the things on your LESS list that sucks the life out of you and, once you've decided on it, close your eyes for a little visualization exercise.

Now, imagine yourself going up to the powers that be in this scenario—maybe it's your boss, mom, or friend—and saying, nope, I'm not going to do that thing. (Of course, we recommend saying it in a nicer way. In the next section. we'll walk you through how to say no with kindness and respect.)

How does it make you feel in your body? Has your heart sped up? Is there a queasy feeling in the pit of your stomach? Maybe, if you're like us, your head is spinning a little. Are you holding tension anywhere in your body? Identify where you're feeling anxiety, and place your hand there. What you're feeling is the very thing that keeps you from saying no.

Now, here's something you're not going to like: We want you to sit with this feeling. It's probably not overly comfortable, which is why, up to this point, it's always been easier to *do more* rather than *give yourself MORE*. We promise you won't implode. Take a few slow, deep breaths.

Now let's say you've ditched that draining thing from your to-do list. Congrats! Think through how you'll use that freed-up time, energy, or money to take better care of yourself and meet *your* needs. Imagine how, after three weeks or three months, the world will probably still be spinning and no one will feel any major impact.

When you think this way, how does your body react? Has your heart rate slowed? Have your glutes, shoulders, or jaws relaxed? It feels good, right?

Perhaps the coolest thing about this switch is that it comes with double benefits: You not only get the good stuff, but you get rid of the bad stuff. You get to enjoy restful moments while also reveling in the fact that you're freed from formerly draining pursuits. You have more physical, mental, and emotional resources to afford to the things that matter. Like you.

BOUNDARIES AND SAYING "NO"

But the problem still stands: Doing less so we can give ourselves MORE isn't automatic, and often, it feels dangerous… at least in the beginning. We don't like to tell others no. We worry what people will think when we raise a boundary between ourselves and their requests.

Getting past this discomfort requires practice—practice thinking about what you really want, assessing what you do out of obligation or fear of not being busy, asking yourself what's the worst that can happen, and politely, but unapologetically, saying no. We find that wading into the waters helps. To do so, start with the things on your LESS list that feel the most doable to ditch, and arm yourself with some boundary-setting strategies.

MAKE A POLICY FOR YOURSELF, AND FOLLOW IT

Creating guidelines can be helpful if you're new to no and are the consummate people-pleaser. Here's what we mean: Maybe you're a freelancer who takes on every client and project that comes your way—forcing you to overwork, skip having a social life, and resent a career that could otherwise be incredibly fulfilling.

To help turn things around, you could look at your calendar and determine a good number of projects or assignments to cap yourself at each month, a number that would allow you to pay the bills and feel good about your accomplishments without burnout. Then, when you hit your limit, you follow your own guidelines and say no to additional work. "Thanks for thinking of me! I have a full workload for October, but I'd be happy to take this on in November," you might say. No trying to figure out how you might be able to finagle things to make it work or stressing over whether you should say yes or no. You've already decided.

Of course, from time to time, opportunities will come along that are so great you'll want to tear your policy into pieces and eat it. "I don't know what policy you're talking about!" It's understandable, and it's totally okay to make exceptions. Just keep them as exceptions rather than the rule.

EXPLAIN, BUT DON'T BE SORRY

"No" is a complete sentence. That's 100% true, but at the same time, leaving your friends, family, or boss with a "no" and zero explanation isn't always (or even usually) the best way to foster healthy, communicative relationships.

Rather, simply and politely state your case. "I'd love to, but I'm not available that day." "I really need some 'me time.'" "Thank you for the invite, but parties make me anxious and you'll be the only person there I know."

It's totally possible to be kind, honest, and not have to apologize for yourself or your feelings. You don't owe anyone an apology… unless you've actually done something that warrants one.

Depending on the situation, it may be beneficial to express your emotions surrounding the decision. Remember, as we covered in Chapter 11, healthy expression involves effective communication, to the right person, at the right time, with the right intensity.

TAKE MENTAL NOTES ON HOW IT GOES

Chances are it will cause far less of an ordeal than you fear. Maybe you'll say no, state your case, and you'll get a "good for you" or "I wish I could set boundaries like that" in return. Seriously. And, if worse comes to worst, you still likely won't end up on anyone's "not getting anything for the holidays this year" list.

As you rack up successful experiences of saying no, each subsequent time will be easier. You'll remember you've done this before, and it went just fine. You've got these experiences on lock.

THINK BEFORE YOU DECIDE

Sure, immediately saying yes is usually easier and way more comfortable in the short term, but knee-jerk answers are a slippery slope to commitments you'll resent later. To better proceed in a way that jives with your values and doesn't encroach on your rest and self-care, take some time to think things over. Ask, "When do you need me to get back to you?"

When mulling things over, consider both your policies and your current balance between your life's stressors and rest. Remember that just because you've said yes to something in the past, you don't have to say yes to it now. You can sometimes say no to babysitting and still happily say yes other times.

FLAKE WITH GRACE

Ideally, you wouldn't skirt your commitments—which, if you practice saying no in the first place, you'll do far less often. But when you do need to back out of something, be honest and empathetic with whomever you have to break the news.

Extend that courtesy to yourself. Show yourself compassion. Beating yourself up doesn't help anyone! Instead, take a few minutes of reflection to evaluate where the wheels came off your intention. Is there anything this experience can teach you? (Growth mindset for the win!)

BODY-LED REST

Just as you learned about body-led eating back in Chapter 12, in this section, you'll cozy up to body-led rest. Body-led rest is about staying attuned to your current balance between stress and rest, understanding that it's natural and perfectly healthy for things to ebb, flow, and teeter-totter. It's the back-and-forth that makes a teeter-totter work, right? Without the up-and-down, one player spends all of recess hovering in the air, while the other's planted on the ground like a cement geranium.

So, no. Stress isn't always a bad thing.

Remember, doing things, managing responsibilities, and exercising all stress your body's systems. As long as these stressors are coupled with appropriate rest, they can foster growth, accomplishment, physical strength, and determination.

Plus, even if stress was all bad (which it isn't), as human beings, we're guaranteed to experience times of immense stress. No matter how much we prioritize rest and recovery, work will get chaotic, family emergencies will happen, we'll have nights when we definitely don't get eight hours of sleep, and we'll get the flu at the most inopportune times. That's life!

During these periods, it becomes extra important to resist the urge to revert to LESS as it relates to emotions, food, movement, and pleasure. If, when we're stressed, we forgo healthy communication, skip meals, don't move, and deny any time for fun, things will just get worse. Much worse. In addition to depriving ourselves of healthy stress-management opportunities, this pattern also robs us of optimal health.

In these times, connecting with our bodies can help guide us toward the rest we need. On its own, it's meditative. And, sometimes, it can involve taking a short pause, evaluating our needs, and rummaging through our toolboxes so that we can care for ourselves amid the stress or in its aftermath.

Here are three favorite methods for checking in with yourself:

1. **Progressive Muscle Relaxation:** Lying or sitting down, tense and tighten your feet as hard as possible for a few seconds, and then let the tension go and completely relax them. Now, move to your calves and continue up your legs. Repeat the process until you've tensed and relaxed every muscle in your body, all the way up through your face.

As you go through each bout of tense-and-relax, pay attention if any parts of your body are holding tension. If at the end of all this relaxing, you notice that some of your muscles have tensed back up, go back and repeat the process there until you feel your entire body relax.

Feels pretty good, right? This quick exercise shouldn't take more than five minutes and has been shown to significantly relieve stress and anxiety and, if you do it at bedtime, it will help improve your sleep and next-day energy levels.[332, 333]

2. **4–7–8 Breathing Meditation:** Take a deep inhale through your nose for four seconds, allowing your belly to inflate and your chest to rise until your lungs are filled to their maximum capacity. Hold your breath for seven seconds, and then exhale through your mouth for eight seconds, pursing your lips to make a forceful *whoosh* sound.

   As you practice this breathing pattern, it can be helpful to focus on inhaling intentions and exhaling any feelings that are holding you down. Repeat them in your head with every inhale and exhale. This is yet another place where being able to identify your emotions comes in handy.

   This diaphragmatic breathing technique, also known as belly breathing, activates the parasympathetic "rest and digest" nervous system while decreasing activity in the sympathetic "fight or flight" one.[334] Adding a meditative component to each breath allows you to turn your attention inward and set intentions.

   You don't have to spend a lot of time to benefit from this. Even five breaths with this technique can work.

3. **5–4–3–2–1 Grounding Technique:** Stop and acknowledge five things you see around you—your hand, a computer, the coffee cup on the table. Notice four things you're touching, such as your feet planted on the floor, or your hair against the back of your neck. Recognize three sounds filling your ears. Is there music playing?

   Take in two smells. Don't smell anything? Grab something around you and get sniffing. Lastly, turn your attention to your sense of taste. What's one thing you taste? Maybe you can taste a hint of the coffee you had at breakfast. *Mmm, coffee breath.*

   The purpose of this activity is to give your mind pause and bring you into the present moment.[335] After all, anxiety typically comes down to ruminating about the past or worrying about the future.

   By engaging in the present, we're able to move from mental paralysis to healthful action.

FLAGS YOUR BODY'S SAYING "HEY, WE NEED SOME REST!"

Hearing our bodies when they're asking for rest (and before they're completely burned out, passed out, or otherwise wrecked) is a critical component of body-led rest. The problem is, in our pursuit to always do more, we've become skilled at tuning out and shhh-ing such pleas for rest.

The three connect-with-your-body exercises we just went through can all help you tune back in to what your body needs. Are your muscles clenched? Is your stomach growling? Are you tired or sleepy? (Yes, there's a difference.)

Of course, if you're naming objects in an attempt to exit a panic attack, it's pretty clear your body needs some R&R. However, we recommend checking in with your body through progressive muscle relaxation, breathing, meditation, and grounding exercises on a regular basis, even when you're feeling pretty good.

After all, some of the ways our bodies prod us for rest are gentle. It's not until we push past their limits that our bodies begin to really push back with attention-grabbing force. Here are some of the less-obvious flags that your body needs rest. Spot them early, and you'll be better able to give your body the rest it needs.

FLAG: YOU'RE CRAVING FOOD, BUT YOU'RE NOT ACTUALLY HUNGRY

As you already know, physical hunger and psychological cravings are anything but the same. Although shortages of rest can increase sensations of physical hunger by influencing the body's hormone levels, they may have an even greater effect on spurring psychological cravings.[336, 337, 338, 339]

For that reason, if you're experiencing strong desires for food without clear stomach-oriented hunger signals, it's possible that fatigue, stress, and a need for rest are contributing. They're probably accompanied by plenty of prickly emotions and maybe even emotion-led eating. You learned about that in Chapter 11. Go ahead and flip back if you need a refresher.

FLAG: YOU'RE ALL ABOUT CAFFEINE

A latte in the morning is one thing. But, a lot of women guzzle several throughout the course of a day, and turn to energy drinks that have ridiculous amounts of caffeine (and B vitamins, as if we'll somehow benefit from drinking more than 20,000% of our RDA in a single shot).[340] But caffeine is no replacement for rest.

And get this: Caffeine doesn't actually give you *energy*. Instead, it blocks receptors in the brain from registering the full force of your fatigue. On caffeine, you're still tired. You're just numb to it.[341]

What's more, it's worth considering what you're consuming along with the caffeine. Common accoutrements include sugar, sugar, and more sugar. An influx of sugar can supply a quick burst of actual energy, but it's typically short-lived. It also has the unfortunate side effect of crowding nutrient-rich foods from your days—foods that could help your body maintain healthy function and immunity in times of stress.

FLAG: YOU'RE CONSISTENTLY EXERCISING— AND SEEING ZERO RESULTS

Your body gets fitter when your body recovers from your workouts. That's why you have rest days, right? Even if you're giving your body enough rest in terms of breaks from intense exercise, it's still possible you're not getting enough total rest and recovery, given your life's current stressors. Physical, emotional, and mental stressors work cumulatively. When you have upticks in any of these three types of stress, you have to increase your rest to get your body's systems back to baseline.

FLAG: EVERYTHING FEELS HARD

Research consistently shows that overworking, lack of rest, and sleep deprivation reduce the brain's ability to focus, process information, and learn new things.[342, 343] Shorting yourself on rest makes everything you do so much harder.

When you're feeling stuck at work or sense your productivity waning, the solution isn't necessarily to push harder. Remember what we said about four-day workweeks? Giving yourself a healthy rest break might be exactly what you need to get a jump on your looming work deadline.

But, no, we aren't advocating that you call in sick every Friday.

PART 4

MAINTAINING YOUR MORE:
TROUBLESHOOTING AND COMMUNITY

CHAPTER 15
RESISTING FORCES THAT ENCOURAGE YOU TO SHRINK BACK

You may have guessed this already, and we have to confirm it: Giving yourself MORE comes with some obstacles.

There's no end to the potential forces that may encourage you to revert back to LESS. Quickly, think back to Part 1 and all of the cultural forces that tricked you into LESS in the first place; they don't just go away!

When you begin changing your thought processes and habits, you won't be 100% consistent. Maybe you'll hit 10%. That's a meaningful start! With every little bit, you're winning and building confidence that you *can* do this. And you will.

As the weeks go by and you continue to practice, you'll uncover new ways to give yourself MORE, and you'll also be intrinsically motivated by the positive benefits you're enjoying. At this stage, you'll become aware that not only *can* you do it, you *are* doing it and it's well worth it. In turn, you'll become even more consistent. As you spend increasing amounts of time in a mindset of MORE, your behaviors and choices will follow suit.

Still, even when you feel like you've really gotten the hang of things, forces will encourage you to shrink back. By simply knowing that, yes, these obstacles can and likely will pop up for you, you'll automatically feel less thrown when it happens. If you also have strategies for dealing with them in your back pocket and ready to go, that's even better.

POTENTIAL THREAT: OTHER PEOPLE

For those who have previously benefited from your pursuit of LESS, your move toward becoming more self-assured, physically strong, and comfortable can feel threatening. Example: A boss and coworkers who depend on you working yourself to death won't love it when you begin to raise boundaries around staying late at the office, opt not to take work home, or begin taking weekends and holidays *off*. Meanwhile, your "pushier" friends might not be too keen on you expressing your desires and opinions, especially when they don't mesh with theirs.

If you belong to an activity group or sports team, you might observe that it has a culture of not resting, or of pushing through injury and illness. It can be hard to resist that way of life and make choices to more lovingly care for yourself.

What you may encounter as most surprising is that family members and friends who truly want the best for you may *still* be hesitant to see you change. After all, they love you as you are! If you have family members or friends who are lifelong dieters, they might be unhappy at losing their calorie-counting support buddy. As you become less interested in debating who's more sleep-deprived, sharing tips from the latest fad diet books, or discussing the best keto frozen entrée, they'll sense your relationship changing. If you used to complain about your appearance or check your reflection every five minutes, they might be uncomfortable when you don't join in their complaints and mirror checks. After all, normative discontent—the social default to complain about our bodies and looks—is a bonding ritual, as unfortunate as that may be.

IT'S NOT ABOUT YOU

The changes you're making to give yourself MORE don't involve giving anyone else short shrift. Expressing your thoughts, opinions, and emotions in personal and professional relationships—rather than clamming up and suppressing them—makes you a more valuable friend and teammate. Most people will welcome your input and be glad that your openness allows them to know you better.

As for the few who respond negatively to your new skills in communicating or balancing your life, the negative response highlights their own insecurity, focus on LESS, or need to be the center of attention or sole decision-maker. This isn't about you, and it's not your responsibility to make them happy. You do you.

Let them know of any push-back you feel. A couple good starter lines to have handy: "I have a concern that _____" or "I'm noticing that I feel _____." These are particularly helpful because they don't challenge or accuse anyone; they're just honest, open, and translate the data in your mind into spoken words.

This becomes more complicated in professional settings. For example, unfortunately, some companies require employees to take calls and answer email at night or on the weekends. Some jobs are mutually exclusive with giving yourself MORE, and if that applies to your current situation, you have a lot to think about. We don't recommend putting this book down to write a resignation letter, but it's important to apply your MORE to your long-term career decisions.

Some people will take issue with your MORE, but most won't. Our clients are often surprised that when they start prioritizing healthy boundaries, they receive accolades instead of criticism. For example, your coworkers might admire you when you leave work on time, seeing how their own struggle to do so is limiting their happiness.

Your personal trainer and workout buddies, if they're the best kind, will also cheer you on for taking a rest day, reminding you that you'll come back stronger for recovering well. And your kids might jump with joy that you aren't going to work while you're on a family beach vacation.

If anyone negatively comments on your "new" or "different" behavior, you can say you're improving your work-life balance, or making sure to get the rest and recovery you need to perform at your best. Note: You absolutely don't have to apologize.

Your new practice of giving yourself MORE is likely to reshape some social interactions. It's unlikely you'll lose any friends, and highly likely the friendships you currently have will grow stronger. This happens in part because, when we start living more fully, we have more interesting things to talk about. When we begin to explore fun new ways of being active (rather than just torching calories with cardio we despise) and savor a wide variety of delicious foods and real-life treats, people want to hear about it. They want to join in.

As you'll read in the next and final chapter, you can be a powerful and positive influence on the women around you. By communicating how you genuinely feel, rather than making mundane small talk or giving always-positive updates even when you're struggling, you'll grow closer to those around you. Allow for others to reciprocate, and you'll find that many people are eager for deeper, more authentic connections.

POTENTIAL THREAT: THE MEDIA

Cognitively, we know that the media and entertainment industries perpetuate the belief that the ideal woman is always LESS. But because their images and messaging are so pervasive in our everyday lives, it can be hard for them to not creep into our consciousness. While helpful, telling ourselves that, "No, this isn't real" isn't always enough to override all their LESS-pushing input in our lives.

GET REGULAR DOSES OF REALITY

Media is a broad topic, but keeping yourself boredom-free certainly doesn't have to be limited to television, movies, social media, and other forms of media. You might find yourself feeling more positive and healthier overall when you entertain yourself by spending your free time with friends, trying new activities, or getting outdoors… and less of it in front of a screen. We're not saying that shows and movies are bad. But we *are* suggesting that you give yourself plenty of reality checks and remain aware that real life is often vastly different from what we see portrayed in the media.

POTENTIAL THREAT: US

When it comes to forces that nudge us to revert to seeking LESS, we may be our own biggest obstacles. It's always easiest to do things the way we're familiar with doing them. And old mentalities and habits can revive themselves and challenge our new way of living. Decades of practice hating our bodies, suppressing emotions, treating exercise as punishment, restricting food, holding back our opinions, and trying to be small and light won't be undone overnight.

Expect plenty of temptation to go back to how you used to do things. For example, if something shakes your confidence, you might reflexively hold in your emotions, restrict your food intake, or forget about your needs for movement, pleasure, and rest.

SHOW YOURSELF COMPASSION

Try to recognize when your old habits resurface, so you can redirect yourself with a reminder that you deserve MORE. Often, some of the best supportive thoughts are reassurances along the lines of "It's safe for me to express myself," "It's okay to need a break," and "Rest and fun are productive and important too." These encouragements work because they counteract sabotaging thoughts like "I ought to just keep my mouth shut," "Don't be lazy," or "You can't take a break when there's still work to do."

POTENTIAL THREAT: THE BEAUTY INDUSTRY

As we've explored, the beauty marketplace is out to make money, and that relies on keeping you unhappy with your appearance. If these messages are impacting you negatively, you might feel like you're spending more money, time, and focus on your looks than you want.

You might notice that your beauty routine and bathroom vanity's array of products keep increasing, yet you're not feeling positive emotions coming from them. Instead, you're trying harder and harder, spending more and more money, and just… failing.

CONSIDER WANTS VERSUS NEEDS

The beauty business isn't all bad. In fact, some self-care rituals that include beauty products or treatments may make you feel wonderful, and we're all for continuing them when that's the case. Our goal isn't to have you empty your makeup drawer and fire your stylist if you don't want to. Rather, we want to help you stay aware that out of the flood of messaging you get surrounding beauty, some of them are rooted in LESS.

We also want to plant the idea in your mind that everything in the field of beauty is *optional*. None of it is required to be a happy, lovable human being, or to live an awesome life. You never *have* to get your brows done. When you hear about a hot new beauty product, don't assume you have to run out or immediately click to purchase it.

Advertisements often imply that you really need it, or that it's taking over by storm and everybody's loving it. But, in reality, you've survived this long without it, and most women probably aren't using it now. Maybe you don't need it after all.

For every 450-step, sped-up makeup tutorial on Instagram, there are thousands of women who walk out the door bare-faced or with a swipe of mascara and lip balm.

Notice where signs that "you need this product!" are most prevalent (magazines, commercials, social media, the cosmetics aisle) and *how they make you feel*. If they make you feel not-pretty-enough and compelled to buy something to fix that, consider how much you want to go along with their deliberate plan, and how frequently this desire occurs. You may want to control your exposure to beauty marketing messages by turning your attention elsewhere, at least some of the time. For instance, you can hide ads from beauty companies in your social media feeds, and when you're at the drugstore to buy tissues, you can bypass the makeup aisle on your way to the cash register.

No matter the beauty culture you find yourself in, a small change to your inner dialog can make a profound difference in how you respond to it. Consider how different it feels to think, *I want to put on makeup* versus *I need to put on makeup*. The same switch is impactful when speaking out loud, so before you say into the mirror, "Boy, do I need a haircut!" consider swapping your language to, "Boy, do I want a haircut!"

If other people are listening, wouldn't it be unfortunate for them to assume you're thinking about the appearance improvements they "need to" make? They may conclude that if you are thinking you need to fix your appearance, you must also be thinking just as critically about their aesthetic defects.

POTENTIAL THREAT: THE WEIGHT-LOSS, "HEALTH," AND FITNESS FIELDS

Like the beauty industry, this category isn't completely bad or always harmful. (After all, we're both in it!) True wellness is about loving and caring for yourself—body and mind—to cultivate your happiest, healthiest, fullest life. Many products and services, food items, and activities are in line with this ethos.

However, many aren't. Even some wellness companies benefit from our smallness. If being slim is your single-greatest goal and it carries a great deal of importance to you, you're more likely to spend your money on it.

Even once you've embraced your MORE, fitness and weight-loss advertisements are likely to keep chasing you around with messages that promote LESS. For that reason, we recommend a healthy dose of caution, knowing that you'll encounter both healthy and unhealthy messages from the field. We encourage you to reject the unhealthy ones.

What parts of the wellness industry can *oppose* giving yourself MORE? Here are some common ones:

- Implications that the ultimate and only goal is looking better or dropping pounds—as fast as possible
- Moral judgments about food and exercise, usually conveyed with terms like "guilt," "good," and "bad"
- Methods of weight loss or extreme exercise that involve significant health risk
- People, products, or advertisements that shame people with larger bodies
- Directives to cut out a food group, or completely avoid fun foods and treats
- Themes of not being capable of making your own food and activity decisions, and needing to "comply" with some expert or program
- False equivalencies between quality, quantity, and intensity (ahem, "no pain, no gain")

SCREW IT!

In addition to not purchasing products or services associated with these messages, we encourage you to oppose them in your mind and also out loud. When an advertisement plasters a "before and after" image in front of your eyes, you can stand up for your MORE by thinking, *That's how she looks, but how does she feel?* You can appreciate her weight loss through an attitude of abundance. You can respond to social media posts about "guilt-free desserts" by sharing your opinion that all desserts can be guilt-free. You never know who might be reading, and be lifted by your healthy outlook.

You can unfollow social media accounts that promote unhealthy ideas. If you want to be inspired by others, look for people who eat meals that look healthy, tasty, and satisfying. Listen to experts who encourage you to be kind to yourself and try your best in your workouts, rather than wreck yourself or chase pain.

And commit to making changes to your nutrition and fitness plans in gradual degrees—not sudden, dramatic shifts. You can always take things a step further in a week or two.

CHAPTER 16
SPREADING YOUR MORE

One of the biggest, most important concepts of this book is coming at you right now. Ready? Here it is:

Giving yourself MORE isn't a zero-sum game.

Let us explain. A zero-sum game is a concept from game theory in which your losses or gains exactly counterbalance someone else's losses or gains.

For example, if you take that valuable center square in a game of tic-tac-toe, your rival loses the ability to claim that square. Poker is also a zero-sum game because for one person to win $250, the other players have to lose $250. The game of chess, too, proceeds with each player losing a piece every time the other gains a piece. If I take your queen, you've lost your queen.

Those are games, but in real life, happiness, love, and health are the opposite. They are endless in supply! We can all pursue greater happiness knowing we're not making someone else sadder as a result. We can love freely, knowing our enamored bliss causes no reduction in someone else's ability to feel love too. The same goes for health. We don't spare anyone else a case of chickenpox by contracting it ourselves, and improving our health thankfully doesn't mean someone else ends up with a flu or broken leg.

Think through the areas in which we've explored giving yourself MORE: body love, movement, emotions, food, pleasure, and rest. All of these share the same limitless bounds as happiness, love, and health. Free refills for everyone. In fact, giving yourself MORE has a positive impact on other people in your life, and even people you don't know.

Everyone wins.

YOU'RE AN INFLUENCER

Whether you know it or not, everything you think, say, and do impacts what the people around you think, say, and do. When we talk about our bodies, movement, emotions, food, pleasure, and rest, our words and tones give other women a glimpse into our mindset and a mindset that could be theirs. We cannot avoid this impact. As humans evolved as social creatures, we developed a subtle but innate tendency to act how we see other humans acting. As such, we're all role models for each other.

For example, consider how it feels when a pal says she "hates her fat thighs." Upon hearing this, your attention instantly flashes to her legs (whatever size they may be), since she just referenced them. Then, your attention rapidly transfers to your own legs (whatever size they may be), because it's natural to mirror other people's concerns, if only for an instant. Subconsciously, your brain does the math: *If her legs are up for circumferential judgment, aren't mine as well? If it's important enough for her to mention, it's important enough to consider about myself.*

You might decide "My legs are awesome," but you also might say something critical about your own body. Whether you truly feel negatively about your body or only mutter commiserating words to help her feel better, doesn't actually matter. Research studies have found that even passively hearing "fat talk" harms a person's body image… and joining in is much more detrimental.[344] Talking critically about your body amplifies and strengthens any negative feelings you have about it.

You hear your own words, after all. She loses, you lose, and everyone else listening takes a hit, too. Cue the communal thigh check, weight shift, and pants tug as every woman within earshot becomes momentarily more insecure about her body.

Is that the change you want to make in the world?

When we hear other women being body-critical, we're more likely to be body-critical ourselves. Worst of all, we anticipate more body-criticism from the world. This leads to increased anxiety and continual body checking, appearance monitoring, and the feeling like we're always on display, being evaluated. It's contagious. We can spread it or we can fight it.

You can reverse the contagion by letting your MORE be seen and heard. You can spread each of the six areas of MORE to other people with your words and actions—and we don't mean by mentioning this book, though we sure would love that too. We're talking about being an example of MORE, even if for a moment here and there. When other people see us living our MORE, they glimpse what their lives can be like if they flip the switch as well; maybe they begin giving themselves MORE.

Each of us is only one person, but we have dozens, hundreds, or even thousands of tiny points of contact with others on a daily basis. If even a few of those start a ripple effect of positivity in place of criticism, or come from abundance instead of scarcity, woman after woman after woman will benefit. And they'll likely begin giving themselves MORE, and spreading it with their circles. Daughters and nieces will get in on the game. As more of us leave the quest for LESS behind, we multiply MORE.

This is how major societal change starts. An initial minority of people becomes inspired to go in a different direction. Because they *don't keep the new ideas to themselves*, they influence the collective majority. The tide turns bit by bit, until the majority of people are moving in the new direction. Girls of today or the next generation will grow up to be healthier, stronger, more resilient, confident women... if we spread MORE now.

Are you working on giving yourself more body love? Give your body a compliment in front of others from time to time, and high-five anyone else who gives herself credit or a kind word. Research shows that while women often expect that conforming to the norm of putting ourselves down boosts our likeability, the opposite is actually true.[345] Women find that women who say positive things about themselves are more likeable, even in a context in which fat talk is already in progress.

A 2012 study explored subjects' responses to hearing women comment on their bodies. In the negative condition, the women said, "I'm pretty unhappy with my weight; I really should go on a diet. I don't think I look good." Subjects heard this type of "fat talk" coming from women of different sizes. In the positive condition, women of varying sizes instead made the positive statement, "I'm very happy with my weight. Why would I diet? I think I look good." Subjects rated the women as being more likable, and expressed a greater desire to know them.[346]

This isn't hard to understand. After all, while it's mildly comforting to have people around us who echo our thoughts and opinions, what's really alluring is someone who sees the world with a bit more positivity. We're drawn to experiences and people who have the potential to make our lives better, expand our horizons, and bring out the best in us. In giving ourselves MORE, we show other women that it's possible to live in a way that's not about shrinking, seeking LESS, or deprivation, but about fullness. And they find it socially desirable!

As you begin to recognize and verbalize your emotions in a genuine way, you pave the way for other women to be real, too. Don't be afraid to share that you're sad, disappointed, frustrated, elated, or proud if that's how you feel. You also don't have to hide your joy, excitement, or energy to placate other people. By taking off your "I'm fine" mask, other women will feel more comfortable setting theirs aside as well.

Spreading MORE also happens at the dinner table. The words you use and the actions you take while eating influence the people who eat with you. Many of our clients tell us happily that once they started referencing hunger and satiety and using them to guide their eating, so did their children. When kids see and hear adults making healthy food decisions, they have a better chance of growing up healthy themselves. No one is too young to learn how to give themselves MORE.

Without you saying a word, your friends are also likely to notice if you bring balanced meals to work, eat lots of fruit and vegetables, and pick up an exercise habit. Women watch what other women do.

And if you do speak about your choices, you can share positivity. Comment on how tasty the food is, or how lucky we are to have fresh strawberries. Mention the great Brussels sprouts recipe you found or fun workout you're doing; maybe another woman will ask for it. You just helped her eat more veggies and move more.

How frequently do you hear people say they "shouldn't be eating this" or that they've "been bad" about their food and need to "work it off"? It's not their fault; they've been soaked in the sea of voices of negativity and judgment about food in the world. They need you to share MORE with them!

You can play a role in neutralizing that trend by being positive and balanced. Responding, "I'm pretty convinced you're still a good person." "You can eat anything you choose to," or "Exercise is meant to be fun, not a punishment" might help someone shed limiting beliefs and feel freer in her relationship with food and exercise.

After all, if you don't feel guilty about ordering anything on the menu, maybe others don't have to either.

Making joyful movement, pleasure, and rest priorities in your own life means making time for them, and those actions speak loudly. Other women will take notice that you're trying new, active hobbies, getting more sleep, doing crafts, enjoying quiet time, or participating in experiences just because they make you happy. Going to a comic convention? Yes! Taking a hip-hop dance class for the first time at 37? That's it!

By pursuing your own joy, you encourage others to do the same. You can also offer kudos to women when you hear they're doing things like going for a walk, getting a massage, hiring a babysitter for a date night, taking a day off from work to be with the kids, or finally going on a vacation.

The power of this book isn't in the hours of entertainment we hope it has provided you. It's in the hope we want to ignite in you. With our work, both in this book and in our coaching, we want to illuminate the innumerable, joyful possibilities you didn't know were there.

You have the power to take these words and make them into something real. We hope you aren't satisfied with simply reading about giving yourself MORE, but that you're galvanized to go out into the world and live it.

We know you can.

REFERENCES

1 Martin, C.B., Herrick, K. A., Sarafrazi, N., Ogden, C. L. Attempts to lose weight among adults in the United States, 2013–2016. NCHS Data Brief, no 313. Hyattsville, MD: National Center for Health Statistics. 2018.

2 LaRose, J. G., Leahey, T. M., Hill, J. O., & Wing, R. R. (2013). Differences in motivations and weight loss behaviors in young adults and older adults in the National Weight Control Registry. Obesity, 21(3), 449-453.

3 O'Brien, K., Venn, B. J., Perry, T., Green, T. J., Aitken, W., & Bradshaw, A. (2007). Reasons for wanting to lose weight: different strokes for different folks. Eating Behaviors, 8(1), 132-135.

4 Jackson, S. E., Steptoe, A., Beeken, R. J., Kivimaki, M., & Wardle, J. (2014). Psychological changes following weight loss in overweight and obese adults: a prospective cohort study. PloS one, 9(8), e104552.

5 Phelan, S., Wing, R. R., Loria, C. M., Kim, Y., & Lewis, C. E. (2010). Prevalence and predictors of weight-loss maintenance in a biracial cohort: results from the coronary artery risk development in young adults study. American journal of preventive medicine, 39(6), 546-554.

6 Rogerson, D., Soltani, H., & Copeland, R. (2016). The weight-loss experience: a qualitative exploration. BMC public health, 16(1), 371.

7 Lose Weight By Focusing On Mental Health First (2015) Orlando Health. Retrieved from: http://oh.multimedia-newsroom.com/index.php/2015/12/01/lose-weight-by-focusing-on-mental-health-first/ [article]

8 Lose Weight By Focusing On Mental Health First (2015) Orlando Health. Retrieved from: http://oh.multimedia-newsroom.com/index.php/2015/12/01/lose-weight-by-focusing-on-mental-health-first/ [article]

9 Lose Weight By Focusing On Mental Health First (2015) Orlando Health. Retrieved from: http://oh.multimedia-newsroom.com/index.php/2015/12/01/lose-weight-by-focusing-on-mental-health-first/ [article]

10 Piers, G., & Singer, M. B. (1953). Shame and guilt: A psychoanalytic and a cultural study (Vol. 86). Springfield, Ill: Thomas.

11 Tice, D. M., Bratslavsky, E., & Baumeister, R. F. (2001). Emotional distress regulation takes precedence over impulse control: If you feel bad, do it!. Journal of personality and social psychology, 80(1), 53.

12 Vartanian, L. R., & Porter, A. M. (2016). Weight stigma and eating behavior: a review of the literature. Appetite, 102, 3-14.

13 Jackson, S. E., Kirschbaum, C., & Steptoe, A. (2016, December). Perceived weight discrimination and chronic stress. UK Society for Behavioural Medicine Annual Scientific Meeting 2016.

14 Vartanian, L. R., & Novak, S. A. (2011). Internalized societal attitudes moderate the impact of weight stigma on avoidance of exercise. Obesity, 19(4), 757-762.

15 Rivera-Hernandez, M. (2014). Depression, self-esteem, diabetes care and self-care behaviors among middle-aged and older Mexicans. Diabetes research and clinical practice, 105(1), 70-78.

16 Bacon, L., Stern, J. S., Van Loan, M. D., & Keim, N. L. (2005). Size acceptance and intuitive eating improve health for obese, female chronic dieters. Journal of the American Dietetic Association, 105(6), 929-936.

17 Carraça, E. V., Silva, M. N., Markland, D., Vieira, P. N., Minderico, C. S., Sardinha, L. B., & Teixeira, P. J. (2011). Body image change and improved eating self-regulation in a weight management intervention in women. International Journal of Behavioral Nutrition and Physical Activity, 8(1), 75.

18 Johnston, B. C., Kanters, S., Bandayrel, K., Wu, P., Naji, F., Siemieniuk, R. A., ... & Jansen, J. P. (2014). Comparison of weight loss among named diet programs in overweight and obese adults: a meta-analysis. Jama, 312(9), 923-933.

19 Dansinger, M. L., Gleason, J. A., Griffith, J. L., Selker, H. P., & Schaefer, E. J. (2005). Comparison of the Atkins, Ornish, Weight Watchers, and Zone diets for weight loss and heart disease risk reduction: a randomized trial. Jama, 293(1), 43-53.

20 Van Cappellen, P., Rice, E. L., Catalino, L. I., & Fredrickson, B. L. (2018). Positive affective processes underlie positive health behaviour change. Psychology & health, 33(1), 77-97.

21 The Theory. (n.d.). Retrieved from https://selfdeterminationtheory.org/the-theory/ [website]

22 Lally, P., & Gardner, B. (2013). Promoting habit formation. Health Psychology Review, 7(sup1), S137-S158.

23 Gardner, B., Lally, P., & Wardle, J. (2012). Making health habitual: the psychology of 'habit-formation' and general practice. Br J Gen Pract, 62(605), 664-666.

24 Pillitteri, J. L., Shiffman, S., Rohay, J. M., Harkins, A. M., Burton, S. L., & Wadden, T. A. (2008). Use of dietary supplements for weight loss in the United States: results of a national survey. Obesity, 16(4), 790-796.

25 Marketdata Enterprises Inc. The U.S. Weight Loss & Diet Control Market (11th Edition).; 2011.

26 Wolf, N. (1991). The beauty myth: How images of beauty are used against women. Random House.

27 MacNeill, L. P., & Best, L. A. (2015). Perceived current and ideal body size in female undergraduates. Eating behaviors, 18, 71-75.

28 Brierley, M. E., Brooks, K. R., Mond, J., Stevenson, R. J., & Stephen, I. D. (2016). The body and the beautiful: health, attractiveness and body composition in men's and women's bodies. PLoS One, 11(6), e0156722.

29 Common Sense Media. At what age does media begin affecting my child's body image? Retrieved from: https://www.commonsensemedia.org/media-and-body-image/ at-what-age-does-media-begin-affecting-my-childs-body-image [article]

30 Common Sense Media. (2015, Jan 21). Children, Teens, Media, and Body Image. Retrieved from https://www.commonsensemedia.org/research/children-teens-media-and-body-image [article]

31 Stice, E., Marti, C. N., Shaw, H., & Jaconis, M. (2009). An 8-year longitudinal study of the natural history of threshold, subthreshold, and partial eating disorders from a community sample of adolescents. Journal of abnormal psychology, 118(3), 587.

32 Mellin, L. M., Irwin Jr, C. E., & Scully, S. (1992). Prevalence of disordered eating in girls: A survey of middle-class children. Journal of the American Dietetic Association (USA).

33 Abramovitz, B. A., & Birch, L. L. (2000). Five-year-old girls' ideas about dieting are predicted by their mothers' dieting. Journal of the American Dietetic Association, 100(10), 1157-1163.

34 Common Sense Media. (2015, Jan 21). Children, Teens, Media, and Body Image. Retrieved from https://www.commonsensemedia.org/research/children-teens-media-and-body-image [article]

35 Boyd, H., & Murnen, S. K. (2017). Thin and sexy vs. muscular and dominant: Prevalence of gendered body ideals in popular dolls and action figures. Body image, 21, 90-96.

36 Brennan, M. A., Lalonde, C. E., & Bain, J. L. (2010). Body image perceptions: Do gender differences exist? Psi Chi Journal of Undergraduate Research, 15(3), 130-138.

37 Fardouly, J., Pinkus, R. T., & Vartanian, L. R. (2017). The impact of appearance comparisons made through social media, traditional media, and in person in women's everyday lives. Body image, 20, 31-39.

38 Fardouly, J., Willburger, B. K., & Vartanian, L. R. (2018). Instagram use and young women's body image concerns and self-objectification: Testing mediational pathways. New Media & Society, 20(4), 1380-1395.

39 Meltzer, A. L., & McNulty, J. K. (2015). Telling women that men desire women with bodies larger than the thin-ideal improves women's body satisfaction. Social Psychological and Personality Science, 6(4), 391-398.

40 Puhl, R. M., Andreyeva, T., & Brownell, K. D. (2008). Perceptions of weight discrimination: prevalence and comparison to race and gender discrimination in America. International journal of obesity, 32(6), 992.

41 Campos-Vazquez, R. M., & Gonzalez, E. (2020). Obesity and Hiring Discrimination. Economics & Human Biology, 100850.

42 Puhl, R. M., & Brownell, K. D. (2006). Confronting and coping with weight stigma: an investigation of overweight and obese adults. Obesity, 14(10), 1802-1815.

43 Hebl, M. R., & Xu, J. (2001). Weighing the care: physicians' reactions to the size of a patient. International journal of obesity, 25(8), 1246.

44 Cavaleri, R., Short, T., Karunaratne, S., & Chipchase, L. S. (2016). Weight stigmatisation in physiotherapy: a systematic review. Physical Therapy Reviews, 21(1), 1-9.

45 Uppot, R. N., Sahani, D. V., Hahn, P. F., Gervais, D., & Mueller, P. R. (2007). Impact of obesity on medical imaging and image-guided intervention. American Journal of Roentgenology, 188(2), 433-440.

46 Mensinger, J. L., Tylka, T. L., & Calamari, M. E. (2018). Mechanisms underlying weight status and healthcare avoidance in women: a study of weight stigma, body-related shame and guilt, and healthcare stress. Body image, 25, 139-147.

47 Singh, M., Sethi, A., Mishra, A. K., Subrayappa, N. K., Stapleton, D. D., & Pellikka, P. A. (2020). Echocardiographic Imaging Challenges in Obesity: Guideline Recommendations and Limitations of Adjusting to Body Size. Journal of the American Heart Association, 9(2), e014609.

48 Schvey, N. A., Sbrocco, T., Bakalar, J. L., Ress, R., Barmine, M., Gorlick, J., ... & Tanofsky-Kraff, M. (2017). The experience of weight stigma among gym members with overweight and obesity. Stigma and Health, 2(4), 292.

49 Puhl, R. M., Himmelstein, M. S., & Quinn, D. M. (2018). Internalizing weight stigma: prevalence and sociodemographic considerations in US adults. Obesity, 26(1), 167-175.

50 Corrigan, P. W., Watson, A. C., & Barr, L. (2006). The self–stigma of mental illness: Implications for self–esteem and self–efficacy. Journal of social and clinical psychology, 25(8), 875-884.

51 Willis, L. E., & Knobloch-Westerwick, S. (2014). Weighing women down: Messages on weight loss and body shaping in editorial content in popular women's health and fitness magazines. Health communication, 29(4), 323-331.

52 Aubrey, J. S., & Hahn, R. (2016). Health versus appearance versus body competence: a content analysis investigating frames of health advice in women's health magazines. Journal of health communication, 21(5), 496-503.

53 Brennan, B. (2015, Jan 21). Top 10 things everyone should know about women consumers. Forbes. Retrieved from: https://www.forbes.com/sites/bridgetbrennan/2015/01/21/top-10-things-everyone-should-know-about-women-consumers/ [article]

54 Marketdata Enterprises (2009). The US weight loss & diet control market. Lynbrook, NY: Marketdata Enterprises.

55 Overweight & Obesity Statistics. August 2017. National Institute of Diabetes and Digestive and Kidney Diseases. Retrieved from : https://www.niddk.nih.gov/health-information/health-statistics/overweight-obesity

56 Marshall, R. (2015, Sept 10). How Many Ads Do You See in One Day? Red Crow Marketing. Retrieved from: https://www.redcrowmarketing.com/2015/09/10/many-ads-see-one-day/ [article]

57 Simpson, J. (2017). Finding brand success in the digital world. Forbes. Retrieved from: https://www.forbes.com/sites/forbesagencycouncil/2017/08/25/finding-brand-success-in-the-digital-world/#7ba91ab0626e [article]

58 Boepple, L., Ata, R. N., Rum, R., & Thompson, J. K. (2016). Strong is the new skinny: A content analysis of fitspiration websites. Body image, 17, 132-135.

59 Tiggemann, M., & Zaccardo, M. (2018). 'Strong is the new skinny': A content analysis of# fitspiration images on Instagram. Journal of Health Psychology, 23(8), 1003-1011.

60 Martin, C. B., Herrick, K. A., Sarafrazi, N., & Ogden, C. L. (2018). Attempts to lose weight among adults in the United States, 2013–2016. NCHS data brief No. 313. Centers for Disease Control and Prevention.

61 Lyubomirsky, S. (2008). The how of happiness: A scientific approach to getting the life you want. Penguin.

62 Latner, J. D., Barile, J. P., Durso, L. E., & O'Brien, K. S. (2014). Weight and health-related quality of life: The moderating role of weight discrimination and internalized weight bias. Eating Behaviors, 15(4), 586-590.

63 Pearl, R. L., Wadden, T. A., Hopkins, C. M., Shaw, J. A., Hayes, M. R., Bakizada, Z. M., ... & Alamuddin, N. (2017). Association between weight bias internalization and metabolic syndrome among treatment-seeking individuals with obesity. Obesity, 25(2), 317-322.

64 Bandura, A. (1994). Self-efficacy. In V. S. Ramachaudran (Ed.), Encyclopedia of human behavior (Vol. 4, pp. 71-81). New York: Academic Press. (Reprinted in H. Friedman [Ed.], Encyclopedia of mental health. San Diego: Academic Press, 1998).

65 Farholm, A., Sørensen, M., Halvari, H., & Hynnekleiv, T. (2017). Associations between physical activity and motivation, competence, functioning, and apathy in inhabitants with mental illness from a rural municipality: a cross-sectional study. BMC psychiatry, 17(1), 359.

66 Liechty, J. M. (2010). Body image distortion and three types of weight loss behaviors among non-overweight girls in the United States. Journal of Adolescent Health, 47(2), 176-182.

67 What Are Eating Disorders? (n. d.) National Eating Disorders Association. Retrieved from: https://www.nationaleatingdisorders.org/what-are-eating-disorders [website]

68 Pillitteri, J. L., Shiffman, S., Rohay, J. M., Harkins, A. M., Burton, S. L., & Wadden, T. A. (2008). Use of dietary supplements for weight loss in the United States: results of a national survey. Obesity, 16(4), 790-796.

69 Dietary Supplements For Weight Loss. (2019, Oct 17) National Institutes of Health. Retrieved from: https://ods.od.nih.gov/factsheets/WeightLoss-HealthProfessional/ [website]

70 Geller, A. I., Shehab, N., Weidle, N. J., Lovegrove, M. C., Wolpert, B. J., Timbo, B. B., ... & Budnitz, D. S. (2015). Emergency department visits for adverse events related to dietary supplements. New England Journal of Medicine, 373(16), 1531-1540.

71 Pankratow, M., Berry, T. R., & McHugh, T. L. F. (2013). Effects of reading health and appearance exercise magazine articles on perceptions of attractiveness and reasons for exercise. PloS one, 8(4), e61894.

72 Craft, B. B., Carroll, H. A., & Lustyk, M. K. B. (2014). Gender differences in exercise Habits and quality of Life Reports: Assessing the Moderating effects of Reasons for exercise. International journal of liberal arts and social science, 2(5), 65.

73 Medvedev, O. N., & Landhuis, C. E. (2018). Exploring constructs of well-being, happiness and quality of life. PeerJ, 6, e4903.

74 Gonzalez, M. C., Correia, M. I. T., & Heymsfield, S. B. (2017). A requiem for BMI in the clinical setting. Current opinion in clinical nutrition and metabolic care, 20(5), 314-321.

75 Leong, D. P., Teo, K. K., Rangarajan, S., Lopez-Jaramillo, P., Avezum Jr, A., Orlandini, A., ... & Rahman, O. (2015). Prognostic value of grip strength: findings from the Prospective Urban Rural Epidemiology (PURE) study. The Lancet, 386(9990), 266-273.

76 Cruz-Jentoft, A. J., Landi, F., Schneider, S. M., Zúñiga, C., Arai, H., Boirie, Y., ... & Sieber, C. (2014). Prevalence of and interventions for sarcopenia in ageing adults: a systematic review. Report of the International Sarcopenia Initiative (EWGSOP and IWGS). Age and ageing, 43(6), 748-759.

77 Roubenoff, R. (2003). Sarcopenia: effects on body composition and function. The Journals of Gerontology Series A: Biological Sciences and Medical Sciences, 58(11), M1012-M1017.

78 Firth, J., Stubbs, B., Vancampfort, D., Firth, J. A., Large, M., Rosenbaum, S., ... & Yung, A. R. (2018). Grip strength is associated with cognitive performance in schizophrenia and the general population: A UK biobank study of 476559 participants. Schizophrenia bulletin, 44(4), 728-736.

79 Kim, J. H. (2019). Effect of grip strength on mental health. Journal of affective disorders, 245, 371-376.

80 Smith, L., Firth, J., Grabovac, I., Koyanagi, A., Veronese, N., Stubbs, B., ... & Jackson, S. E. (2019). The association of grip strength with depressive symptoms and cortisol in hair: a cross-sectional study of older adults. Scandinavian journal of medicine & science in sports.

81 Salvatore, J., & Marecek, J. (2010). Gender in the gym: Evaluation concerns as barriers to women's weight lifting. Sex Roles, 63(7-8), 556-567.

82 Dworkin, S. L. (2003). A woman's place is in the... cardiovascular room? Gender relations, the body, and the gym. Athletic intruders: Ethnographic research on women, culture, and exercise, 131-158.

83 Nuckols, G. (2018, Apr 9) Strength Training For Women: Setting the Record Straight. Stronger By Science. Retrieved from: https://www.strongerbyscience.com/strength-training-women/

84 Markula, P. (1995). Firm but shapely, fit but sexy, strong but thin: The postmodern aerobicizing female bodies. Sociology of sport journal, 12(4), 424-453.

85 Salvatore, J., & Marecek, J. (2010). Gender in the gym: Evaluation concerns as barriers to women's weight lifting. Sex Roles, 63(7-8), 556-567.

86 Salvatore, J., & Marecek, J. (2010). Gender in the gym: Evaluation concerns as barriers to women's weight lifting. Sex Roles, 63(7-8), 556-567.

87 Workout Worries: A Look At What Causes Gym Aversion and Anxiety. (n. d.) Fitrated. Retrieved from: https://www.fitrated.com/resources/workout-worries/#the-many-faces-of-gym-anxiety [website]

88 Cutler, T. S., DeFilippis, E. M., Unterbrink, M. E., & Evans, A. T. (2016). Increasing incidence and unique clinical characteristics of spinning-induced rhabdomyolysis. Clinical Journal of Sport Medicine, 26(5), 429-431.

89 Teixeira, P. J., Carraça, E. V., Markland, D., Silva, M. N., & Ryan, R. M. (2012). Exercise, physical activity, and self-determination theory: a systematic review. International journal of behavioral nutrition and physical activity, 9(1), 78.

90 Nazem, T. G., & Ackerman, K. E. (2012). The female athlete triad. Sports Health, 4(4), 302-311.

91 Statuta, S. M., Asif, I. M., & Drezner, J. A. (2017). Relative energy deficiency in sport (RED-S). Br J Sports Med, 51(21), 1570-1571.

92 MacNeill, L. P., & Best, L. A. (2015). Perceived current and ideal body size in female undergraduates. Eating behaviors, 18, 71-75.

93 Vohs, K. D., & Baumeister, R. F. (Eds.). (2016). Handbook of self-regulation: Research, theory, and applications. Guilford Publications.

94 Cutrona, C. E., & Russell, D. W. (2017). Autonomy promotion, responsiveness, and emotion regulation promote effective social support in times of stress. Current opinion in psychology, 13, 126-130.

95 Sloan, E., Hall, K., Moulding, R., Bryce, S., Mildred, H., & Staiger, P. K. (2017). Emotion regulation as a transdiagnostic treatment construct across anxiety, depression, substance, eating and borderline personality disorders: A systematic review. Clinical psychology review, 57, 141-163.

96 Fasciano, L. C., Dale, L. P., Shaikh, S. K., Little Hodge, A. L., Gracia, B., Majdick, J. M., ... & Ford, J. D. (2020). Relationship of childhood maltreatment, exercise, and emotion regulation to self-esteem, PTSD, and depression symptoms among college students. Journal of American College Health, 1-7.

97 Aparicio, E., Canals, J., Arija, V., De Henauw, S., & Michels, N. (2016). The role of emotion regulation in childhood obesity: implications for prevention and treatment. Nutrition research reviews, 29(1), 17-29.

98 Isasi, C. R., Ostrovsky, N. W., & Wills, T. A. (2013). The association of emotion regulation with lifestyle behaviors in inner-city adolescents. Eating behaviors, 14(4), 518-521.

99 Prefit, A. B., Cândea, D. M., & Szentagotai-Tătar, A. (2019). Emotion regulation across eating pathology: A meta-analysis. Appetite, 104438.

100 Ruscitti, C., Rufino, K., Goodwin, N., & Wagner, R. (2016). Difficulties in emotion regulation in patients with eating disorders. Borderline personality disorder and emotion dysregulation, 3(1), 3.

101 Dingemans, A., Danner, U., & Parks, M. (2017). Emotion regulation in binge eating disorder: A review. Nutrients, 9(11), 1274.

102 Whiteside, U., Chen, E., Neighbors, C., Hunter, D., Lo, T., & Larimer, M. (2007). Difficulties regulating emotions: Do binge eaters have fewer strategies to modulate and tolerate negative affect? Eating behaviors, 8(2), 162-169.

103 Westerberg, D. P., & Waitz, M. (2013). Binge-eating disorder. Osteopathic Family Physician, 5(6), 230-233.

104 Hudson, J. I., Hiripi, E., Pope Jr, H. G., & Kessler, R. C. (2007). The prevalence and correlates of eating disorders in the National Comorbidity Survey Replication. Biological psychiatry, 61(3), 348-358.

105 Heatherton, T. F., & Baumeister, R. F. (1991). Binge eating as escape from self-awareness. Psychological bulletin, 110(1), 86,

106 Morin, A. (2003). Self-awareness review part 2: Changing or escaping the self. *Science & Consciousness Review, 1.*

107 Leehr, E. J., Krohmer, K., Schag, K., Dresler, T., Zipfel, S., & Giel, K. E. (2015). Emotion regulation model in binge eating disorder and obesity-a systematic review. Neuroscience & Biobehavioral Reviews, 49, 125-134.

108 Van Strien, T. (2018). Causes of emotional eating and matched treatment of obesity. Current diabetes reports, 18(6), 35.

109 Nasirzadeh, Y., Kantarovich, K., Wnuk, S., okayrainec, A., Cassin, S. E., Hawa, R., & Sockalingam, S. (2018). Binge eating, loss of control over eating, emotional eating, and night eating after bariatric surgery: results from the Toronto Bari-PSYCH Cohort Study. Obesity surgery, 28(7), 2032-2039.

110 Goldschmidt, A. B., Lavender, J. M., Hipwell, A. E., Stepp, S. D., & Keenan, K. (2017). Emotion regulation and loss of control eating in community-based adolescents. Journal of abnormal child psychology, 45(1), 183-191.

111 Telch, C. F. (1997). Skills training treatment for adaptive affect regulation in a woman with binge-eating disorder. International Journal of Eating Disorders, 22(1), 77-81.

112 Robinson, A. (2013). Integrative response therapy for binge eating disorder. Cognitive and behavioral practice, 20(1), 93-105.

113 Deaver, C. M., Miltenberger, R. G., Smyth, J., Meidinger, A. M. Y., & Crosby, R. (2003). An evaluation of affect and binge eating. Behavior Modification, 27(4), 578-599.

114 Haedt-Matt, A. A., & Keel, P. K. (2011). Revisiting the affect regulation model of binge eating: a meta-analysis of studies using ecological momentary assessment. Psychological bulletin, 137(4), 660.

115 Deaver, C. M., Miltenberger, R. G., Smyth, J., Meidinger, A. M. Y., & Crosby, R. (2003). An evaluation of affect and binge eating. Behavior Modification, 27(4), 578-599.

116 Christou-Champi, S., Farrow, T. F., & Webb, T. L. (2015). Automatic control of negative emotions: evidence that structured practice increases the efficiency of emotion regulation. Cognition and Emotion, 29(2), 319-331.

117 Haga, S. M., Kraft, P., & Corby, E. K. (2009). Emotion regulation: Antecedents and well-being outcomes of cognitive reappraisal and expressive suppression in cross-cultural samples. Journal of Happiness Studies, 10(3), 271-291.

118 Low, R. S., Overall, N. C., Hammond, M. D., & Girme, Y. U. (2017). Emotional suppression during personal goal pursuit impedes goal strivings and achievement. Emotion, 17(2), 208.

119 Spokas, M., Luterek, J. A., & Heimberg, R. G. (2009). Social anxiety and emotional suppression: The mediating role of beliefs. Journal of behavior therapy and experimental psychiatry, 40(2), 283-291.

120 English, T., Lee, I. A., John, O. P., & Gross, J. J. (2017). Emotion regulation strategy selection in daily life: The role of social context and goals. Motivation and Emotion, 41(2), 230-242.

121 Impett, E. A., Kogan, A., English, T., John, O., Oveis, C., Gordon, A. M., & Keltner, D. (2012). Suppression sours sacrifice: Emotional and relational costs of suppressing emotions in romantic relationships. Personality and Social Psychology Bulletin, 38(6), 707-720.

122 Cameron, L. D., & Overall, N. C. (2018). Suppression and expression as distinct emotion-regulation processes in daily interactions: Longitudinal and meta-analyses. Emotion, 18(4), 465.

123 Smith, C. V., Lair, E. C., & O'Brien, S. M. (2019). Purposely stoic, accidentally alone? Self-monitoring moderates the relationship between emotion suppression and loneliness. Personality and Individual Differences, 149, 286-290.

124 Srivastava, S., Tamir, M., McGonigal, K. M., John, O. P., & Gross, J. J. (2009). The social costs of emotional suppression: A prospective study of the transition to college. Journal of personality and social psychology, 96(4), 883.

125 Smith, C. V., Lair, E. C., & O'Brien, S. M. (2019). Purposely stoic, accidentally alone? Self-monitoring moderates the relationship between emotion suppression and loneliness. Personality and Individual Differences, 149, 286-290.

126 Spokas, M., Luterek, J. A., & Heimberg, R. G. (2009). Social anxiety and emotional suppression: The mediating role of beliefs. Journal of behavior therapy and experimental psychiatry, 40(2), 283-291.

127 Simpson, C. C., & Mazzeo, S. E. (2017). Skinny isn't enough: A content analysis of fitspiration on Pinterest. Health communication, 32(5), 560-567.

128 Kilpatrick, M., Hebert, E., & Bartholomew, J. (2005). College students' motivation for physical activity: differentiating men's and women's motives for sport participation and exercise. Journal of American college health, 54(2), 87-94.

129 Mega Ice Cream Egypt (2020, Jan 21) https://www.facebook.com/megaicecream. eg/posts/2620263911354112 [Facebook post]

130 Ambassadors Ice Cream (2019, Aug 8) https://www.facebook.com/ambassadorsicecream/photos/a.284706402224523/354847718543724/ [Facebook post]

131 6 Times Ben & Jerry's Has Been There For You. (2016) Ben & Jerry's UK. https://www.benjerry.co.uk/whats-new/2016/there-for-you [Blog Post]

132 Dozois, D. J., & Rnic, K. (2015). Core beliefs and self-schematic structure in depression. Current Opinion in Psychology, 4, 98-103.

133 Fenn, K., & Byrne, M. (2013). The key principles of cognitive behavioural therapy. InnovAiT, 6(9), 579-585.

134 Mayhew, R., & Edelmann, R. J. (1989). Self-esteem, irrational beliefs and coping strategies in relation to eating problems in a non-clinical population. Personality and Individual Differences, 10(5), 581-584.

135 Möller, A. T., & Bothma, M. E. (2001). Body dissatisfaction and irrational beliefs. Psychological Reports, 88(2), 423-430.

136 Nolan, L. J., & Jenkins, S. M. (2019). Food Addiction Is Associated with Irrational Beliefs via Trait Anxiety and Emotional Eating. Nutrients, 11(8), 1711.

137 McComb, S. E., & Mills, J. S. (2019). Orthorexia nervosa: A review of psychosocial risk factors. Appetite.

138 Kim, H., & D'Andrea, A. D. (2012). Regulation of DNA cross-link repair by the Fanconi anemia/BRCA pathway. Genes & development, 26(13), 1393-1408.

139 Reingruber, H., & Pontel, L. B. (2018). Formaldehyde metabolism and its impact on human health. Current opinion in toxicology, 9, 28-34.

140 Burgos-Barragan, G., Wit, N., Meiser, J., Dingler, F. A., Pietzke, M., Mulderrig, L., ... & Monks, P. S. (2017). Mammals divert endogenous genotoxic formaldehyde into one-carbon metabolism. Nature, 548(7669), 549-554.

141 Ashurst, J. V., & Nappe, T. M. (2019). Methanol toxicity. StatPearls Publishing.

142 Hou, C. Y., Lin, Y. S., Wang, Y. T., Jiang, C. M., & Wu, M. C. (2008). Effect of storage conditions on methanol content of fruit and vegetable juices. Journal of food composition and analysis, 21(5), 410-415.

143 COT (UK Committee on toxicity of chemicals in food, consumer products and the environment). (2011). COT Statement on the effects of chronic dietary exposure to methanol.

144 WHO (1997). Environmental Health Criteria196: Methanol. World Health Organization, Geneva.

145 WHO (1997). Environmental Health Criteria196: Methanol. World Health Organization, Geneva.

146 Stegink, L. D., Filer Jr, L. J., Bell, E. F., Ziegler, E. E., & Tephly, T. R. (1989). Effect of repeated ingestion of aspartame-sweetened beverage on plasma amino acid, blood methanol, and blood formate concentrations in normal adults. Metabolism, 38(4), 357-363.

147 Leech, J. (2017) The Military Diet: A Beginner's Guide (with a meal plan) Health-line. Retrieved from:
https://www.healthline.com/nutrition/the-military-diet-101 [Article]

148 The Five Day Bikini Blitz Diet (2012, Jan 28) Retrieved from: https://www.mirror.co.uk/lifestyle/dieting/five-day-bikini-blitz-diet-408723?service=responsive [article]

149 Pomroy, H. Lose 5lb in 5 days: It's the diet, by a top nutritionist, celebrities use to get results fast. Today, we reveal how to trim your tum to fit into that Christmas party dress. (2014, Dec 1) The Daily Mail. Retrieved from https://www.dailymail.co.uk/femail/article-2855188/Lose-5lb-5-days-diet-nutritionist-celebrities-use-results-fast-Today-reveal-trim-tum-fit-Christmas-party-dress.html [article]

150 48 Hour Miracle Diet. Retrieved from: https://hollywooddiet.com/48-hour-miracle-diet.html [product website]

151 The Five Day Bikini Blitz Diet (2012, Jan 28) Retrieved from: https://www.mirror.co.uk/lifestyle/dieting/five-day-bikini-blitz-diet-408723?service=responsive [article]

152 McBride, J. J., Guest, M. M., & Scott, E. L. (1941). The storage of the major liver components; emphasizing the relationship of glycogen to water in the liver and the hydration of glycogen. Journal of Biological Chemistry, 139, 943-952.

153 Saris, W. H. (2001). Very-low-calorie diets and sustained weight loss. Obesity research, 9(S11), 295S-301S.

154 Durbán, A., Abellán, J. J., Latorre, A., & Moya, A. (2013). Effect of dietary carbohydrate restriction on an obesity-related prevotella-dominated human fecal microbiota. Metagenomics, 2(235722).

155 Saris, W. H. (2001). Very-low-calorie diets and sustained weight loss. Obesity research, 9(S11), 295S-301S.

156 Kirschner, M. A., Schneider, G., Ertel, N. H., & Gorman, J. (1988). An eight-year experience with a very-low-calorie formula diet for control of major obesity. International journal of obesity, 12(1), 69-80.

157 Eckert, E. D., Gottesman, I. I., Swigart, S. E., & Casper, R. C. (2018). A 57-year follow-up investigation and review of the Minnesota study on human starvation and its relevance to eating disorders. Archives of Psychology, 2(3).

158 Higginson, A. D., & McNamara, J. M. (2016). An adaptive response to uncertainty can lead to weight gain during dieting attempts. Evolution, medicine, and public health, 2016(1), 369-380.

159 Dulloo, A. G., Jacquet, J., & Girardier, L. (1997). Poststarvation hyperphagia and body fat overshooting in humans: a role for feedback signals from lean and fat tissues. The American journal of clinical nutrition, 65(3), 717-723.

160 Dulloo, A. G., Jacquet, J., Montani, J. P., & Schutz, Y. (2015). How dieting makes the lean fatter: from a perspective of body composition autoregulation through adipostats and proteinstats awaiting discovery. Obesity reviews, 16, 25-35.

161 Levinson, C. A., Fewell, L., & Brosof, L. C. (2017). My Fitness Pal calorie tracker usage in the eating disorders. Eating behaviors, 27, 14-16.

162 Keller, C., & Siegrist, M. (2014). Successful and unsuccessful restrained eating. Does dispositional self-control matter?. Appetite, 74, 101-106.

163 van Strien, T. (1997). Are most dieters unsuccessful? An alternative interpretation of the confounding of success and failure in the measurement of restraint. European Journal of Psychological Assessment, 13(3), 186-194.

164 Norris, C. J., Do, E., Close, E., & Deswert, S. (2019). Ambivalence toward healthy and unhealthy food and moderation by individual differences in restrained eating. Appetite, 140, 309-317.

165 Polivy, J., Coleman, J., & Herman, C. P. (2005). The Effect of Deprivation on Food Cravings and Eating Behavior in Restrained and Unrestrained Eaters. International Journal of Eating Disorders, 38(4), 301–309.

166 Meule, A., Lutz, A., Vögele, C., & Kübler, A. (2012). Food cravings discriminate differentially between successful and unsuccessful dieters and non-dieters. Validation of the Food Cravings Questionnaires in German. Appetite, 58(1), 88-97.

167 Hill, A. J., Weaver, C. F., & Blundell, J. E. (1991). Food craving, dietary restraint and mood. Appetite, 17(3), 187-197.

168 Schumacher, S., Kemps, E., & Tiggemann, M. (2019). The food craving experience: Thoughts, images and resistance as predictors of craving intensity and consumption. Appetite, 133, 387-392.

169 Tapper, K. (2018). Mindfulness and craving: effects and mechanisms. Clinical psychology review, 59, 101-117.

170 Hollitt, S., Kemps, E., Tiggemann, M., Smeets, E., & Mills, J. S. (2010). Components of attentional bias for food cues among restrained eaters. Appetite, 54(2), 309-313.

171 Neimeijer, R. A., de Jong, P. J., & Roefs, A. (2013). Temporal attention for visual food stimuli in restrained eaters. Appetite, 64, 5-11.

172 Lopez, A. L. O., & Johnson, L. (2016). Associations between restrained eating and the size and frequency of overall intake, meal, snack and drink occasions in the UK adult national diet and nutrition survey. PLoS One, 11(5), e0156320.

173 Boon, B., Stroebe, W., Schut, H., & IJntema, R. (2002). Ironic processes in the eating behaviour of restrained eaters. British Journal of Health Psychology, 7(1), 1-10.

174 Hofmann, W., Rauch, W., & Gawronski, B. (2007). And deplete us not into temptation: Automatic attitudes, dietary restraint, and self-regulatory resources as determinants of eating behavior. Journal of Experimental Social Psychology, 43(3), 497-504.

175 Ogden, J., Oikonomou, E., & Alemany, G. (2017). Distraction, restrained eating and disinhibition: An experimental study of food intake and the impact of 'eating on the go'. Journal of health psychology, 22(1), 39-50.

176 Polivy, J., & Herman, C. P. (1976). Effects of alcohol on eating behavior: Influence of mood and perceived intoxication. Journal of Abnormal Psychology, 85(6), 601–606.

177 Polivy, J., & Herman, C. P. (1976). The effects of alcohol on eating behavior: Disinhibition or sedation. Addictive Behaviors.

178 Koenigstorfer, J., Groeppel-Klein, A., Kettenbaum, M., & Klicker, K. (2013). Eat fit. Get big? How fitness cues influence food consumption volumes. Appetite, 65, 165-169.

179 Polivy, J., & Herman, C. P. (2017). Restrained eating and food cues: recent findings and conclusions. Current obesity reports, 6(1), 79-85.

180 Koenigstorfer, J., & Baumgartner, H. (2016). The effect of fitness branding on restrained eaters' food consumption and postconsumption physical activity. Journal of Marketing Research, 53(1), 124-138.

181 Irmak, C., Vallen, B., & Robinson, S. R. (2011). The impact of product name on dieters' and nondieters' food evaluations and consumption. Journal of consumer research, 38(2), 390-405.

182 Cavanagh, K. V., Kruja, B., & Forcstell, C. A. (2014). The effect of brand and caloric information on flavor perception and food consumption in restrained and unrestrained eaters. Appetite, 82, 1-7.

183 Cools, J., Schotte, D. E., & McNally, R. J. (1992). Emotional arousal and overeating in restrained eaters. Journal of Abnormal Psychology, 101(2), 348–351

184 Jansen, A. (1996). How restrained eaters perceive the amount they eat. British Journal of Clinical Psychology, 35(3), 381-392.

185 Herman, C. P., & Mack, D. (1975). Restrained and unrestrained eating. Journal of personality, 43(4), 647-660.

186 Waugh, E. J., Polivy, J., Ridout, R., & Hawker, G. A. (2007). A prospective investigation of the relations among cognitive dietary restraint, subclinical ovulatory disturbances, physical activity, and bone mass in healthy young women. The American journal of clinical nutrition, 86(6), 1791-1801.

187 Heatherton, T. F., & Wagner, D. D. (2011). Cognitive neuroscience of self-regulation failure. Trends in cognitive sciences, 15(3), 132-139.

188 de Witt Huberts, J. C., Evers, C., & de Ridder, D. T. (2013). Double trouble: restrained eaters don't eat less and feel worse. Psychology & health, 28(6), 686-700.

189 Heatherton, T. F., Polivy, J., & Herman, C. P. (1991). Restraint, weight loss, and variability of body weight. Journal of Abnormal Psychology, 100(1), 78–83.

190 Tiggemann, M. (1994). Dietary restraint as a predictor of reported weight loss and affect. Psychological reports, 75(3_suppl), 1679-1682.

191 Klesges, R. C., Isbell, T. R., & Klesges, L. M. (1992). Relationship between dietary restraint, energy intake, physical activity, and body weight: A prospective analysis. Journal of Abnormal Psychology, 101(4), 668–674.

192 Gilhooly, C. H., Das, S. K., Golden, J. K., McCrory, M. A., Dallal, G. E., Saltzman, E., ... & Roberts, S. B. (2007). Food cravings and energy regulation: the characteristics of craved foods and their relationship with eating behaviors and weight change during 6 months of dietary energy restriction. International Journal of Obesity, 31(12), 1849.

193 Delahanty, L. M., Meigs, J. B., Hayden, D., Williamson, D. A., Nathan, D. M., & Diabetes Prevention Program (DPP) Research Group (2002). Psychological and behavioral correlates of baseline BMI in the diabetes prevention program (DPP). Diabetes care, 25(11), 1992–1998. doi:10.2337/diacare.25.11.1992.

194 Fitzgibbon, M. L., Stolley, M. R., & Kirschenbaum, D. S. (1993). Obese people who seek treatment have different characteristics than those who don't seek treatment. Health Psychology, 12(5), 342–345.

195 Koenders, P. G., & van Strien, T. (2011). Emotional eating, rather than lifestyle behavior, drives weight gain in a prospective study in 1562 employees. Journal of Occupational and Environmental Medicine, 53(11), 1287-1293.

196 Polivy, J. (1996). Psychological consequences of food restriction. Journal of the American Dietetic Association, 96(6), 589.

197 Tiggemann, M. (1994). Dietary restraint as a predictor of reported weight loss and affect. Psychological reports, 75(3_suppl), 1679-1682.

198 Codina, N., & Pestana, J. V. (2019). Time Matters Differently in Leisure Experience for Men and Women: Leisure Dedication and Time Perspective. International journal of environmental research and public health, 16(14), 2513.

199 Beville, J. M., Umstattd Meyer, M. R., Usdan, S. L., Turner, L. W., Jackson, J. C., & Lian, B. E. (2014). Gender differences in college leisure time physical activity: application of the theory of planned behavior and integrated behavioral model. Journal of American College Health, 62(3), 173-184.

200 Craig, L., & Mullan, K. (2010). Parenthood, gender and work-family time in the United States, Australia, Italy, France, and Denmark. Journal of Marriage and Family, 72(5), 1344-1361.

201 Average hours per day spent in selected activities by sex and day. US Bureau of Labor Statistics. Retrieved from : https://www.bls.gov/charts/american-time-use/activity-by-sex.htm#

202 Sullivan, O. (2019). Gender inequality in work-family balance. Nature Human Behaviour, 3(3), 201-203.

203 Krueger, A. B. (2007). Are we having more fun yet? Categorizing and evaluating changes in time allocation. Brookings Papers on Economic Activity, 2007(2), 193-215.

204 Krueger, A. B. (2007). Are we having more fun yet? Categorizing and evaluating changes in time allocation. Brookings Papers on Economic Activity, 2007(2), 193-215.

205 Bakan, D. (1966). The duality of human existence. Chicago, IL: Rand McNally.

206 Sczesny, S., Nater, C., & Eagly, A. H. (2018). Agency and communion: Their implications for gender stereotypes and gender identities. In Agency and communion in social psychology (pp. 103-116). Routledge.

207 Helgeson, V. S., Swanson, J., Ra, O., Randall, H., & Zhao, Y. (2015). Links between unmitigated communion, interpersonal behaviors and well-being: A daily diary approach. Journal of Research in Personality, 57, 53-60.

208 Fritz, H. L., & Helgeson, V. S. (1998). Distinctions of unmitigated communion from communion: Self-neglect and overinvolvement with others. Journal of Personality and Social Psychology, 75(1), 121.

209 Fritz, H. L., & Helgeson, V. S. (1998). Distinctions of unmitigated communion from communion: Self-neglect and overinvolvement with others. Journal of Personality and Social Psychology, 75(1), 121.

210 Doell, S. R., & Hawkins II, R. C. (1982). Pleasures and pounds: An exploratory study. Addictive Behaviors, 7(1), 65-69.

211 Amy, E.A. and Kozak, A.T. (2012), "The More Pain I Have, the More I Want to Eat": Obesity in the Context of Chronic Pain. Obesity, 20: 2027-2034.

212 Tyler Boden, M., J Heinz, A., & B Kashdan, T. (2016). Pleasure as an overlooked target of substance use disorder research and treatment. Current drug abuse reviews, 9(2), 113-12.

213 Metzl, J. M. (2003). 'Mother's Little Helper': The Crisis of Psychoanalysis and the Miltown Resolution. Gender & History, 15(2), 228-255.

214 Grant, B. F., Chou, S. P., Saha, T. D., Pickering, R. P., Kerridge, B. T., Ruan, W. J., ... & Hasin, D. S. (2017). Prevalence of 12-month alcohol use, high-risk drinking, and DSM-IV alcohol use disorder in the United States, 2001-2002 to 2012-2013: results from the National Epidemiologic Survey on Alcohol and Related Conditions. JAMA psychiatry, 74(9), 911-923.

215 Contois, E. J. (2015). Guilt-free and sinfully delicious: A contemporary theology of weight loss dieting. Fat Studies, 4(2), 112-126.

216 Chao, Y. H., Yang, C. C., & Chiou, W. B. (2012). Food as ego-protective remedy for people experiencing shame. Experimental evidence for a new perspective on weight-related shame. Appetite, 59(2), 570-575.

217 Lefebvre, S., Hasford, J., & Wang, Z. (2019). The effects of guilt and sadness on sugar consumption. Journal of Business Research, 100, 130-138.

218 Lindeman, M., & Stark, K. (2000). Loss of pleasure, ideological food choice reasons and eating pathology. Appetite, 35(3), 263-268.

219 Kuijer, R. G., & Boyce, J. A. (2014). Chocolate cake. Guilt or celebration? Associations with healthy eating attitudes, perceived behavioural control, intentions and weight-loss. Appetite, 74, 48-54.

220 Weinberg, R. S. (1978). Relationship between extrinsic rewards and intrinsic motivation. Psychological Reports, 42(3_suppl), 1255-1258.

221 Deci, E. L., & Ryan, R. M. (2008). Self-determination theory: A macrotheory on human motivation, development, and health. Canadian Psychology, 49, 182–185.

222 Cutright, K. M., & Samper, A. (2014). Doing It the Hard Way: How Low Control Drives Preferences for High-Effort Products and Services. Journal of Consumer Research, 41(3), 730–745. doi:10.1086/677314.

223 Dr. Brene Brown On Joy: It's Terrifying. (n. d.) Project Meditation. Retrieved from: https://www.project-meditation.org/pm/why-joy-terrifies-us/ [article]

224 Time spent in unpaid, paid and total work, by sex. Organisation for Economic Co-operation and Development. Retrieved from: https://www.oecd.org/gender/data/time-spent-in-unpaid-paid-and-total-work-by-sex.htm [website]

225 American Time Use Survey-2018 Results. (2019, June 19) US Bureau of Labor Statistics. Retrieved from: https://www.bls.gov/news.release/pdf/atus.pdf?mod=article_inline

226 Insomnia. (2015, April 15) Cleveland Clinic. Retrieved from: https://my.clevelandclinic.org/health/diseases/12119-insomnia [website]

227 Gender and Stress (n.d.) American Psychological Association. Retrieved from: https://www.apa.org/news/press/releases/stress/2010/gender-stress [website]

228 Short Sleep Duration Among US Adults (2017, May 2). Centers for Disease Control and Prevention. Retrieved from: https://www.cdc.gov/sleep/data_statistics.html [website]

229 Do Women Need More Sleep Than Men? Piedmont Healthcare. Retrieved from: https://www.piedmont.org/living-better/do-women-need-more-sleep-than-men [website]

230 Diekelmann, S., & Born, J. (2010). The memory function of sleep. Nature Reviews Neuroscience, 11(2), 114-126.

231 Jackson, S. E., Kirschbaum, C., & Steptoe, A. (2017). Hair cortisol and adiposity in a population-based sample of 2,527 men and women aged 54 to 87 years. Obesity, 25(3), 539-544.

232 Epel, E. S., McEwen, B., Seeman, T., Matthews, K., Castellazzo, G., Brownell, K. D., ... & Ickovics, J. R. (2000). Stress and body shape: stress-induced cortisol secretion is consistently greater among women with central fat. Psychosomatic medicine, 62(5), 623-632.

233 Britton, K. A., Massaro, J. M., Murabito, J. M., Kreger, B. E., Hoffmann, U., & Fox, C. S. (2013). Body fat distribution, incident cardiovascular disease, cancer, and all-cause mortality. Journal of the American College of Cardiology, 62(10), 921-925.

234 Brain Basics: Understanding Sleep. (2019, Aug 13) National Institute of Neurological Disorders and Stroke. Retrieved from: https://www.ninds.nih.gov/Disorders/Patient-Caregiver-Education/Understanding-Sleep [website]

235 Krause, A. J., Simon, E. B., Mander, B. A., Greer, S. M., Saletin, J. M., Goldstein-Piekarski, A. N., & Walker, M. P. (2017). The sleep-deprived human brain. Nature Reviews Neuroscience, 18(7), 404.

236 Stress In America: Are Teens Adopting Adults' Stress Habits? American Psychological Association. Retrieved from: https://www.apa.org/news/press/releases/stress/2013/stress-report.pdf [website]

237 Leproult, R., & Van Cauter, E. (2010). Role of sleep and sleep loss in hormonal release and metabolism. In Pediatric Neuroendocrinology (Vol. 17, pp. 11-21). Karger Publishers.

238 Raspopow, K., Abizaid, A., Matheson, K., & Anisman, H. (2014). Anticipation of a psychosocial stressor differentially influences ghrelin, cortisol and food intake among emotional and non-emotional eaters. Appetite, 74, 35-43.

239 Björntorp, P. (2001). Do stress reactions cause abdominal obesity and comorbidities? The International Association for the Study of Obesity, Obesity Reviews, 2 (2), 73–86.

240 Escoto, K. H., Laska, M. N., Larson, N., Neumark-Sztainer, D., & Hannan, P. J. (2012). Work hours and perceived time barriers to healthful eating among young adults. *American journal of health behavior*, *36*(6), 786–796. https://doi.org/10.5993/AJHB.36.6.6

241 Devine, C. M., Jastran, M., Jabs, J., Wethington, E., Farell, T. J., & Bisogni, C. A. (2006). "A lot of sacrifices:" work-family spillover and the food choice coping strategies of low-wage employed parents. Social science & medicine (1982), 63(10), 2591–2603.

242 Stress In America: Are Teens Adopting Adults' Stress Habits? American Psychological Association. Retrieved from: https://www.apa.org/news/press/releases/stress/2013/stress-report.pdf [website]

243 Robinson, E., Aveyard, P., Daley, A., Jolly, K., Lewis, A., Lycett, D., & Higgs, S. (2013). Eating attentively: a systematic review and meta-analysis of the effect of food intake memory and awareness on eating. *The American journal of clinical nutrition*, *97*(4), 728-742.

244 Ogden, J., Oikonomou, E., & Alemany, G. (2017). Distraction, restrained eating and disinhibition: An experimental study of food intake and the impact of 'eating on the go'. Journal of health psychology, 22(1), 39-50.

245 Clark J. (2003). Women too busy to exercise. BMJ (Clinical research ed.), 326(7387), 467. doi:10.1136/bmj.326.7387.467

246 Clark J. (2003). Women too busy to exercise. BMJ (Clinical research ed.), 326(7387), 467. doi:10.1136/bmj.326.7387.467

247 Stults-Kolehmainen, M. A., & Bartholomew, J. B. (2012). Psychological stress impairs short-term muscular recovery from resistance exercise. Medicine & Science in Sports & Exercise, 44(11), 2220-2227.

248 Stults-Kolehmainen, M. A., & Sinha, R. (2014). The effects of stress on physical activity and exercise. *Sports medicine*, 44(1), 81-121.

249 Selfcare Products. Lululemon. Retrieved from: https://shop.lululemon.com/c/selfcare/ [website]

250 Pressed Juicery (2019, Feb 17) https://www.facebook.com/watch/?v=458475281637624 [Facebook Post]

251 Therabox https://www.mytherabox.com/ [website]

252 Eveleth, R. (2013, Oct 24) There are 37.2 Trillion Cells in Your Body. Smithsonian Magazine. Retrieved from https://www.smithsonianmag.com/smart-news/there-are-372-trillion-cells-in-your-body-4941473/ [website]

253 Haff, G. G., & Triplett, N. T. (Eds.). (2015). Essentials of strength training and conditioning 4th edition. Human kinetics.

254 Purves, D., Augustine, G.J., Fitzpatrick, D., et al., editors. (2001) Neuroscience. 2nd edition. Sunderland (MA): Sinauer Associates; The Regulation of Muscle Force. Available from: https://www.ncbi.nlm.nih.gov/books/NBK11021/

255 Haff, G. G., & Triplett, N. T. (Eds.). (2015). Essentials of strength training and conditioning 4th edition. Human kinetics.

256 Koch, C. (Chief Scientific Officer, Allen Institute for Brain Science). (2013, June 14) Decoding the Most Complex Object In The Universe. NPR.org

257 Cuddy, A. J., Schultz, S. J., & Fosse, N. E. (2018). P-curving a more comprehensive body of research on postural feedback reveals clear evidential value for power-posing effects: reply to Simmons and Simonsohn (2017). Psychological Science, 29(4), 656-666.

258 Fardouly, J., Pinkus, R. T., & Vartanian, L. R. (2017). The impact of appearance comparisons made through social media, traditional media, and in person in women's everyday lives. Body image, 20, 31-39.

259 Mensinger, J. L., Calogero, R. M., Stranges, S., & Tylka, T. L. (2016). A weight-neutral versus weight-loss approach for health promotion in women with high BMI: A randomized-controlled trial. Appetite, 105, 364-374.

260 Duhigg, Charles. (2012) The power of habit: why we do what we do in life and business. New York : Random House,

261 Nadler, R. T., Rabi, R., & Minda, J. P. (2010). Better mood and better performance: Learning rule-described categories is enhanced by positive mood. *Psychological Science*, 21(12), 1770-1776.

262 Puetz, T. W. (2006). Physical activity and feelings of energy and fatigue. Sports medicine, 36(9), 767-780.

263 Sparling, P. B., Giuffrida, A., Piomelli, D., Rosskopf, L., & Dietrich, A. (2003). Exercise activates the endocannabinoid system. Neuroreport, 14(17), 2209-2211.

264 Sharma, A., Madaan, V., & Petty, F. D. (2006). Exercise for mental health. Primary care companion to the Journal of clinical psychiatry, 8(2), 106. doi:10.4088/pcc. v08n0208a

265 Ekelund, U., Tarp, J., Steene-Johannessen, J., Hansen, B. H., Jefferis, B., Fagerland, M. W., ... & Larson, M. G. (2019). Dose-response associations between accelerometry measured physical activity and sedentary time and all cause mortality: systematic review and harmonised meta-analysis. bmj, 366, l4570.

266 Gill, D. L., Hammond, C. C., Reifsteck, E. J., Jehu, C. M., Williams, R. A., Adams, M. M., ... Shang, Y. T. (2013). Physical activity and quality of life. Journal of preventive medicine and public health = Yebang Uihakhoe chi, 46 Suppl 1(Suppl 1), S28–S34.

267 Oppezzo, M., & Schwartz, D. L. (2014). Give your ideas some legs: The positive effect of walking on creative thinking. Journal of experimental psychology: learning, memory, and cognition, 40(4), 1142.

268 Stenson, J. (2005) Exercise May Make You A Better Worker. NBC News.com Retrieved from: http://www.nbcnews.com/id/8160459/ns/health-fitness/t/exercise-may-make-you-better-worker/#.Xh-HJlOPbVp [article]

269 Vance, D. E., Marson, D. C., Triebel, K. L., Ball, K. K., Wadley, V. G., & Cody, S. L. (2016). Physical Activity and Cognitive Function in Older Adults: The Mediating Effect of Depressive Symptoms. The Journal of neuroscience nursing : journal of the American Association of Neuroscience Nurses, 48(4), E2–E12.

270 Loprinzi, P. D., Frith, E., Edwards, M. K., Sng, E., & Ashpole, N. (2018). The effects of exercise on memory function among young to middle-aged adults: systematic review and recommendations for future research. American Journal of Health Promotion, 32(3), 691-704.

271 Crochiere, R. J., Kerrigan, S. G., Lampe, E. W., Manasse, S. M., Crosby, R. D., Butryn, M. L., & Forman, E. M. (2020). Is physical activity a risk or protective factor for subsequent dietary lapses among behavioral weight loss participants?. Health psychology: official journal of the Division of Health Psychology, American Psychological Association.

272 Working Off Depression (2014, March) Harvard Health Publishing. Retrieved from: https://www.health.harvard.edu/mind-and-mood/working-off-depression [article]

273 Strickland, J. C., & Smith, M. A. (2014). The anxiolytic effects of resistance exercise. Frontiers in psychology, 5, 753. doi:10.3389/fpsyg.2014.00753.

274 Seguin, R. A., Eldridge, G., Lynch, W., & Paul, L. C. (2013). Strength Training Improves Body Image and Physical Activity Behaviors Among Midlife and Older Rural Women. Journal of extension, 51(4), 4FEA2.

275 Ahmed, C., Hilton, W., & Pituch, K. (2002). Relations of strength training to body image among a sample of female university students. The Journal of Strength & Conditioning Research, 16(4), 645-648.

276 Stoll, O. (2018). Peak Performance, the Runner's High and Flow. In Handbook of sports and exercise psychology. American Psychology Association Washington, DC.

277 Csikszentmihályi, M.; Abuhamdeh, S. & Nakamura, J. (2005), "Flow", in Elliot, A. (ed.), Handbook of Competence and Motivation, New York: The Guilford Press, pp. 598–698.

278 Department of Health and Human Services (2018) Physical Activity Guidelines for Americans, 2nd edition. Washington, DC: U.S. Department of Health and Human Services.

279 Schoenfeld, B. J., Grgic, J., Ogborn, D., & Krieger, J. W. (2017). Strength and hypertrophy adaptations between low-vs. high-load resistance training: a systematic review and meta-analysis. The Journal of Strength & Conditioning Research, 31(12), 3508-3523.

280 Prichard, I., & Tiggemann, M. (2008). Relations among exercise type, self-objectification, and body image in the fitness centre environment: The role of reasons for exercise. Psychology of Sport and Exercise, 9(6), 855-866.

281 Strelan, P., & Hargreaves, D. (2005). Reasons for exercise and body esteem: Men's responses to self-objectification. Sex Roles, 53(7-8), 495-503.

282 Zijlstra, H., van Middendorp, H., Devaere, L., Larsen, J. K., van Ramshorst, B., & Geenen, R. (2012). Emotion processing and regulation in women with morbid obesity who apply for bariatric surgery. Psychology & Health, 27(12), 1375-1387.

283 Zeeck, A., Stelzer, N., Linster, H.W., Joos, A. and Hartmann, A. (2011), Emotion and eating in binge eating disorder and obesity. Eur. Eat. Disorders Rev., 19: 426-437.

284 Conti, C, Di Francesco, G, Lanzara, R, et al. Alexithymia and binge eating in obese outpatients who are starting a weight-loss program: A structural equation analysis. Eur Eat Disorders Rev. 2019; 27: 628– 640.

285 Becker-Stoll, F. and Gerlinghoff, M. (2004), The impact of a four-month day treatment programme on alexithymia in eating disorders. Eur. Eat. Disorders Rev., 12: 159-163.

286 Casagrande, M., Boncompagni, I., Forte, G., Guarino, A., & Favieri, F. (2019). Emotion and overeating behavior: effects of alexithymia and emotional regulation on overweight and obesity. Eating and Weight Disorders-Studies on Anorexia, Bulimia and Obesity, 1-13.

287 Kajanoja, J., Karukivi, M., Scheinin, N. M., Tuulari, J. J., Ahrnberg, H., Karlsson, L., & Karlsson, H. (2019). Alexithymia, body mass index and gestational diabetes in pregnant women—FinnBrain birth cohort study. Journal of psychosomatic research, 124, 109742.

288 Bernstein, E. E., & McNally, R. J. (2017). Acute aerobic exercise helps overcome emotion regulation deficits. Cognition and emotion, 31(4), 834-843.

289 Bowler, D. E., Buyung-Ali, L. M., Knight, T. M., & Pullin, A. S. (2010). A systematic review of evidence for the added benefits to health of exposure to natural environments. BMC public health, 10(1), 456.

290 Kaimal, G., Ray, K., & Muniz, J. (2016). Reduction of cortisol levels and participants' responses following art making. Art therapy, 33(2), 74-80.

291 Drake, J. E., Coleman, K., & Winner, E. (2011). Short-term mood repair through art: Effects of medium and strategy. Art therapy, 28(1), 26-30.

292 Eaton, J., & Tieber, C. (2017). The effects of coloring on anxiety, mood, and perseverance. Art Therapy, 34(1), 42-46.

293 Smolarski, K., Leone, K., & Robbins, S. J. (2015). Reducing negative mood through drawing: Comparing venting, positive expression, and tracing. Art Therapy, 32(4), 197-201.

294 Cameron, L. D., & Overall, N. C. (2018). Suppression and expression as distinct emotion-regulation processes in daily interactions: Longitudinal and meta-analyses. Emotion, 18(4), 465.

295 McRae, K., Ciesielski, B., & Gross, J. J. (2012). Unpacking cognitive reappraisal: goals, tactics, and outcomes. Emotion, 12(2), 250.

296 Jamieson, J. P., Nock, M. K., & Mendes, W. B. (2012). Mind over matter: Reappraising arousal improves cardiovascular and cognitive responses to stress. Journal of Experimental Psychology: General, 141(3), 417.

297 Keng, S. L., Tan, E. L. Y., Eisenlohr-Moul, T. A., & Smoski, M. J. (2017). Effects of mindfulness, reappraisal, and suppression on sad mood and cognitive resources. Behaviour research and therapy, 91, 33-42.

298 Wolgast, M., Lundh, L. G., & Viborg, G. (2011). Cognitive reappraisal and acceptance: An experimental comparison of two emotion regulation strategies. Behaviour research and therapy, 49(12), 858-866.

299 Svaldi, J., Caffier, D., & Tuschen-Caffier, B. (2010). Emotion suppression but not reappraisal increases desire to binge in women with binge eating disorder. Psychotherapy and Psychosomatics, 79(3), 188.

300 Christou-Champi, S., Farrow, T. F., & Webb, T. L. (2015). Automatic control of negative emotions: evidence that structured practice increases the efficiency of emotion regulation. Cognition and Emotion, 29(2), 319-331.

301 Reader, S. W., Lopez, R. B., & Denny, B. T. (2018). Cognitive reappraisal of low-calorie food predicts real-world craving and consumption of high-and low-calorie foods in daily life. Appetite, 131, 44-52.

302 Giuliani, N. R., Calcott, R. D., & Berkman, E. T. (2013). Piece of cake. Cognitive reappraisal of food craving. Appetite, 64, 56-61.

303 Hennecke, M. and Freund, A.M. (2016), Age, Action Orientation, and Self-Regulation during the Pursuit of a Dieting Goal. Appl Psychol Health Well-Being, 8: 19-43.

304 Chatterjee, M. B., Baumann, N., Osborne, D., Mahmud, S. H., & Koole, S. L. (2018). Cross-Cultural Analysis of Volition: Action Orientation Is Associated With Less Anxious Motive Enactment and Greater Well-Being in Germany, New Zealand, and Bangladesh. Frontiers in psychology, 9, 1043.

305 Budde, H., & Wegner, M. (Eds.). (2018). The exercise effect on mental health: neurobiological mechanisms. CRC Press.

306 Dayan, P. H., Sforzo, G., Boisseau, N., Pereira-Lancha, L. O., & Lancha Jr, A. H. (2019). A new clinical perspective: Treating obesity with nutritional coaching versus energy-restricted diets. Nutrition, 60, 147-151.

307 O'Reilly, G. A., Cook, L., Spruijt-Metz, D., & Black, D. S. (2014). Mindfulness-based interventions for obesity-related eating behaviours: a literature review. Obesity reviews, 15(6), 453-461.

308 Veit, R., Horstman, L. I., Hege, M. A., Heni, M., Rogers, P. J., Brunstrom, J. M., ... & Kullmann, S. (2019). Health, pleasure, and fullness: changing mindset affects brain responses and portion size selection in adults with overweight and obesity. International Journal of Obesity, 1.

309 Tapper, K. (2018). Mindfulness and craving: effects and mechanisms. Clinical psychology review, 59, 101-117.

310 O'Reilly, G. A., Cook, L., Spruijt-Metz, D., & Black, D. S. (2014). Mindfulness-based interventions for obesity-related eating behaviours: a literature review. Obesity reviews : an official journal of the International Association for the Study of Obesity, 15(6), 453–461. doi:10.1111/obr.12156

311 Knekt, P., Kumpulainen, J., Järvinen, R., Rissanen, H., Heliövaara, M., Reunanen, A., ... & Aromaa, A. (2002). Flavonoid intake and risk of chronic diseases. The American journal of clinical nutrition, 76(3), 560-568.

312 Kumar, G. P., & Khanum, F. (2012). Neuroprotective potential of phytochemicals. Pharmacognosy reviews, 6(12), 81.

313 Leiherer, A., Mündlein, A., & Drexel, H. (2013). Phytochemicals and their impact on adipose tissue inflammation and diabetes. Vascular pharmacology, 58(1-2), 3-20.

314 Agus, M. S., Swain, J. F., Larson, C. L., Eckert, E. A., & Ludwig, D. S. (2000). Dietary composition and physiologic adaptations to energy restriction. The American journal of clinical nutrition, 71(4), 901-907.

315 Zhang, L., Pagoto, S., Olendzki, B., Persuitte, G., Churchill, L., Oleski, J., & Ma, Y. (2018). A nonrestrictive, weight loss diet focused on fiber and lean protein increase. Nutrition, 54, 12-18.

316 van Baak, M. A., & Mariman, E. (2019). Dietary strategies for weight loss maintenance. Nutrients, 11(8), 1916.

317 Sheflin, A. M., Melby, C. L., Carbonero, F., & Weir, T. L. (2017). Linking dietary patterns with gut microbial composition and function. Gut Microbes, 8(2), 113-129.

318 Menni, C., Jackson, M. A., Pallister, T., Steves, C. J., Spector, T. D., & Valdes, A. M. (2017). Gut microbiome diversity and high-fibre intake are related to lower long-term weight gain. International Journal of Obesity, 41(7), 1099-1105.

319 Carfora, V., Caso, D., & Conner, M. (2016). Randomized controlled trial of a messaging intervention to increase fruit and vegetable intake in adolescents: Affective versus instrumental messages. British journal of health psychology, 21(4), 937-955.

320 Vaillancourt, C., Bédard, A., Bélanger-Gravel, A., Provencher, V., Bégin, C., Desroches, S., & Lemieux, S. (2019). Promoting Healthy Eating in Adults: An Evaluation of Pleasure-Oriented versus Health-Oriented Messages. Current developments in nutrition, 3(5), nzz012.

321 Cornil, Y., & Chandon, P. (2016). Pleasure as a substitute for size: How multisensory imagery can make people happier with smaller food portions. Journal of Marketing Research, 53(5), 847-864.

322 Cornil, Y., & Chandon, P. (2016). Pleasure as an ally of healthy eating? Contrasting visceral and Epicurean eating pleasure and their association with portion size preferences and wellbeing. Appetite, 104, 52-59.

323 Gilovich, T., Kumar, A., & Jampol, L. (2015). A wonderful life: experiential consumption and the pursuit of happiness. Journal of Consumer Psychology, 25(1), 152–165.

324 MacKerron, G., & Mourato, S. (2013). Happiness is greater in natural environments. Global Environmental Change, 23(5), 992–1000.

325 Frühauf, A., Niedermeier, M., Elliott, L. R., Ledochowski, L., Marksteiner, J., & Kopp, M. (2016). Acute effects of outdoor physical activity on affect and psychological well-being in depressed patients – A preliminary study. Mental Health and Physical Activity, 10, 4–9.

326 Gidlow, C. J., Randall, J., Gillman, J., Smith, G. R., & Jones, M. V. (2016). Natural environments and chronic stress measured by hair cortisol. Landscape and Urban Planning, 148, 61–67.

327 Gidlow, C. J., Jones, M. V., Hurst, G., Masterson, D., Clark-Carter, D., Tarvainen, M. P., ... Nieuwenhuijsen, M. (2015). Where to put your best foot forward: Psychophysiological responses to walking in natural and urban environments. Journal of Environmental Psychology, 45, 22–29.

328 Amabile, T.M., & Kramer S.J. (2011) The power of small wins. Harvard Business Review, 89, pp. 71–80.

329 How Sleep Can Help You Be More Productive At Work. (n. d.) National Sleep Foundation. Retrieved from: https://www.sleep.org/articles/sleep-and-productivity-at-work/ [website]

330 Yang, R., Hale, L., Branas, C., Perlis, M., Gallagher, R., Killgore, W., ... & Grandner, M. (2018). 0189 Work Productivity Loss Associated with Sleep Duration, Insomnia Severity, Sleepiness, and Snoring. Sleep, 41(suppl_1), A74-A74.

331 Published the results of measuring the effects of the "Work Life Choice Challenge 2019 Summer" in-house project, "4 days a week & 3 days a week" (2019, Oct 31). Microsoft News Center. Retrieved from: https://news.microsoft.com/ja-jp/2019/10/31/191031-published-the-results-of-measuring-the-effectiveness-of-our-work-life-choice-challenge-summer-2019/ [article]

332 Nasiri, S., Akbari, H., Tagharrobi, L., & Tabatabaee, A. S. (2018). The effect of progressive muscle relaxation and guided imagery on stress, anxiety, and depression of pregnant women referred to health centers. Journal of education and health promotion, 7.

333 Dayapoğlu, N., & Tan, M. (2012). Evaluation of the effect of progressive relaxation exercises on fatigue and sleep quality in patients with multiple sclerosis. The Journal of Alternative and Complementary Medicine, 18(10), 983-987.

334 Zaccaro, A., Piarulli, A., Laurino, M., Garbella, E., Menicucci, D., Neri, B., & Gemignani, A. (2018). How breath-control can change your life: a systematic review on psycho-physiological correlates of slow breathing. Frontiers in human neuroscience, 12, 353.

335 5, 4, 3, 2, 1: Countdown to make anxiety blast off. (2017, May 24) Mayo Clinic Health System. Retrieved from: https://www.mayoclinichealthsystem.org/hometown-health/speaking-of-health/5-4-3-2-1-countdown-to-make-anxiety-blast-off [article]

336 Alonso-Alonso, M., Woods, S. C., Pelchat, M., Grigson, P. S., Stice, E., Farooqi, S., ... & Beauchamp, G. K. (2015).

337 Chao, A. M., Jastreboff, A. M., White, M. A., Grilo, C. M., & Sinha, R. (2017). Stress, cortisol, and other appetite-related hormones: Prospective prediction of 6-month changes in food cravings and weight. Obesity, 25(4), 713-72.

338 Leproult, R., & Van Cauter, E. (2010). Role of sleep and sleep loss in hormonal release and metabolism. In Pediatric Neuroendocrinology (Vol. 17, pp. 11-21). Karger Publishers.

339 Raspopow, K., Abizaid, A., Matheson, K., & Anisman, H. (2014). Anticipation of a psychosocial stressor differentially influences ghrelin, cortisol and food intake among emotional and non-emotional eaters. Appetite, 74, 35-43.

340 How To Use. (n. d.) 5 hour energy. Retrieved from: https://5hourenergy.com/facts/how-to-use/ [website]

341 Nehlig, A., Daval, J. L., & Debry, G. (1992). Caffeine and the central nervous system: mechanisms of action, biochemical, metabolic and psychostimulant effects. Brain Research Reviews, 17(2), 139-170.

342 Virtanen, M., Singh-Manoux, A., Ferrie, J. E., Gimeno, D., Marmot, M. G., Elovainio, M., ... & Kivimäki, M. (2009). Long working hours and cognitive function: the Whitehall II Study. American Journal of Epidemiology, 169(5), 596-605.

343 Killgore, W. D. (2010). Effects of sleep deprivation on cognition. Progress in brain research (Vol. 185, pp. 105-129). Elsevier.

344 Lin, L., & Soby, M. (2017). Is listening to fat talk the same as participating in fat talk?. Eating disorders, 25(2), 165-172.

345 Tompkins, K. B., Martz, D. M., Rocheleau, C. A., & Bazzini, D. G. (2009). Social likeability, conformity, and body talk: Does fat talk have a normative rival in female body image conversations?. Body Image, 6(4), 292-298.

346 Barwick, A., Bazzini, D., Martz, D., Rocheleau, C., & Curtin, L. (2012). Testing the norm to fat talk for women of varying size: What's weight got to do with it?. Body Image, 9(1), 176-179.

347 Cain, M. (2019, Nov 7) I Was the Fastest Girl in America, Until I Joined Nike. The New York Times. Retrieved from: https://www.nytimes.com/2019/11/07/opinion/nike-running-mary-cain.html [article]

348 Krane, V., Choi, P. Y., Baird, S. M., Aimar, C. M., & Kauer, K. J. (2004). Living the paradox: Female athletes negotiate femininity and muscularity. Sex roles, 50(5-6), 315-329.

349 Rothenburg, B. (2015, July 10) Tennis's Top Women Balance Body Image With Ambition. The New York Times. Retrieved from: https://www.nytimes.com/2015/07/11/sports/tennis/tenniss-top-women-balance-body-image-with-quest-for-success.html [article]

350 Savage, B. M., Lujan, H. L., Thipparthi, R. R., & DiCarlo, S. E. (2017). Humor, laughter, learning, and health! A brief review. Advances in physiology education, 41(3), 341-347.

351 Atroszko, P. A. (2012). Research on behavioural addictions: Work addiction. Modern research trends of young scientists: Current status, problems and prospects, 11-24.

INDEX